THE FOUR SEASON GUIDE TO NEW ENGLAND

A YANKEE BOOKS TRAVEL GUIDE

THE FOUR SEASON GUIDE TO NEW ENGLAND

by Michael A. Schuman

YANKEE BOOKS

Camden, Maine

We would like to thank the following for the use of their photographs:

Blithewold Gardens and Aboretum, Michael Schuman, Vermont Travel Division, Robert S. Arnold, Vermont Maple Festival Council, Inc., Northern Outdoors, Springfield Newspapers, Michael Gordon, Bob Perry, Stratton Mountain, Hubert Schriebl, Greenfield Hill Congregational Church, Shelburne Museum, John A. Lynch, Clemens Kalischer, Nancy Forest, Lexington Minutemen, Rhode Island Department of Economic Development, Dick Hamilton, Bob Story, Walter H. Scott, Charles Ives Center for the Arts, Connecticut Department of Economic Development, Saint-Gaudens National Historic Site, Lisa Bourdon, Hartford Downtown Council, Claire White-Peterson, Rockland Courier Gazette, Norwalk Seaport Association, Mary Anne Stets, Fort Fairfield Chamber of Commerce, Bill Finney Photography, Photography by Swenson, Rhode Island Tourist Promotion Division, Rhode Island Red Sox, New Hampshire Farm Museum, Inc., Eric Francis, Bill Hennefrund, Maine Office of Tourism, Tom Hindman, Les Campbell, Edaville Railroad, Dick Smith, Balloon Inn Vermont, Stuart Bratesman, Dartmouth College, John Foraste, Brown University, Salem Witch Museum, Plimoth Plantation, Bank of Boston Balloon Parade, The Balsams Grand Resort Hotel, Jack Spratt, Jason Threlfall, Strawbery Banke Museum, First Night Boston, Tubbs Snowshoes, Old Sturbridge Village, Rangeley Lakes Region Chamber of Commerce, Witch's Dungeon Museum, Salem Cross Inn, Mystic Seaport.

Cover photograph credits:

Winter — © State of New Hampshire, David Brownell; *Fall* — Vermont Travel Division, Dr. John C. Weaver; *Summer* — Massachusetts Office of Travel and Tourism, Kindra Clineff; *Spring* — New Hampshire Office of Vacation Travel, Bob Grant.

Cover Design • Dale Swensson, Mt. Desert, Maine
Composition • High Resolution, Inc., Camden, Maine

Printed in the United States

Library of Congress Cataloging-in-Publication Data

Schuman, Michael A.
    The four season guide to New England/by Michael A. Schuman.
       p. cm. — (A Yankee Books travel guide)
    ISBN 0-89909-327-2
    1. New England—Description and travel—1981- —Guide-books.
I. Title. II. Series.
F2.3.S383 1991
917.404'43—dc20
                                  91-12515
                                  CIP

10 9 8 7 6 5 4 3 2 1

To the memory of Kelila Fay-Bernice Schuman

CONTENTS

ACKNOWLEDGMENTS

Many people were of invaluable help in researching this book. Special thanks go to Barbara Beeching at the Connecticut Department of Economic Development, the people at the Maine Publicity Bureau, Kim Thompson and Ashley McCown at the Massachusetts Office of Travel and Tourism, Ann Kennard at the New Hampshire Office of Vacation Travel, Kay Tucker and Kerry Ann Malloy at the Rhode Island Department of Economic Development, and John Cashman at the Vermont Travel Division. Also, some copy was written for and appeared in different form in the *Keene Sentinel*, Keene, New Hampshire.

Introduction

Residents of southern California or Florida can only determine the current season by looking at a calendar. Here in New England, however, we have the gift of four, distinct changing seasons, each with its own special qualities.

So they have Mickey Mouse. We have old-fashioned sleigh rides and hills of crimson and gold.

When you have seen one palm tree you have seen them all. Not so for our carpets of daffodils and lilacs, panoramas of color in the spring air, or our mountains and lakes, bold and striking in the morning sun, subdued and subtle in the evening shade.

Our traditions transcend the glorification of roses and oranges. We can boast clambakes and sugaring off and jonnycake breakfasts and mammoth sculptures of packed and shaped granular powder — beguiling behemoths or cabalistic creatures made of chicken wire and snow, firmly implanted in the winter chill on college campuses and town greens. We have annual events well into their second and third centuries of continuity.

We toast our foods — our lobsters, our apples, our quahogs, our clams, our blueberries, our syrup, our scallops, our potatoes, our oysters.

There is plenty to do all year long, even during that stretch of the year when nightfall seems to engird New England by mid-afternoon and warm, balmy days seem a billion light years away.

The purpose of this book is to reintroduce New England to New Englanders and to put out the welcome mat to our visitors. Practically speaking, it will afford you an abundance of ideas about the places to go and things to do throughout the year. In doing so, this book celebrates our changing seasons, our natural resources, and our people.

On the pages within I discuss the many forms of recreation, entertainment, and leisure activity peculiar to each season. Summer doesn't have to be limited to a trip to the same ocean beach every year. It could mean a concert in the moonlight, or a scallop festival, or a visit to an inland beach, one with water temperatures that are quite palatable.

Winter doesn't have to mean hibernation. It might instead be a sleigh ride across the open fields, or a viewing of snow sculptures on parade. Springtime could consist of a trip to see dogwoods in bloom or a rafting excursion even a non-outdoors type could favor. Fall could be the colors seen from inside a gondola.

One final note — we are deliberately being evasive about dates of festivals, admission costs, and specific features of tours. They can and do change readily. Before arranging your vacation around a special event, please call or write the reference contacts listed for latest up-to-date information.

SPRING

S pring in New England is nebulous. It can be two weeks in May, or it can last from Easter into June. Or it might not exist at all; many are the springs that vanish, squeezed out between an endless winter and the first sweats of summer.

There's one certainty: our spring never starts when the calendar says it does. The azaleas and wisteria in Charleston and Savannah might be in full bloom in March, but one will find New England still white and barren and cold. So we wait and wait. The first warm day of spring is like the first bite of a tantalizing pizza fresh from the oven; it always tastes the best.

Spring is also the season in which many of our holidays fall. Massachusetts, known as the home of the Irish-American, is the setting for the liveliest St. Patrick's Day commemorations: from the streets of South Boston to the slopes of the Berkshires, the spirit of the green lingers in the air and the shamrocks of green are painted on the sidewalks, and there is no need to be Irish to share in the celebrations.

A CARPET OF BLOSSOMS AT THEIR PEAK CAN BE SEEN AT BLITHEWOLD GARDENS AND ARBORETUM'S ANNUAL SPRING BULB DISPLAY.

The midnight ride of Paul Revere is recreated annually, although to accommodate twentieth-century work schedules it begins several hours after midnight. And the Easter/Passover season means sunrise services and a recreated egg roll at a genuine summer White House.

Spring is the season of our first harvest; the wisps of smoke curling above our sugarhouses are the first harbingers of warmth to come. The recreation-minded can head to the slopes, where our ski season extends well into May, or the spirited can take on the rockiest whitewater rapids in Maine. The hungry might venture to Rhode Island, whose long-standing May breakfasts welcome the spring with feasts of jonnycakes, clam cakes, grits, pancakes, and eggs. For a feast for your eyes, meanwhile, visit Connecticut's Dogwood Festival, or any of several other events marking the return of the blossoms.

With flowers and food, shamrocks and sugaring, who needs to wait until summer to have fun?

MAPLE SUGARING

We once arrived at the retail store of Harry and David of mail order fame in Medford, Oregon. We hoped to meet two guys named Harry and David. Harry, we idealized, would be bringing in a bushel of freshly picked apples, and David would be chatting with some friendly patrons.

We met only a cashier named Linda, and we peered inside an elongated wing of the building to see endless rows of typewriters and filing cabinets and office desks.

In this day, when mail order firms with folksy names turn out to be major conglomerates, and corporations are buying up family farms like summer squash, maple syrup is a product of primarily family-run operations. There is a sincerity among New England's maple product producers that is rarely encountered elsewhere nowadays.

A visitor to Hollywood would be hard pressed to find any original Warner Brothers and you won't see any Proctor and Gamble still making detergent.

You will find sons and daughters helping their parents in tedious labor in hundreds of sugarhouses across New England. One such enterprise that goes all out for visitors during maple season is Harlow's, in Putney, Vermont.

There is a sincerity among New England's maple product producers that is rarely encountered elsewhere nowadays.

Harlow's Sugar House

ALTHOUGH IT IS a well-stocked Vermont maple and souvenir shop throughout the year, Harlow's in Putney, a short jaunt north of Brattleboro in the southeastern corner of the Green Mountain State, is at its best on sugaring season weekends, when a maple snack bar is operated.

Here you can try all the Vermont snacks typical of the sugaring season. There are doughnuts adorned with maple butter, maple syrup on ice cream, maple fritters, maple candies, and of course, sugar on snow, perhaps the most traditional sugaring treat.

Not to be found on any restrictive diet or as part of your doctor's orders, *sugar on snow* consists of caramel-like maple syrup literally poured over snow; in years of little snowfall, crushed ice makes a suitable substitute. Authentic sugar on snow is always topped with a pickle to offset the sweetness.

To appreciate the labor involved in producing maple syrup, step into Harlow's boiling-off room, where you can watch the experts at work. One city-bred sugar maker once admitted she grew up thinking syrup flowed directly from trees. Here you will discover the hard facts.

Sap, not syrup, flows from trees, and to make one

IF YOU VISIT SUGARHOUSES
AT THE RIGHT TIME, YOU
CAN STILL SEE WORKERS
TAPPING MAPLE TREES.

gallon of syrup, approximately 40 gallons of sap must be boiled down. A typical tree produces only ten gallons of sap, which means that millions of trees must be tapped yearly.

At Harlow's, you are invited to ask questions of the workers as they toss logs in the furnace to keep the evaporator fired up, or as they tend the boiling sap. Yet progress and modern technology have made inroads into the backwoods of New England. Just as a tourist looking for the Old West of Zane Grey would be disappointed upon visiting late twentieth-century Denver, and just as a first-time traveler to

Atlanta would hardly recognize the city as it was depicted in *Gone with the Wind*, so sentimentalists searching for the traditional team of oxen hauling in buckets of sap from a maple grove will be in for a surprise. (By the way, call a grove of sugar maples a "sugar bush" and you will pass for an expert.)

The majority of producers, including Harlow's, have swapped those oh-so-picturesque galvanized steel buckets for plastic tubing—though not as scenic, the tubing saves hours of drudgery. However, many still hang buckets on isolated trees by the roadside. Says Doug Harlow: "True, it's not practical, but it is what people want to see when they drive the back roads of Vermont in April."

Harlow's Sugar House is located on Route 5 in Putney. To reach Harlow's, take exit 4 off Interstate 91. The store is open daily, whereas the maple snack bar is only open weekends during sugaring season. (802) 387–5852.

Sugaring at Old Sturbridge Village

ACTUALLY, THERE IS still one place where you can be sure to witness a scene, the likes of which will satisfy the history buff. Old Sturbridge Village, the archetypal recreation from the 1830s in Sturbridge, Massachusetts, celebrates the thawing of New England with its demonstrations of early nineteenth-century sugaring.

Plastic tubing is unheard of at Sturbridge. So are galvanized steel buckets and sugarhouses. State of the art in the 1830s meant equipment of wood and iron, and a makeshift outdoor sugar camp.

In late February or early March, when ideal sugaring weather—warm during the day and below freezing at night—arrives, costumed interpreters set up their sugar camp, and, using augers, drill holes in the maple trees near the Asa Knight Store. They then insert *spiles* (spouts made from sumac wood) into the holes, and wait as the sap drips into wooden troughs at the bases of the trees.

When the troughs are filled, the sap is gathered into wooden buckets, fashioned of staves at the village's cooper shop. There are no giant-sized evaporators here. The sap is brought to the outdoor sugar camp and poured into an iron kettle, then boiled over a blazing fire until it reaches a sugar-like texture. Because maple sugar was less costly than cane sugar

AT OLD STURBRIDGE VILLAGE COSTUMED INTERPRETERS
BOIL SAP THE NINETEENTH-CENTURY WAY.

in the 1830s, sugar, not syrup, was the end result. Maple syrup wouldn't become popular for another 50 years.

How could early nineteenth-century sugar makers tell when the their product reached the right consistency? The resident interpreters at Sturbridge, like their ancestors, place a bit of sugar on a cold ax head; if it can be peeled off, it's ready. Or, they may

A YOUNG VERMONTER GETS HER FIRST LESSON IN MAPLE SUGARING FROM A SEASONED EXPERT ON AN EARLY SPRING MORNING.

put it in a bubble wand and blow on it; if it hardens on the stick, then it's also ready.

Lastly, the sugar is poured into cone-shaped molds in which it hardens. It takes about 40 gallons of sap to equal four pounds of sugar.

Old Sturbridge Village is open daily except Monday in sugaring season. Admission is charged for all but children under six. The village is on Route 20 west in Sturbridge; take exit 9 off the Massachusetts Turnpike or exit 2 off Interstate 84. (508) 347–3362.

A GUIDE TO FAVORITE SUGARHOUSES

THE OMNIPRESENT curl of steam that hangs over the stark woods any time from late February through late April signifies to those within eyeshot that syrup is being made. John Matthews of **Stuart & John's Sugarhouse** in Westmoreland, New Hampshire, believes that many are attracted to the sight and smell of boiling sap mainly because it's the first precursor of spring.

Offers Matthews: "When you see a robin on the lawn in the summer you don't think anything of it. But the first one is always special. People like to see the wood fire and steam and smell the sap for the same reason. It's the first sign of springtime."

If you want to celebrate spring's arrival by indulging your sweet tooth, take note that there are literally hundreds of sugarhouses in New England, many of which open their doors to visitors during this busy season. Following is a list of a few sugar shacks that make a point of welcoming the curious and/or hungry. Most are in full swing on weekends, although others may sell their products only on weekdays. Quirky New England weather can cause the sugaring season to vary by weeks from one year to the next. Therefore, please call first before making a special trip.

Massachusetts

SOUTH FACE FARM, Ashfield. Owner Tom McCrumm says: "I'd like people to leave here with something in their heads as well as in their stomachs. We have a sign that says: 'We like to answer questions,' since some people might be shy or self-conscious when it comes to asking things."

That in mind, Tom gives tours when things are not too busy, answers all questions from novices and experts alike, and lets visitors embark on a self-guided tour into the sugar bush. South Face Farm also maintains a restaurant on weekends in season, offering French toast with homemade bread, doughnuts with maple cream, and breakfast meats. South Face has about 4,000 taps. (413) 628–3268.

DAVENPORT MAPLE FARM, Shelburne.

Owner Martha Davenport operates a restaurant here specializing in syrup-topped entrées, like waffles, pancakes, and Finnish pancakes ("more like a custard," she states). Patrons can see sap being boiled down as they dine. Private tours can be arranged. Davenport has 3,500 taps and uses tubing, but also hangs about 1,200 buckets. (413) 625–2866.

GOULD'S SUGARHOUSE, Shelburne.

No tours are offered, but Helen Gould's restaurant serves up corn fritters drenched in syrup, as well as pancakes, waffles, and sandwiches. Evaporator workers are on hand to answer your questions. The Goulds have about 1,000 taps and use both tubing and buckets. (413) 625–6170.

RED BUCKET SUGAR SHACK, Worthington.

The red buckets by the roadside indicate the presence of this cozy little restaurant and sugarhouse deep in the Berkshire woods. Patrons dine on pancakes, doughnuts with maple cream, eggs, and breakfast meats. And they can drink *maple milk* (like chocolate milk but with maple syrup instead of chocolate). The floor is stone, the walls are of weathered wood, the windows offer views into the sugar bush, and you dine in the same room where the evaporator is hard at work. There are no formal tours, but you can chat with the workers. There are about 5,600 taps. (413) 238–7710.

MT. TOBY SUGARHOUSE, Sunderland.

Sugar on snow (with pickle) is the primary offering for visitors with a maple craving, although doughnuts and coffee are also on tap. You can stroll through the sugar bush, examining both tubing and buckets at this operation, which utilizes about 1,000 taps. You can talk with the folks tending the evaporator and purchase syrup, maple candy, or maple cream, all produced here. (413) 665–3127 during sugaring season; (413) 773–8301 rest of the year.

For a complete list of Massachusetts sugarhouses

open to the public, contact the Massachusetts Maple Producers Association, P.O. Box 377, Ashfield, MA 01330; (413) 628–3912.

New Hampshire

SUNNYSIDE MAPLES, Loudon. Sundaes, pancakes, homemade baked beans with ham, and jams and jellies—all made with, garnished with, or covered with some form of maple product—are available in the restaurant here. There are no formal tours, but visitors can watch sap being boiled and can ask questions. There are 3,000 taps, and tubing rather than buckets is mainly used. (603) 783–9961 or (603) 267–8217.

ABBOTT FARM SUGAR HOUSE, Tilton. The specialty here is maple candy making. Onlookers watch as sugar is poured into old-fashioned molds in order to become solid sweets. Unlike most other sugarhouses, Abbott Farm is as busy on weekdays as weekends. There is a small store on the premises and visitors can chat with the workers sugaring off or, with a reservation, can take a tour. Buckets hang by the roadside, but tubing is used deep in the sugar bush. (603) 286–4095.

STUART & JOHN'S SUGARHOUSE, Westmoreland. The restaurant here thrives on spring and fall weekends, with diners happily feasting on French toast, homemade doughnuts topped with maple butter, pancakes, corn fritters in syrup, maple sundaes, and maple frappes. You can watch and talk with the folks hard at work boiling down. Depending on the year, Stuart & John's maintains from 7,000 to 8,000 taps. (603) 399–4486.

PEASE'S SCENIC VALLEY, Orford. The Pease family runs a loose ship. There is no formal restaurant, but on sugaring season Sundays Toni Pease cooks pancakes served with syrup that are yours for a donation. Doughnuts with syrup or maple candies might also be offered. ("Our candies are made fresh and sold fresh. They don't sit around for a month or two like they do in some stores," says Toni.) There are some buckets, some tubing, and up to 600 taps. Gerald Pease tends the evaporator and is happy to explain his sugaring operation. (603) 353–9070.

For a complete list of New Hampshire sugarhouses open to the public, contact the New Hampshire Maple Producers Association, Inc., New Hampshire Department of Agriculture, 105 Loudon Road, Building 1, Concord, NH 03301; (603) 271-3788.

Vermont

GREEN MOUNTAIN SUGAR HOUSE, Ludlow.
Guided tours are offered and samples of hot syrup ("Emphasize the *hot*," says owner Ann Rose) as it is being made are yours when you visit. A gift shop with maple products is on the grounds of this high-production operation boasting 18,000 taps. (802) 228-7151.

COUTURE'S SUGARHOUSE, Westfield. Sugar on snow parties are the highlight of this sugarhouse on the rooftop of Vermont near the Canadian border. Also, sugar on snow is always served on the first

SYRUP MAKERS TENDING THE EVAPORATOR IS A COMMON SIGHT FOR THOSE WHO VISIT AN OPERATING SUGARHOUSE.

Sunday of the sugaring season. Guided tours are offered regularly, and a shop is home to lollipops, candies, spreads, jellies—all maple flavored, of course; in addition, 11-ounce blocks of maple sugar are sold. The Coutures also have a mobile sugarhouse that they bring to fairs and other special events. They have about 4,000 taps. (802) 744–2733.

BUTTERNUT MOUNTAIN FARM, Johnson.

Owner David Marvin says: "My operation is a high-tech one. There is nothing old-fashioned here." That stated, this is the place to visit to see a new slant on an age-old tradition. Marvin boils down sap with both oil and steam fires, and offers tours by pre-arrangement. He also owns a shop with an extraordinary variety of maple products. The list includes the expected, like pancake and muffin mixes, and the unexpected, including maple salad dressing, maple beet pickles, cucumber pickles, and maple granola. Marvin has about 16,000 taps. (802) 635–7483.

GOODRICH'S SUGARHOUSE, West Danville.

Glenn and Ruth Goodrich are the sixth generation of a family that has been producing maple products for over 150 years. They offer tours through their new sugarhouse, explaining steps from boiling down sap to packaging, and they also present a slide show. For sale is a potpourri of maple products from syrup and candy to maple granola, maple fudge, and maple popcorn. The sugarhouse is open to visitors through sugaring season into December. The Goodriches have about 5,000 taps. (802) 563–9917.

GREEN MOUNTAIN AUDUBON NATURE CENTER, Huntington.

This is an educational center first and a syrup producer second, and therefore is a perfect place to learn and do. On the last Saturday in February you can lend a hand tapping trees or just watch others at work. Boiling goes on most weekends, guided and self-guided walks are offered, a videotape can be screened, and sugar on snow parties are regularly slated during peak sugaring season. There are about 740 taps here, all buckets. (802) 434–3068.

For a complete list of Vermont sugarhouses open to the public, contact the Vermont Department of Agriculture, State Office Building, 116 State Street, Montpelier, VT 05602; (802) 828–2416.

Maine

IF MAINE WERE filled with maple trees, it wouldn't be known as the Pine Tree State. Still, Maine does have a small but active sugaring industry, and the fourth Sunday in March is cause for celebration. This is Maine Maple Sunday, when upwards of 20 state sugarhouses open their doors to visitors, offering tours of their operations and tastes of their products. It's a good excuse for a trip out of the house on these early spring days when you're just dying for it to warm up.

For a list of the sugarhouses open on Maine Maple Sunday, write the Division of Marketing Development, Department of Agriculture, State House Station 28, Augusta, ME 04333, or call (207) 289-7636.

In addition, there are sugarhouses in Maine welcoming visitors throughout the season.

It's a good excuse for a trip out of the house on these early spring days when you're just dying for it to warm up.

JILLSON'S SUGARHOUSE, Sabattus. This enterprise near Lewiston serves up sugar parties which are really feasts for those who had better be hungry. On the menu when you visit are likely to be jonnycakes, baked beans, ham, pancakes, home fries, fried salt pork, sugar on snow, and other traditional New England victuals, and you can expect nearly all to have some kind of maple connection.

The parties are really a Canadian custom with an American slant, and sometimes a Franco-American band shows up to provide musical entertainment. Visitors can take a self-guided tour of the sugarhouse and watch a videotape, and children are welcome to pet the barn animals. The Jillsons use buckets and tubing and have about 1,000 taps. (207) 375-4486.

HALL FARMS, East Dixfield. The Hall family leads the curious on guided tours explaining the sugaring process from tapping to the finished product. Says Gloria Hall: "They can last from 20 to 45 minutes depending on the size of the group and their ages. We get people who think the syrup flows thick from the trees so we'll give them a taste of sap since they have no idea what it's like." Tours are by chance or reservation, but you are more likely to find someone home in the early morning or late afternoon. They will also explain the whole sugaring process—through displays and pictures—when it's not sugaring season. The Halls have about 1,800 taps. (207) 645-4608.

MAPLE HILL FARM, Farmington. You can sample syrup, buy maple taffy, or take an informal tour when the sap is running of what owner Donna Tracy calls "one of the oldest sap houses in Franklin County." She adds, "We use both tubing and buckets, so people can see both the old and new ways." Tours are given by chance or appointment. Maple Hill Farm uses about 2,700 taps. (207) 778–4506.

Connecticut

ROBERT AND JEAN LAMOTHE, Burlington. "You'd be surprised how many people don't know maple syrup is made in Connecticut," marvels Jean Lamothe, "and how many think maple sap flows in the fall, not the spring. We've had many calls for tours in the fall." The Lamothes give regularly scheduled tours of their sugarhouse on weekends from the beginning of February through the end of March, and offer mid-week tours by appointment. They have from 900 to 1,000 taps, and use both buckets and tubing. (203) 582–6135.

Rhode Island

COGGESHALL FARM, Bristol. Demonstrations of old-fashioned sugaring methods are scheduled on specified weekends at the farm museum, off Poppasquash Road, adjacent to Colt State Park. Visitors can help farm workers collect sap, transport it by oxen cart, and boil it down by using handmade spiles and wooden buckets. A blacksmith or woodworker might be on hand. Admission is charged. (401) 253–9062.

FESTIVALS

The Annual Vermont Maple Festival

THE HOT-SELLING snack items here are not cotton candy or popcorn. This festival is maple flavored through and through. It is where Vermont's best known agricultural product is shown off and put on a pedestal, not to mention on pancakes, fritters, crushed ice, and snow.

Actually, Saint Albans, Vermont, site of the fest, is an otherwise unassuming town of 8,000 just 15 chilly miles south of the Canadian border. But because it is the seat of the largest maple producing county in the country, it is an apt setting for this tribute to all things maple.

Sugar on snow might be the bestselling victual, but it is hardly the sole one. A pancake breakfast is held each morning and you are allowed seconds and thirds. Of course, all the maple syrup is locally produced and unless you want to risk being tarred and feathered, don't ask anyone for Mrs. Butterworth's.

Maple sugar candies are made as visitors watch, and they are on sale alongside sundry pastries adorned with maple butter. And there is no better venue to purchase a pint, quart, or gallon of the bona fide product to use on your own pancakes at home.

After sampling the best-tasting sweets Vermont has to offer, take a walk to Taylor Park to check out alternative sights, like a local craftsman who takes cumbersome logs and chunks of wood, and, with a big chain saw, carves out images of brown bears,

SUGAR ON SNOW IS THE HOTTEST SELLING SNACK ITEM AT THE ANNUAL VERMONT MAPLE FESTIVAL.

owls, sea captains, and Indian chiefs. On Saturday night the festival takes on an international air, as the best fiddlers from New England and Quebec take the stage for an annual concert. It's a popular event, so plan to arrive 30 minutes early for a good seat. Early arrivals also get the best location at the parade that marches through the center of Saint Albans on Sunday morning.

The Vermont Maple Festival takes place over a weekend in early April. For information, contact the Vermont Maple Festival, Box 255, Saint Albans, VT 05478; (802) 524–5800.

Inn on Lake Waramaug Maple Sugaring Festival

SHOULD YOU BE unable to make the trip to the North Country, you can avail yourself of a smaller, one-day-long festival at the homey, white Inn on Lake Waramaug in Connecticut's Litchfield Hills.

As in Saint Albans, you can become a dean of sugaring knowledge as you view demonstrations of the labor involved in harvesting New England's noteworthy nectar. Sugar makers from nearby environs set up networks of tubing connecting the inn's maples and explain different stages of the sugaring process through charts and placards.

Young people can expect a chance to tap maple stumps brought especially for this purpose and watch the sap flow. (One boy and girl will be also be honored as the festival young king and queen.)

You can then royally stuff yourself during brunch with waffles topped with Connecticut-made maple syrup, or can wait until the afternoon when dessert— syrup over homemade ice cream—is served. Sugar on snow and maple candies and jellies are also served, and arts and crafts such as leather goods, quilts, and paintings are for sale.

The event takes place on a Sunday in March. For more information, contact The Inn on Lake Waramaug, 107 North Shore Road, New Preston, CT 06777; (203) 868–0563.

Maple Days at Norlands

NORLANDS LIVING HISTORY Center in Livermore, Maine, is a working nineteenth-century farm that hosts live-in experiences for those who are willing to sleep on a corn husk mattress at night and work in the fields or churn butter during the day. For those requesting a less active look at the 1800s, Norlands schedules special festivals and events. **Maple Days**, a weekend in March, consists of a pancake breakfast, maple sundaes, and horse-drawn sled rides into the nearest sugar bush. You can lend a hand and help gather the sap or tend the boiler in the farm's little sugarhouse. A full country meal is usually served twice daily. Norlands Living History Center, RD 2, Box 3395, Livermore Falls, ME 04254; (207) 897–2236.

WHITEWATER RAFTING

Bumping along the Kennebec River on a raft in the wilds of interior Maine isn't for everyone, but experts in the sport of whitewater rafting testify that it's for many more people than some would think. Some say it is the ideal outdoor recreational sport for city folks; a way to meet the outdoors head on, to tackle Mother Nature and emerge victorious, then unwind in the less hostile swirling waters of a hot tub or in a lounge seat.

How can you tell if whitewater rafting is for you? One veteran guide says: "Ask yourself, 'Do you mind getting wet? Are you afraid of the water? Can you swim?' If you answer yes to either of the first two questions, or no to the last, don't get involved."

Another goes so far as to say that the need to swim isn't essential. Kevin Russell of Eastern River Expeditions says: "You can't swim anyway in this water and you wear lifejackets all the time." But Russell concedes, "If you are afraid of the water, you are not meant to do this."

Representatives of rafting companies throughout New England say the bulk of their customers are not outdoors-oriented but rather are out for a day trip, albeit an adventurous one. Kevin Russell says rafting is analogous to New England's favorite winter sport. "Rafting is not that much unlike skiing," says Russell, "in that there are rivers that are like bunny slopes for beginners, and we don't put people in something they can't handle. We tailor their trips to their experience and advance them as they progress." White water is categorized in classes ranging from I to V,

with the most difficult water at the high end of the scale.

Carolann Ouelette, a guide at Maine's New England Whitewater Center, stresses, "We don't like to say that it's a safe trip because there are risks that are inherent in this type of sport, but we emphasize that we are safety-conscious." New England Whitewater, like all other licensed rafting companies, makes certain that all rafts include a licensed, trained guide and stresses that it's most important for people to listen to their guides. And like all reputable companies, they begin each day with a safety talk lasting about a half hour.

Says Ouelette: "We tell how to paddle, how to get people back into the raft if they fall out, how to swim in the river, and what to do if you capsize."

A typical whitewater rafting day trip runs in the following manner, although there are variations among companies. About the time you would be normally starting your work day, you gather with your fellow raft riders to hear the important safety presentation. You will be asked to sign a waiver stating basically that you realize that you are getting involved in a physical sport and are aware that risks exist.

Then you are shuttled by bus or van from the base camp to the river, where your guide might run through a practice round of paddling commands. After that you're on the water, and depending on

MAJESTIC SCENERY SURROUNDS WHITEWATER RAFTERS AS THEY CRUISE THE RIVER.

your river and guide, you can expect to spend three to five hours that day coasting along, bouncing and bashing and bounding along the waves, smashing into swirling swells, paddling with the flow and revelling in the exhilaration of letting the waters take you. A break to take a hike into adjacent woods, or a refreshing swim in a quiet spot, is sometimes thrown in.

About noon or, depending on the rafting company, when the water riding is over, expect to replenish your batteries with an obligatory cookout, where steak is grilled by the water or under the spreading branches in the open outdoors. Vegetables, a side dish like rice, potatoes, or cole slaw, cookies, and lemonade usually accompany the main course.

Some rafting outfits substitute chicken or lobster for steak, and at least one, Zoar Outfitters in Charlemont, Massachusetts, takes an exclusive non-meat route. Explains Zoar's Karen Blom: "Most of our customers are vegetarians, so midway on the trip, on an island, we have a catered picnic lunch with seafood, pasta, or some other kind of salad, sandwiches, chips, and salsa."

And then there is the coffee—served a special way at Northern Outfitters, Inc.'s cookouts. Says Manager Jim Yearwood: "We serve only camp coffee, the way Maine guides have made it for ages. We add two raw eggs for every pound, mixing in the shell and everything. It takes the bitterness out of the coffee and makes a smooth cup."

Hard to say which could be more challenging, the rapids of the West Branch of the Penobscot or Maine guide coffee. Regardless, when the rafting is finished, you are shuttled back to the base lodge where, depending on the facilities, you are welcome to collect your thoughts or soothe tired muscles in the sheer decadence of a hot tub or sauna. (Some companies also offer two-day rafting and camping trips in which you end the first day sleeping under the pines.)

Then it's show time. Just about every whitewater company provides its customers with a slide or videotape presentation—or a combination of both—recapping the day's events.

Such a viewing might be necessary to convince yourself beyond a shadow of a doubt that you actually did it, or it could simply be a warm, dry way of reliving a fun and memorable outing. At least one lodge has a large screen television, and seeing yourself larger than life rollicking in the river might make the whole experience worthwhile.

Other than that, what is the lure? The answer you get depends on the expert you ask. Some emphasize the exclusivity and the fact that journeying the river admits people to scenery that is otherwise inaccessible. Cliff Borgeson of Saco Bound/Downeast Whitewater in New Hampshire's White Mountains offers: "It's a once in a lifetime experience, with the wild water and world-class beautiful scenery. Rafting is not available everywhere in the world—up here, Alaska, Jamaica, out West, Costa Rica."

Others mention the sense of community, good conversation with like-minded people, and a closeness that grows from sharing trust with your guide and fellow rafters, a feeling of togetherness not found in more casual outings.

But answers from guides and other masters almost always include the words "challenge" and "thrill." Karen Blom of Zoar Outfitters sums it up with, "It's the challenge of putting yourself in a situation that's a little scary, and the thrill of getting splashed and bounced around."

Kevin Russell at Eastern River Expeditions notes, "It's the thrill of running the rapids themselves. This is not a roller coaster ride where you end up on the same track you started on. There is an element of risk here. But there is also the confidence in knowing you have completed the trip."

RAFTING FANS SAY THE SENSE OF COMMUNITY WITH FELLOW RAFTERS IS A PRIME LURE OF THE SPORT.

THE RIVERS AND THE COMPANIES

SPRING IS THE natural season for whitewater rafting. Melting snow and April rains add up to heavy river flows in May and June. In addition, some rivers sputter out between Mother's and Father's Days, and before the kids are out of school, the thrill of those waterways can be gone.

However, because many of New England's rivers are dam controlled, their rafting seasons extend into October. Some companies report summer to be their busiest season, though they acknowledge that serious rafters usually take to the water in spring. They also find wet suits are required wear in the spring, since water temperatures of 45 to 50 degrees are, depending on one's point of view, excitingly brisk or downright cold in May and June. Common rafting attire in summer, when the water can range around 70 degrees, is the casual bathing suit.

In New England, Maine is the state best known for whitewater rafting.

Maine

IN NEW ENGLAND, Maine is the state best known for whitewater rafting. However, all but Rhode Island offer rafting and companies that will guide you along the waves.

In Maine, most action takes place on three rivers: the **Kennebec**, the **West Branch of the Penobscot**, and the **Dead**, all in the central part of the state. The Kennebec and the Dead bisect in a village appropriately named The Forks, giving this little town notoriety among whitewater enthusiasts; it is home to about a dozen commercial rafting enterprises. The West Branch of the Penobscot, further east, skirts the southern edge of Baxter State Park.

Because the dams on the Kennebec and Penobscot are used to create hydro power, the water releases are regular and rafting on those rivers takes place all summer. The dam on the Dead River is for flood control purposes, so there are few releases, making it mainly a spring rafting river. (However, a usual fall release prompts enthusiasts to wear T-shirts emblazoned with "I'll be there when they raise the Dead.")

Once used by the logging industry as an express lane for cyclopean trees, the Kennebec is today the Northeast's most popular rafting river. Much of it passes through imposing 12-mile-long Kennebec Gorge, scene of crashing billows and splashing waves which make for Class IV and V white water.

Because the Kennebec is deep enough to cover boulders and other impediments, it's recommended for non-experts as well as thrill seekers. Below Magic Falls, the roughest rapids on the Kennebec, is a put-in spot called Carry Brook; from here on down the river calms down, becoming Class II and III white water. It's a good place for those with small children to give whitewater rafting a whirl, and it's also a welcome spot for seasoned rafters to try their hands at guiding inflatable kayaks, available from most rafting companies.

The West Branch of the Penobscot is classified as a *drop-pool river*, meaning that it is characterized by deep drops through chutes, followed by calmer pools of water. Mount Katahdin and the other visual treats of Baxter State Park ensure that riders of this river avail themselves of the most dramatic and rugged scenery of inland Maine. It's also not unusual to see moose, bald eagles, and other wildlife along the riverbanks.

Most rafting companies begin trips on the West Branch of the Penobscot at Ripogenus Gorge, where the first two miles consist of the most turbulent churning Class V white water in the East. In this vertical-walled, rocky canyon, the river drops over 70 feet per mile and features one series of rapids known as "The Exterminator." One company recommends that only those with plenty of experience and "an aggressive 'go- for-it' nature" take on the upper section of the West Branch.

The lower section, or the next ten miles of the West Branch, is gentler, but still prone to steep drops, making for Class III and IV rapids. Although the Penobscot is especially high in May and June, it is a shallower river than the Kennebec, with exposed boulders and other obstacles throughout the rafting season.

The Dead River comes to life in early May when spring runoff makes for hefty volumes of water. The Dead is best known for its 16 miles of continuous Class III and IV white water with hardly any slow-moving stretches. It's also a remote river, far from vestiges of civilization like paved roads—in the midst of true Maine wilderness. To get a spot on a Dead guided rafting trip in spring, it is best to reserve it in January or February.

There are well over a dozen commercial rafting companies in Maine. Some of the biggest are:

Eastern River Expeditions, P.O. Box 1173, Moosehead Lake, Greenville, ME 04441: (800) 634–7238 or (207) 695–2411;

Northern Outdoors, P.O. Box 100, The Forks, ME 04985; (800) 765–7238 or (207) 663–4466;

New England Whitewater Center, Box 21, Caratunk, ME 04925; (800) 766–7238 or (207) 672–5506.

For a complete list of Maine's whitewater rafting companies, contact the Maine Publicity Bureau, Inc., 97 Winthrop Street, Hallowell, ME 04347: (207) 289–2423.

Other States

IN NEW HAMPSHIRE, Saco Bound/Downeast Whitewater leads spring trips down the Class IV Swift River in the Granite State's White Mountains. Flowing parallel to the famous Kancamagus Highway, the Swift is fed by natural watersheds as opposed to lakes, making raft trips dependent on winter runoff and spring rainfall. The Swift doesn't offer the high water volume of Maine's rivers, but its steep grades and exposed rocks offer technical whitewater expeditions.

Saco Bound/Downeast also embarks on the remote and steep Class III and IV Rapid River in the Rangeley Lakes region of western Maine, in addition to the Kennebec, Dead, and West Branch of the Penobscot. Saco Bound/Downeast Whitewater, P.O. Box 119, Center Conway, NH 03813; (603) 447–2177 or (603) 447–3801.

One or two spring water releases on the dam-controlled West River provide Class IV whitewater rafting in the town of Jamaica in southern Vermont. (There is usually a release scheduled in fall, too.) Independent rafters can take a two-mile-long shuttle ride from a state park parking lot to a put-in point on the river. There is a charge both for the shuttle and for park admission. Contact the Park Regional Manager, RR 1, Box 33, North Springfield, VT 05150; (802) 886–2215 for release dates.

Guided rafting adventures on the West are led by North American Whitewater Expeditions, with offices in both Maine and Connecticut, and by Zoar Outdoors in Charlemont, Massachusetts. Both also lead trips on the comparatively placid but rocky Deerfield River, with its Class III rapids. The Deerfield, which begins in southwestern Vermont and empties into the Connecticut River in northern Massachusetts, is an ideal beginner and intermediate-level river. North American Whitewater Expeditions,

663–4439 or (203) 245–8860; Zoar Outdoors, P.O. Box 245, Charlemont, MA 01339; (413) 339–4010.

Connecticut residents who don't wish to travel far from home can embark on rapid-riding trips from mid-March through April on the Class IV and V Housatonic River at Bulls Bridge Gorge. The run is short but technical, best for experienced rafters, and is located in a quiet corner of the state. North American Whitewater Expeditions (a staff member called this part of the Housatonic "a last gem in Connecticut, as close as it is to New York City") and Riverrunning Expeditions, Ltd., Main Street, Falls Village, CT 06031; (203) 824–5579 lead rafting tours here.

Keep in mind that many of these rafting centers also offer aquatic adventures on canoes and kayaks, as well as hiking, biking, or horseback riding trips.

Saint Patrick's Day

Saint Patrick was born late in the fourth century in a part of the sprawling Roman Empire that is in present-day Wales. Chances are he never raised the dead or drove the snakes from Ireland.

Sorry to be the bearer of such disagreeable news, but when you are swigging a mug of green beer, listening to an authentic Celtic air played on cittern and fiddle, or watching the rhinestone and feather-bedecked Mummers parade down Beech Street in Holyoke, what difference will historical facts make anyway?

Trish Murphy, an Irish-American craftswoman who makes and sells Claddagh rings (which have a unique design consisting of hands, a heart, and a crown), once stated to me at an Irish fair, "We have an expression—For an Englishman it could be serious, but it's never hopeless; for an Irishman it could be hopeless, but it's never serious." This Murphy's law sums up the spirit of St. Patrick's Day in New England.

For an Englishman it could be serious, but it's never hopeless; for an Irishman it could be hopeless, but it's never serious.

For the record, the man who would become known as St. Patrick was a fervent sinner kidnapped from Wales by Irish invaders when he was in his mid-teens, then sold into slavery. While working as a shepherd in County Antrim, he renounced his sinful past and expressed his faith in God. He later escaped from Ireland and studied in a monastery in Gaul before returning to the Emerald Isle years later as its second bishop. Gifted with an engaging personality,

Patrick was successful in gaining converts, and for three decades he traveled up and down the island establishing churches and monasteries. Patrick is said to have died in County Down on March 17, in the year 461.

The St. Patrick's Parade in Holyoke, Massachusetts

THE BADGE OF Irish pride in western New England, this parade annually draws 15,000 participants and a quarter of a million spectators (never mind that it's televised locally to another 100,000 observers). Dominic Kiernan, Lord Mayor of Wexford, Ireland, a frequent visitor, was asked why he returns. "I've seen quite a few parades around the world and the United States and at home and this is really a whole family celebration. That's what's so great about Holyoke and why Holyoke stands above all other parades."

What started as a single-day event in 1952 has grown into a three-month-long festivity, with dinners and pageants preceding the big three-hour-long procession the Sunday after St. Patrick's Day. About 30 bands, pared down from a potential list of over 100, participate. Don't be surprised to hear numerous ren-

PHILADELPHIA'S RENOWNED SPLASHY MUMMERS ARE AN ANNUAL SIGHT AT HOLYOKE'S ST. PATRICK'S PARADE.

ditions of "When Irish Eyes are Smiling" over the course of the day—from kilted pipers, precise drum and bugle corps, and Philadelphia's splashy Mummers—before the last float makes its way up High Street.

The parade begins its long trek on Northampton Street near the intersection with South Street. It turns right onto Beech Street, then right onto Hampden Street and right once more onto High Street, where it ends near the corner with Appleton Street. You will have the luck of the Irish if you find a bleacher seat in front of the television booth and broadcasting area on Beech Street, since most bands can be counted on to perform for the cameras.

Parking is never an easy chore. Recommended parking areas are the lot at Holyoke High School near the broadcasting area and the garages on Dwight Street (east of High Street) and High Street (between Suffolk and Appleton Streets). From Interstate 91, take exit 17 or 16 east to the parade route. For more information, contact (413) 533–1700.

Boston's Parade

THE BAY STATE'S other famous St. Patrick's Day caravan tramps down the streets of South Boston and commemorates both the neighborhood's Irish heritage and Evacuation Day, for it was on March 17, 1776, when the British were forced out of Boston. About a third of a million from Southie and elsewhere line the parade route, down West and East Broadway, along East Fourth Street, around Thomas Park, and on Telegraph Street, finally ending at Andrew Square.

You can tell you are approaching the parade route when you see the green, white, and orange flags of Ireland supplementing the American flags hanging outside South Boston homes. Blues Brothers imitators and celebrants with green hair lend further hints that you are closing in on the action. For further information, contact the Boston Mayor's Office at (617) 725–3911.

The St. Patrick's Day Celebration at Brodie Mountain

GREEN SNOW, GREEN beer, and green eggs and ham are there for your viewing and dining pleasure, and if your name is Kelly, no greenbacks are necessary to enjoy all three. Any place known as **Kelly's Irish Alps** is a natural setting for a major league St. Patrick's Day blowout and this Berkshire Mountains ski area in New Ashford, just north of Pittsfield, is home to perhaps the biggest in New England, lasting up to a week.

Leprechauns are everywhere, and there are shamrocks painted on faces and on the snow, says spokesman Matt Kelly, one of several Kellys employed at this family-run ski area, where the trails bear names like Irish Stew, Harp's Hump, Killarney, and Paddy's Promenade.

For the athlete, the **Irish Olympics** is the premier attraction. Entrants glide, slide, and coast down hills on everything but skis; dinner trays, inner tubes, and canoes are common vehicles. They also take part in several obstacle races, and in a display of sheer derangement, hurl themselves into what could be described as a giant melting snowcone, in **Brodie's Slush Jumping Contest**. The object is to ski down a hill and create the biggest and best splash in a five-foot-deep hole of slush. It's not unusual to get 400 entrants to toss themselves into this mammoth slush hole. Why? According to Matt Kelly, "because it's there."

The green snow that blankets a big section of the base area and other sporadic spots was once produced with green dye. After skiers complained of irremovable stains on their clothing, the dye was replaced with a secret formula which, says Matt Kelly, washes right off. Adding to the atmosphere is "T-Bear the lepre-hound," a dog weighing in at about five pounds who dons a green suit including vest and a hat marked with shamrocks. Another dog, named Otis, has been known to ski down the slopes while humans bearing green, white, or orange flares take part in the torchlight parade down mile-long Shamrock Trail.

Serious skiers, meanwhile, compete in the **Brodie Mountain Pro Cup Race**, also on Shamrock Trail, a regular event since 1967 and reported by Brodie personnel to be the oldest continuously running professional ski race in North America. Over $1,500 in cash and prizes are awarded, with special categories for ski school instructors, women, and amateurs.

On the cultural side of the blotter, the country ballads and minstrels of the Emerald Isle can be heard live on the holiday itself—and depending on when the seventeenth falls, on the day before or after, too—in the Blarney Room and in Kelly's Irish Pub, both located in the main lodge. Entertainers adept on the pipes, fiddle, and guitar have annually made the cross-Atlantic leap from Dublin and Cork to perform at Brodie during this festive event.

An Irish jig demonstration is often scheduled, and those who haven't shown their stuff on the slopes can try their luck in the Irish jig contest. The Brodie Colleen Contest, a search for "a pure morsel of feminine pulchritude," according to Brodie staff, is open to women over 21; the winner will be on hand to give out awards following contests and will also receive day passes.

On the menu in Kelly's Cafe, straight from the pages of Dr. Seuss, are green eggs and ham (first thing in the morning, yet!) while an Irish corned beef and cabbage dinner is the main course at the gala St. Paddy's Day Party in the Blarney Room. And don't forget the endless shades of green beer.

And don't forget the endless shades of green beer.

Skiers wearing green receive discounts on their lift tickets while those named Kelly are truly gifted. If they can prove their name with a picture ID card, they ski free all day. Brodie Mountain, Route 7, New Ashford, MA 01237; (413) 443–4752.

Smugglers' Notch

BRODIE MAY HAVE the biggest St. Patrick's Day bash, but it is hardly the only one. **Smugglers' Notch** in Vermont has also boasted green snow in past years, and often honors the holiday with a silly slalom featuring participants in appropriate green hats. Smugglers' Notch lounges are the sites of live Irish music, and there is usually a special St. Patrick's Day brew or cocktail on hand concocted for revellers. (802) 644–8851.

Irish History Tour of Boston

Uncommon Boston, a purveyor of specialized tours and customized events, offers an annual St. Patrick's trek tracing the history of the Irish in the place perceived as the most Irish city west of Dublin. It lasts from two to two and a half hours and leaves its guests filled with information, as well as corned beef and cabbage, a refrain from an Irish lilt, and perhaps an Irish ale or two.

The tour has traditionally traced Boston's Irish history chronologically, starting in the North End—the premier Irish neighborhood following the potato famine that devastated Ireland in the late 1840s—and ending at an Irish tavern like the Black Rose in Quincy Market. In between, stops are likely at the L Street Bathhouse, Carson Beach, Rose Fitzgerald Kennedy's birthplace, and the statue of Mayor James Michael Curley, outside Faneuil Hall Marketplace. If Boston's St. Patrick's Day parade is taking place, that is also fitted into the schedule.

You hear tales of Boston's Irish past imparted by knowledgeable tour guides such as Alan Winecour, who states that the L Street Bathhouse was created out of necessity at a time when many newly arrived Irish immigrants in South Boston lacked bathtubs and toilets in their homes. Winecour also stops in the financial district, once a teeming Irish neighborhood known as Fort Hill. It was around the year 1868, offers Winecour, that Fort Hill was demolished so the city would have needed space for expansion. Since the timing coincidentally followed an influx of about 50,000 Irish immigrants, one theory has always been that it was a ploy among the establishment to rid the city of the Irish.

In addition to satisfying his guests' appetites for knowledge, Winecour doesn't overlook their biological appetites. A stop for food and music at a pub like the Black Rose, a gathering spot for Boston's newest crop of Irish residents, is a fitting ending for the tour. Uncommon Boston, 437 Boylston Street, 4th floor, Boston, MA 02116; (617) 731-5854.

You hear tales of Boston's Irish past imparted by knowledgeable tour guides.

SPRING SKIING

Don't be misled by temperatures in the 40s or even the 50s. Rain falling on the streets where you live can mean half a foot of new snow on the ski slopes.

But if you feel as comfortable wearing skis as you would driving a tank, you don't need to feel left out. Several athletic events, like mogul contests and slaloms, draw hundreds of non-skiing spectators. The rising mercury in March and April makes the wide white outdoors a much more comfortable arena than you would have found just weeks earlier. And there are food festivals and other annual pastimes for which the grandeur of the mountains provides a stunning setting and you don't even need to look at a single pair of skis.

Of course, those out for skiing action have been heading to Tuckerman Ravine in New Hampshire's

White Mountains since the days when skis were made of wood—only wood. It is one of the few places in the country where people can expect to ski into June.

Sunday River

TODAY JUST ABOUT any ski area boasting snow-making ability—and most of the bigger areas apply—promises skiing after the calendar announces the vernal equinox. How long afterwards can vary greatly. Some, like **Sunday River** in Bethel, Maine, deliver skiing well into May. In fact, Sunday River offers free skiing to all comers on May 1. They also attract springtime visitors with an array of special events drawing the likes of both skillful skiers and chili chefs.

The powder flies as bump-bashers maneuver themselves over moguls on Sunday River's slopes at the **Bust 'n' Burn Mogul Competition** in April. You can expect over 150 skiers, from loyal regulars to experts from out West, to take part in this contest, and hundreds more are usually on hand to watch. Skiers are categorized by age and gender and take part in a qualifying round on Saturday. On Sunday, qualifiers are seeded and ski one-on-one in a "bump-off." Thousands of dollars of ski equipment are awarded to winners. The performances are choreographed to music from the last two decades, and trailside barbecues keep spectators from going hungry.

No one starves at the **"Eat the Heat" Chili Cook-off** in late March, either. A few dozen entrants, appropriately bedecked in costumes relating to themselves or their chili, have their offerings judged on taste, aroma, texture, spiciness, and other categories. To paraphrase an old political adage, if you can't stand the heat, stay out of the chili cook-off.

Heat of another kind brings Ski Patrol members from across New England to the slopes of Bethel. This is **White Heat,** where you will find Sunday River's steepest and widest trails, and the home of the **Toboggan Challenge**. In this relay event, teams race down trails in both loaded and unloaded sleds, and are judged on speed and technique (the proper way to bring a seriously injured skier down a hill). Spectators are encouraged and a "wound-licking party" follows. Sunday River, P.O. Box 450, Bethel, ME 04217; (207) 824–2187.

Vermont

FOR SPRINGTIME POPULARITY at **Mount Snow**, it's hard to beat the **"Glade-iator of the Year" Contest**, another showcase for bump skiers. Grouped accord-

ing to age, participants tackle the steepest and most difficult trails, and are awarded points for aerials (the total number of jumps they accomplish) and speed. Judges subtract points for each fall, and any skier who loses his or her skis is disqualified. Preliminaries take place on Saturday and the finals are on Sunday. About 800 spectators watch this early April competition.

A ski with a seat mounted on it might sound like the winter equivalent of a rider lawn mower, but it takes a great deal of skill to propel yourself downhill on one. These specially fitted skis are called *jack jumps*, and are used by lumberjacks and ski lift operators. In the **Paul Holland Memorial Jack Jump Racc**, an annual March event, competitors race through a dual slalom course and are clocked just as conventional skiers would be. Trophies and cash prizes are awarded to the winners.

Should you wish to take home something other than sore muscles as a remembrance of your ski trip, plan a visit during Mount Snow's **Vermont Products Day**, held in late March. About five or ten venders sell foods and crafts, all made in the Green Mountain State. The expected, like cheese and maple syrup, are supplemented by the less typical, such as chocolate sauce or ketchup. For a teasing taste of the upcoming warm weather, take to the slopes during **Daylight Skiing Time** in April when the lifts stay open until 6 P.M. and an outdoor barbecue is on the menu. Mount Snow, Mount Snow, VT 05356; (802) 464-3333.

The longer days of March make for some of the biggest bumps on **Mount Mansfield**, where the **Stowe Bump Contest** takes place on a late March or early April Sunday. Some of the best hotdog skiers in the East head north for this event.

However, Mount Mansfield is also home to one of New England's most long-standing spring ski meets. The **Stowe Sugar Slalom** coincides with Vermont's maple sap harvest in early April. Since 1940 this race has drawn skiers to Stowe, and the number of entrants today approaches 450 racers. Qualifying runs are held Saturday morning on North Slope, cutting the field to about 100 skiers who compete Sunday. You will find some entrants purely out for fun, while others are dead serious and out to improve their Federation Internationale des Ski (the governing body for ski racers) standings. All racers and spectators are invited afterwards to the sugarhouse just off the Nosedive Trail, where free sugar on snow is offered.

Mount Mansfield, P.O. Box 1310, Stowe, VT 05672; (802) 253–7311.

Another showcase for the best of the bump artists gets underway at **Killington** in early April. This weekend event, **the Bear Mountain Mogul Challenge**, is a favorite that annually lures over 1,000 spectators. It is held on Bear Mountain, Killington's steepest, and about 200 top mogul competitors match skills. Qualifying rounds are held Saturday with the field whittled down to 32 men and 16 women for the Sunday finals.

Not everything at Killington is so serious. Late April's **Superstar Weekend** finds skiers out for fun locking horns with each other, as well as moguls and other obstacles. You may have to ski around railroad ties or barrels, or doff your skis and high-step through a dozen big, fat tires in the obstacle race. Snow volleyball is another likely event, as are a mogul competition and a talent show.

To leave no doubts regarding the longevity of their ski season, Killington has hosted a **May Day Fun Slalom** every year since 1962. For this race, intermediate and advanced skiers take on either Sky Peak or Killington Peak. The first 200 skiers who register and complete the course receive a mid-week day-long lift ticket for the following season. When the gods of winter have been especially generous, Killington also entertains guests at the **June First Fun Slalom** with similar competitions and a complimentary barbecue. Killington, Ltd., Killington, VT 05751; (802) 422–3333.

Okemo Mountain in Ludlow extols the oncoming spring in mid-March with its **Ski and Swing Spring Spree** (try and say that three times fast), for which ski boots and dancing shoes are required footwear.

In the daytime is the **Bumps and Bamboo Contest**, an event popular in the western United States. Skiers first race in the morning in a timed giant slalom run, which is the "bamboo" portion of the meet, named for the sticks. In the afternoon they partake in a freestyle mogul run for the "bump" part. Combined scores from the two races produce the winner. At nighttime is a shake-the-winter-blahs beach party. Wear your straw hat, flip flops, and bathing suits, and compete for best dance honors. Okemo Mountain, RFD 1, Ludlow, VT 05149; (802) 228–4041.

A taste of bayou country is yours at **Burke Mountain** in Lyndonville. For mid-March's **Cajun Crawfish Festival**, this ski area in northern Vermont ships in upwards of 500 pounds of crawfish from south Louisiana. They are boiled outdoors, and

TARA EBERHARD, A U.S. OPEN SNOWBOARD CHAMPION, IS SUSPENDED HIGH ABOVE
THE SLOPES OF STRATTON MOUNTAIN, SITE OF THE ANNUAL CHAMPIONSHIPS.

patrons dine under a tent to live Cajun or zydeco music.

Later in March is Burke Mountain's **Surf's Up Beach Party**. A massive, man-made puddle, about 30 by 20 feet, is built at the bottom of the area's training hill. Skiers—most garbed in beach outfits—begin their descent high on the hill and try to jump over the puddle. After the first round, the combatants try again from a lower starting point, making it harder to build up speed. As the race proceeds, skiers start closer and closer to the base, until just one remains. The winner gets a small prize, like a record or a gift certificate. The losers go splash. Burke Mountain, P.O. Box 247, East Burke, VT 05832; (802) 626–3305.

Stratton Mountain, a pioneer among eastern ski areas in welcoming snowboarders to its slopes, hosts the **U.S. Open Snowboarding Championships** in either late March or early April. For three days crowds, which in the past have numbered in the thousands, come to watch the country's top men and women show their best efforts in what might be called the closest thing to surfing on snow. Participants vie for fastest finishing times in meets like the dual slalom and giant slalom, whereas they are judged on the difficulty and fluidity of their turns and flips in a competition called the half pipe. The Stratton Corporation, Stratton Mountain, VT 05155; (802) 297–2200.

New Hampshire

CIVIL ENGINEERS MIGHT make the best competitors at **Loon Mountain**'s Cardboard Box Classic at their **Spring Fling Weekend.** The rules are simple. Take a cardboard box, and using only tape, fashion yourself a vehicle that will slide fast down a snow-covered hill. Use no staples, no wood, no metal, nothing other than tape and cardboard.

A Loon Mountain spokesperson says entries for this . . . well . . . loony event range from the sophisticated to the basic. Creations all depend on which awards their creators are gunning for. Prizes are given for both appearance—mainly originality and design—and time. Often a simple design makes for the fastest box.

That doesn't stop many of the 30 or 40 contestants from plugging their creativity into high gear. One entrant carved out a cardboard shark with a cardboard leg in its mouth; the concoction was labeled: "Jaws III—The Great White Shark Meets the Great

White Mountain." There have also been giant skiing cardboard beer cans, jets, and railroad locomotives. Since the vehicles lack brakes, they coast down a fairly small portion of the hill. A good time is about nine seconds; a slow mover can take up to a minute.

Break from the Cardboard Box Classic with a hot dog or hamburger fresh from an outdoor barbecue grill. Then watch or take part in other events, like a NASTAR race, a mogul contest, and a children's race.

For serious, but not necessarily expert skiers, Loon offers its **Governor Adams Cup Race** on a late March Saturday. It's a non-sanctioned citizen giant slalom that usually draws a couple hundred racers. Loon Mountain, Lincoln, NH 03251; (603) 745–8111.

Loon Mountain has no monopoly on looniness. Things get pretty wild over at **Wildcat** during its **Corn Snow Caper**, named for common springtime snow that has melted and refrozen a number of times to form a rough, granular texture. The two-day snow ball is family oriented and designed for both parents and children. However, one Wildcat staffer says, "Many adults seem to wimp out of the costume parade, but I think it's good for kids to see their parents cut loose."

Parade entrants need only to dress in any costume they can wear while skiing. A Wildcat employee in a cat outfit serves as a pseudo-grand marshal and leads the pack. Children have been known to masquerade as anything from Cinderella to a Big Mac with an accompanying tot decked as a French fry. And one time six adults encased themselves in a cardboard container and wore tin foil caps, impersonating a six-pack.

The **Silly Slalom**, another Corn Snow Caper activity, is a snow-borne obstacle race. Those who enlist must complete a course, sans skis but on snow, that will take them up and down hill, over and under slalom poles, and across hay bales, for example. They might also be requested to toss a basketball into a bucket, or whirl a hula hoop over a cone. It always ends with a toboggan run.

Also part of the Caper weekend are a mogul contest and a standard slalom. You can enter any or all of the quartet of activities, but only those who enter all four are eligible to be named king, queen, prince, or princess of the weekend, qualifying them for small prizes awarded when it's all finished. Wildcat Mountain, Pinkham Notch, Route 16, Jackson, NH 03846; (603) 466–3326.

Pigskin meets powder with the annual New England Patriots **Rites of Spring** fund raiser in March. The Pats take to the slopes at both Wildcat and Attitash, managing to find time for a bit of tackle in the snow and autograph signing, too.

The **Old Man of the Mountains** isn't just a White Mountains landmark. It's the name of an April race in **Attitash** attracting, shall we say, more mature skiers. Only those over 40 qualify, and thanks to an age-handicapped scoring system, the oldest have the best chances of winning. In previous years, winners of the Old Man race have been 67, 75, and 89 years old.

And yes, though she doesn't merit her own rock formation, Attitash acknowledges an Old Lady of the Mountains winner. Additional honors are the Feisty Lady Award, judged on aggressiveness, the Rookie of the Year Award to 40-year-old kids, and the Caterpillar Award for the slowest skier.

One Attitash staff member, who has many years to go until he qualifies, said of the Old Man of the Mountains race: "It sounds as if these guys are old and slow but I wouldn't want to compete against some of them. A lot are former champions."

New England businesses go head to head at Attitash's **Eastern Corporate Ski Championships** in mid-March. Four-person teams representing their companies race in a slalom and giant slalom, with winners copping top prizes including vacations and ski equipment. Following the lead of other ski centers, Attitash now presents **Spring Mania**, with snow volleyball, barbecues, live music, and plenty of skiing. Spring Mania is held in early April. Attitash, Route 302, Bartlett, NH 03812; (603) 374–2368.

Their neighbors at **Waterville Valley** keep a low profile. One spokesperson says, "We have impromptu festive events as the mood strikes us." Skiing can continue into late April here, and spring barbecues in the base lodge are likely. Waterville Valley, Inc., Waterville Valley, NH 03215; (603) 236–8311.

RETURN OF THE BLOSSOMS

R elishing the arrival of spring is like taking off a pair of too-tight shoes.

The first signs of spring might be the melting snow

and the flowing sap. The second sign is likely the budding trees. The third sign could be the greening grass.

But spring really hasn't sprung until the blossoms come out of hiding. With the blooming plants out come the short pants. And the short sleeves. Or no sleeves. The mercury hits the 70s, and life seems worth living once more. Men and women fall in love all over again and want to do something crazy . . . I mean really crazy . . . like wash the car or clean the garage, something no person in his or her right mind would find appealing any other time of year.

Should you want to partake in something safer or less messy, head to any of the special events in New England that celebrate the return of the blossoms. There are many showcasing the lilacs, the daffodils, and assorted other flowers. Perhaps the most long-standing, however, is the Dogwood Festival, a tradition in Fairfield, Connecticut, since 1936, and still run entirely by volunteers.

DOGWOOD FESTIVAL

APPROXIMATELY 30,000 DOGWOODS in the Greenfield Hill section of Fairfield are the true stars of this eight-day-long, mid-May event. For what seems like ages, nature lovers paraded through Greenfield Hill to see the white and pink dogwoods in full bloom. So many came, in fact, that in 1936 some area women decided to sell handmade crafts and pickles on a card table in front of the tall-spired Greenfield Hill Congregational Church. Responding to requests from the dogwood peepers, they later offered punch, cookies, and sandwiches. As the years went by, increasing numbers of visitors meant more and more crafts and food for sale, until finally the festival was spawned.

Today you will find at the Dogwood Festival everything but pickles. Handcrafts, for example, are both sold and demonstrated. Perhaps you can observe a weaver, a blacksmith, or a sheep shearer on the village green when you visit.

There is art for both sale and display from local professionals like Steven Dohanos, Jo Michael Polseno, Hillary Longmuir, Evelyn Butterfield, and Heidi Lindy.

There are special activities. The year we visited, the fest took on a medieval air as a young woman joined hands with visiting children and danced around a flower-topped maypole on the green. Then we chat-

A MEDIEVAL TOUCH AT FAIRFIELD'S DOGWOOD FESTIVAL
IS THIS FLOWER-CROWNED MAYPOLE ON THE GREEN.

SOME DOGWOODS ARE NATIVE WHILE OTHERS ARE JAPANESE IMPORTS.
THE GREENFIELD HILL CONGREGATIONAL CHURCH, HOWEVER, IS ALL-AMERICAN.

ted with a gardening author who was signing books in the plant tent.

There is food: picnic lunches are for sale and a seated luncheon is scheduled on weekdays.

There is a children's tent, where youngsters can delight in making tissue flowers or having their faces used as canvases.

And there are the blossoms, blossoms, everywhere, on the village green and along the neighboring residential streets. One festival spokeswoman says the best area thoroughfares on which to see dogwoods in bloom are Bronson Road, Old Academy Road, and Congress Street. The pure white dogwoods you see are native to Fairfield and were growing wild in the woods when this area was settled in the seventeenth century. But they didn't line roadsides until 1795, when a Dr. Isaac Bronson transplanted several from the woods.

There is no such long heritage for the pink dogwoods which, in what might be considered foreshadowing, are Japanese imports, brought to Fairfield around the turn of the twentieth century. In fact, a festival spokeswoman told how it was a status symbol to have Japanese dogwoods in your yard back then, the way wearing a Rolex watch or driving a Mercedes-Benz is today.

History here transcends flower plantings, though. To get a grasp on the early American legacy of this present-day bedroom community, you can take a heritage walking tour into the neighborhood's private gardens and backyards, led by guides dressed in colonial fashions.

None other than Frederick Law Olmstead, America's best-known landscape architect and designer of New York City's Central Park and Boston's Common, designed and built the formal English garden in back of the nearby Varick Dey House, seen on the 30-minute-long tour. Typically English, it consists of a boxwood hedge symmetrically placed around lawn paths, statuary, and fountains.

The garden's tulips are reminiscent of the seventeenth century, when "tulipmania" overtook Europe and tulips were traded like corporate stocks, commodities, or real estate. You will hear on the walking tour that two bulbs were adequate for a dowry and a man once sold his factory for a pair of bulbs. There is also the tale of the hungry sailor who while at sea mistook a tulip bulb for an onion and ate it. He was put to death.

The delicately balanced Varick Dey House contains a Palladian window, a common touch on area homes. The house was the residence of a popular minister who served at the Greenfield Hill Congregational Church for six years in the 1820s. The best known of the church's leaders, however, was Timothy Dwight, Revolutionary War chaplain, Yale University president, and progressive educator.

The Dogwood Festival always takes place in mid-May. Admission to the majority of festival events is free. Greenfield Hill Congregational Church, 1045 Old Academy Road, Fairfield, CT 06430; (203) 259–5596.

OTHER FESTIVALS

FOLLOWING ARE SOME other special festivals in honor of the returning blossoms of late spring.

Massachusetts

THOUSANDS OF DAFFODILS highlight **Brewster in Bloom**, a weekend-long late April bash in this former sea captains' community on Cape Cod. A full array of floral activities include flower arranging demonstrations, bulb displays, and the judging of daffodil plantings. Brewster's distinctive bed and breakfast inns open up for a home tour, lobsters and clams are baked, and wine, cheese, and herb-seasoned delicacies are tasted. And what would a small town fiesta be without a Main Street parade? The Brewster Board of Trade, P.O. Box 1241, Brewster, MA 02631; (508) 896–8088.

A parade of antique cars decked with daffodils is one annual occurrence during Nantucket's **Daffodil Festival**, a late April celebration on this combination resort island and living museum. The mobile, floral procession takes place on Saturday of the festival weekend, as cars motor their way from the town of Nantucket to Siasconset, where they set up elaborate tailgate picnics; judges award ribbons for originality, beauty, and design. Storekeepers decorate their windows with daffodils and are also awarded honors.

If you simply wish to view the fields of yellow bulbous flowers backed by the briny sea, you might want to visit when the festival isn't taking place and there are fewer crowds to contend with. Nantucket Chamber of Commerce, Nantucket, MA 02554; (508) 228–1700.

A Victorian pace of life is also the rule at the Arnold Arboretum's **Lilac Sunday** in the Jamaica Plain section of Boston. Usually the third Sunday in May, this is the only day in the year when the arboretum staff permits picnicking on the grounds; food venders selling fresh-squeezed lemonade, salads to go, or hot dogs are there almost to emphasize the permissiveness. (One year the arboretum even tried offering lilac sundaes with purple ice cream, but nasty weather prevailed and the staff was stuck with a glut of the stuff.) Morris dancers and musicians are often on hand as visitors stroll among the lilacs or gather information from experts regarding the planting and caring of lilacs. The Arnold Arboretum of Harvard University, 125 Arborway, Jamaica Plain, MA 02130; (617) 524–1718.

The folks at Nashoba Valley Winery in Bolton, Massachusetts, have one clear goal—to inform wine snobs that fruit wines are to be taken as seriously as grape wines. They produce dry white, red, semisweet, and dessert wines made from apples, pears, blueberries, cranberries, plums, and other regionally grown fruits. To show off their grounds as well as their distinctive spirits, the Nashoba Valley people schedule several one-day festivals throughout the year.

The biggest treat for the eyes might be May's **Apple Blossom Festival**, when the hillside apple orchard is in full bloom. Complementing the winery's blessed blossoms might be craftpersons weaving wall hangings or caning chairs, or morris dancers stepping up a storm. Traditional or folk music is usually performed, and wine making and tasting is, of course, a natural. Later on, Nashoba Valley celebrates the berries, with a **Strawberryfest** in June and a **Raspberryfest** in July. Nashoba Valley Winery, 100 Wattaquadoc Hill Road, Bolton, MA 01740; (508) 779–5521.

Want to add some spice to your life? The Thornton Burgess Society in East Sandwich on Cape Cod presents its annual **Herb Festival** in mid-May. The clichéd quartet of parsley, sage, rosemary, and thyme make way for less famous herbs, like chocolate mint, sweet cicely, baby's breath, and lungwort, the latter a source of blue and pink flowers despite the odious name. Herbs are made into crafts, tea, and salads and are added into main courses and desserts. They are offered for sale and tasting and are the topics of lectures. The event lasts two weekend days.

The Thornton W. Burgess Society is a non-profit nature and conservation association named in honor of Burgess, a children's author and creator of Peter Rabbit of the Briar Patch. Year-round, the society maintains the Green Briar Nature Center & Jam Kitchen, with walking trails, a wildflower garden, and art and natural history exhibits, as well as a museum devoted to the life and creations of the author. Thornton W. Burgess Society, 6 Discovery Hill Road, East Sandwich, MA 02537; (508) 888–6870.

Vermont

IF YOU HAVE ever wondered what it would have been like to step into a Victorian-era garden party, you should plan a visit to **Lilac Sunday**, scheduled for late May at the Shelburne Museum in Shelburne, just south of Burlington, Vermont. You can stand among the idle wealthy dressed in their nineteenth-century best and take mallet to ball in genteel games like croquet and lawn bowling. Then take a ride in a horse-drawn antique carriage led by a driver in period clothing. Or sip a cup of tea as the tender tones of a string quartet soothe your twentieth-century frazzled soul.

All this is in honor of the Shelburne Museum's renowned lilac gardens. (Of course, the term "museum" for this multi-building complex is a bit of a misnomer, since this is a museum like Windsor castle is a split-level.) The gardens contain 400 plants representing more than 90 varieties of one of museum founder Electra Havemeyer Webb's favorite plants. Walking tours through the fragrant lilac gardens—as well as through the museum's apple tree and herb gardens—are also on tap. For information on this foray into the days when presidents all had beards and it was an insult not to be titled a lady or gentleman, contact Shelburne Museum, Shelburne, VT 05482; (802) 985–3346.

Connecticut

HAMDEN, CONNECTICUT, CELEBRATES goldenbells, a.k.a. forsythia, radiant yellow in color and blooming by the thousands in late April and early May. The **Goldenbells Festival**, a happening since 1971, covers three weeks beginning mid-April and showcases the arts, athletics, and nature. Join a hiking expedi-

GUIDES DRESSED IN THEIR VICTORIAN BEST POPULATE THE GROUNDS AT SHELBURNE MUSEUM'S LILAC SUNDAY.

tion into Sleeping Giant Park, or view wildflowers on a guided tour. Then it might be show time at a concert given by the Hamden Symphony Orchestra, Town Hall, Hamden, CT 06518; (203) 248–3077.

Connecticut's Bartlett Arboretum offers a trio of guided walks designed to show off its extensiveness. The **Wildflower Walk** in May will acquaint you with their carpets of bright yellow lesser celandine and delicate white wood anemone, in addition to other profuse flowers. In late May is a **Rhododendron and Azalea Walk**, while June is the time for the **Conifer Walk**, when the arboretum's collections of dwarf conifers and witches'-broom are the center of attention. Bartlett Arboretum, University of Connecticut, 151 Brookdale Road, Stamford, CT 06903; (203) 322–6971.

Dinosaur State Park in Rocky Hill hosts its own **Spring Wildflower Walk** in May, along its nature trails. A slide show can accompany the walk. (203) 529–8423.

Maine

FIDDLEHEADS ARE NOT violin addicts. They are fern fronds that grow coiled and are an upcountry delicacy. At the Maine State **Fiddlehead Festival** in Unity, held in May, this little green morsel is eaten in quiche, ravioli, doughnuts, soup, bread, cupcakes, and other forms. One year a standard three-bean salad was transformed into a two-bean and fiddle-head salad. Meanwhile, live bluegrass music, a craft exhibition and sale (slate art and pack baskets have been sold in the past), and a talent show keep the assembled fiddlehead heads entertained between bites. Public Relations, Unity College, HC 78, Box 1, Unity, ME 04988; (207) 948–3131, ext. 235.

Fiddleheads are not violin addicts.

NEW ENGLAND'S NOTEWORTHY GARDENS

SPRING MIGHT BE the most symbolic time to appreciate nature's floral bonanza, but most of New England's gardens bloom into early fall. Some, in fact, are at their peak in summer, while others merit an inspection several times a year. Here are several of the most respected garden spots in our six states.

BLITHEWOLD GARDENS AND ARBORETUM The
anxiously awaited bulb display at this mansion and grounds near Newport, Rhode Island, shines for visi-

A WALK IN THE SPRINGTIME AT GARDEN IN THE WOODS MEANS KEEPING COMPANY
WITH PRIMROSES, PHLOX, SWEET WOODRUFF, AND CRESTED IRIS.

tors from mid-April through mid-May when over 20,000 crocuses, daffodils, and tulips bloom. In late April, Arbor Day is celebrated with grounds tours and outdoor activities for children. In May is an annual plant sale of annuals, perennials, vegetables, and herbs.

An array of exotic trees and shrubs supplement the rose, rock, and water gardens. Included among the odd specimens are a Chinese toon tree, ginkgos, a bamboo grove, and a giant sequoia, eighty feet tall and the largest of this type east of the Rockies. There is also a trio of beeches on the north lawn resembling members of the Van Wickle family that originally owned the mansion and gardens. The grounds are open year-round. The mansion may be visited mid-April through October, but is closed Mondays and holidays. Admission is charged. Ferry Road, Bristol, RI; (401) 253–2707.

GARDEN IN THE WOODS

At the botanical garden of the New England Wild Flower Society, 45 acres burst with 1,500 varieties of plants. May and early June explode with yellow, white, or crimson primroses, blue wood phlox, sweet-scented sweet woodruff,

THERE IS A VISTA OF FLORAL COLOR AT THE BERKSHIRE BOTANICAL GARDENS IN SPRING.

and crested iris. First to appear for the year, however, is showy trillium, one of 22 varieties of trillium blooming throughout the garden. In spring the floral show changes about every two weeks. Visit in early May, mid-May, and early June, and you will see varied blossoms on parade each time. Guided walks are offered throughout the season, lasting into October. Admission is charged. Hemenway Road, Framingham, MA; (508) 877–6574 for a recording listing events and hours; (617) 237–4924 to speak with a human.

BERKSHIRE BOTANICAL GARDENS

Set among the hills of western Massachusetts are the Berkshire Botanical Gardens. In springtime walk the center's primrose path for a vista of floral color. Late spring and summer is the time for the day lilies to show off. The center also maintains landscaped gardens, a terraced herb garden, a rose garden, and a wooded walking path while herbs, begonias, and vegetables are shown in raised beds and window boxes. Admission is charged. Routes 102 and 183, Stockbridge, Massachusetts; (413) 298–3926.

VERMONT WILDFLOWER FARM

This is a cousin of Massachusetts's Garden in the Woods, with six acres of wildflowers adorning the grounds in Charlotte, 12 miles south of Burlington. In May this garden is a sea of white, thanks to the great white trillium in bloom, which crave the limy soil found here near the shore of Lake Champlain. Head to the farm in June to inspect the buttercups, daisies, red poppies, and numerous other flowers. There are hundreds of wildflowers in bloom here throughout summer and into the fall, but hybrids—flowers concocted by man—are nowhere to be seen. You can watch a multi-media presentation when you visit, and buy seeds and other gifts in person or through the mail. Admission is charged. Route 7, Charlotte, Vermont; (802) 425–3500.

ELIZABETH PARK

Highly regarded for its rose gardens, over 15,000 bushes of some 1,100 varieties cover the grounds. Orderliness is the rule, with rows of arbors and arches and roses in a carpet of colors. The centerpiece is a little gazebo, offering a splendid overall view of the flowers. The All-American Rose Selections Committee has declared this a demonstration garden, meaning that the latest varieties of roses are shown here before they are introduced nationwide. Also in the park is a rock garden, a perennial garden, and an annual garden. Lawn bowling takes place here in warm weather, ice skating in the winter. 915 Prospect Avenue, Hartford, Connecticut; (203) 722–6541.

EASTER AND PASSOVER

The first Easter egg roll at the White House took place in 1878 during the administration of President Rutherford B. Hayes, the nineteenth president. Girls in long Victorian dresses and boys in jaunty hats and suits ran and rollicked, rolling decorated hard-boiled Easter eggs down the grassy lawn on the White House's south grounds.

One newspaper of the day reported, "In rolling down with their eggs the girls—some of them pretty good size, too—were totally regardless of the extent of striped stockings displayed."

In spite of such a lascivious display of girls' striped stockings, just about every year since then the White House has invited all Washington children to join in an official egg rolling party on the day after Easter Sunday. That initial rolling in 1878 drew several hundred youngsters. Over a century later upwards of 30,000 young egg rollers and their adult escorts keep this tradition alive. On this one day, rolling eggs might even surpass flinging mud as the favored pastime in the nation's capital.

The "Summer White House" Easter Egg Roll

EVEN THE MOST accommodating New England parent is entitled to feel hesitant about driving half a day down Interstate 95 so their young ones can roll eggs on the White House lawn. Luckily, **Hammersmith Farm** in Newport, Rhode Island, has the next best thing.

This seaside "cottage," which could be described as exuding a rustic opulence, was the home of the mother and stepfather of the little girl who would grow up to be First Lady of the United States, Jacqueline Bouvier Kennedy. During his administra-

HAMMERSMITH FARM, A
REAL "SUMMER WHITE
HOUSE," IS THE SETTING
FOR A PRESIDENTIAL-STYLE
EASTER EGG ROLL.

tion, President John F. Kennedy periodically took his family here to escape the pressures of the Oval Office, earning Hammersmith Farm the nickname of the "Summer White House."

The folks at Hammersmith invite all children six and under and their escorts to join in New England's version of the Easter egg roll. As is done at the other White House nowadays, the young ones line up side by side and are given a wooden egg and spoon. At the sound of a whistle, they roll their eggs with their spoon and keep rolling—and in some cases, rolling and rolling and rolling—until they reach the finish line.

There are no winners or losers at this Easter Sunday event. Several rolls are scheduled throughout the afternoon, and all participants receive a sticker and some Easter goodies after completing their turns. Sometimes the Easter bunny makes a guest appearance to hand out prizes.

Prior to the rolling, all are encouraged to take the guided tour of Hammersmith Farm decorated for the holiday. Most first-time visitors find that compared to the more famous, imposing Newport mansions like The Breakers and Marble House, this place is downright humble. There are no miles of marble or Flemish tapestries in Hammersmith Farm; here the furniture is attractively cushy and the rooms are practical. Even those of us who shop at K-Mart would feel at home at Hammersmith Farm.

During Easter week, including Sunday, you can expect to see ornaments such as an Easter tree complete with dyed eggs on the children's table in the dining room, and plants or candies in baskets in the bedrooms. On Easter even Pedro, the resident miniature donkey, dons the proper attire and poses for pictures in his bonnet. With an eye toward accuracy, the staff here notes that all floral decorations are traditional in nature and reflect the taste of Janet Bouvier Auchincloss, Jackie Kennedy's mother, in the early 1960s.

All events are limited to children six and under. Admission is charged for adults but is free for children. Hammersmith Farm, Ocean Drive, Newport, RI 02840; (401) 846–7346.

Easter Sunrise Service at Cathedral of the Pines

THE VIEW ALONE at this outdoor shrine in Rindge, New Hampshire, is inspiring. The cathedral is a nondenominational outdoors place of worship used yearly by area churches and synagogues. It is open to the public any time when there is no service, and you are welcome to take a seat on a wooden bench under the trees-and gaze beyond the stone altar into the misty distance.

On Easter morning, this sumptuous setting is the site of a very early sunrise service. It usually commences about a half hour prior to sunrise. The early bird gets the view here, but even if you can't see Mount Monadnock and the far-reaching rows of hills from where you sit, you will be surrounded by scores of lofty pines. Sit here under a blue New Hampshire sky and savor this singular setting.

The hilltop location can be chilly, especially in the wee hours of a March or April morning, so come dressed for winter. In pleasant weather you can expect to be one of 1,500 worshippers. The service lasts about 45 minutes and is followed by a buffet breakfast held by the nearby Rindge Congregational Church.

If you have time to explore this natural sanctuary afterward, wander over to the Altar of the Nation, containing a stone from every state and four territories, or examine the four bronze relief tablets above

WITH MOUNT MONADNOCK
IN THE DISTANCE, CATHEDRAL
OF THE PINES IS A TRULY
INSPIRATIONAL SETTING.

the arches on the Memorial Bell Tower. The tablets depict women in history, and were designed by Norman Rockwell and sculpted by his son Peter. The tower contains carillon chimes and two Sheffield steel bells, which resound every half hour and after the sunrise service. There is also an indoor chapel with flags from around the world, as well as artifacts, including a Congressional Medal of Honor.

The cathedral was built in 1946 by Dr. and Mrs. Douglas Sloane as a memorial to their son, Sanderson Sloane, who died in action during World War II. The location is the site the young man had chosen for his future home. Cathedral of the Pines, RR 2, Box 2700, Rindge, NH 03461; (603) 899–3300.

EASTER AT SKI AREAS

THE EASTER BUNNY schussing down a mountainside is one of the common if comical spectacles you can expect to see at several of New England's large ski areas on Easter Sunday. From the ridiculous to the sublime, you can also count on sunrise services in some majestic settings.

Maine

THE SUMMIT OF Locke Mountain, 1,865 feet high, is the venue of the Easter sunrise service at **Sunday River** in Bethel, Maine. You are invited to take the lift up and either ski or take the lift down at the conclusion of the service. About 60 to 200 worshippers attend, and many can be found immediately afterwards at an all-you-can-eat buffet breakfast, where you can have your fill of crêpes, quiche, home fries, and other morning sustenance.

The chase is on a few hours later, with children in search of Easter eggs. About 500 eggs are hidden in the garden near the children's ski school, where an egg might be found under the wooden lobster or beside some other odd props. Inside all the plastic eggs are treats, ranging from wrapped chocolate eggs to cash to one free junior season's pass for the next year. Also in residence is the floppy-eared Easter bunny, skiing alongside youngsters on the novice slopes or handing out candy. (207) 824–2187.

New Hampshire

Festivities are underway the day before Easter at Town Square in New Hampshire's **Waterville Valley**. The Easter bonnet parade and contest lures owners of both frivolous and elegant holiday hats, who march through town and are judged for appearance. Anticipate seeing anything, like bonnets sprouting moose antlers or topped with humongous sunflowers. On Easter morning you can join a few hundred others who ride the ski lift up Mt. Tecumseh to the 3,900-foot elevation point for the sunrise service. Breakfast is an option immediately afterwards. Mid-morning is time for the Easter egg hunt on the mountain. Those who find the most eggs in their particular age categories win prizes, while a special reward awaits the finder of the one golden egg. (603) 236–8311.

Easter at **Attitash** is a happening with youngsters in mind. The slope by the learning center is the site of the action, like an Easter egg hunt, a visit from the Easter bunny and sweet treats. (603) 374–2368.

THE EASTER BUNNY, COMPLETE WITH SPRING HAT, BOW TIE, AND FLOPPY EARS, IS
THE STAR ATTRACTION AT MAINE'S SUNDAY RIVER SKI AREA ON EASTER SUNDAY.

Vermont

UP AND DOWN Vermont, kids and adults spend Easter similarly. At **Mt. Snow** in West Dover the sunrise service is held atop the 3,600-foot-high summit, and usually lasts 45 minutes to an hour, attracting both skiers and non-skiers. In adverse conditions like heavy winds, Mt. Snow retail manager and ordained minister Paul Mello and the four or five singers and instrumentalists who accompany him conduct the service in the summit lodge; in rain, it is held in the base lodge. The necessary antidotes to a chilly spring Vermont morning service—hot coffee and filling doughnuts—are complimentary, though there is a full breakfast offered in the base lodge.

During Mt. Snow's version of the Easter egg hunt, young ones go in search of about 100 plastic eggs, each filled with treats and labeled with numbers corresponding to prizes like chocolate bunnies, T-shirts or caps.

There is one king-sized prize, a season's pass for the next year, stuffed inside a golden egg hidden somewhere on the mountain and the target of both children and adults. If it has not been found by noon, hourly clues are announced at the ski school desk. The golden egg is always placed in plain sight, but it is often easily camouflaged among brown leaves on the ground. (802) 464–3333.

The commanding vista of the Stowe Valley and the Green and White Mountains from the summit of **Mt. Mansfield** further north can force even the most frazzled of persons to turn reflective.

The idea of a sunrise service atop Mt. Mansfield was first proposed by Reverend Douglas Brayton in 1955. Those of little faith told Brayton he would never get cooperation from the owners, but Mt. Mansfield Company General Manager Sepp Ruschp was pleased to work with Brayton, who would go on to deliver the first service that year. In an Edmund Hillary-esque answer to the question: "Why the mountain top?" Brayton replied, "It was a lovely place, so why not do it."

The service takes place at the summit in rain, snow, or shine, unless weather conditions are extreme, and is open to all, whether or not on skis. The Easter bunny is known to put in an occasional appearance. There is also the possibility of an Easter buffet breakfast following the service. (802) 253–7311.

Okemo Mountain in Ludlow also hosts a sunrise service in the Sugar House, a mid-mountain lodge, that is intended mainly for skiers. On the secular side, adults and children compete in an Easter bonnet contest, with headgear decorated in ski-related designs.

Bonnets with puffs of cotton and toothpick skiers typically show up on young heads, while their grown-up counterparts have adorned bonnets with old lift tickets or gone for the outrageous, attaching an old pair of skis to their Easter headpiece, or dangling poles from it. For the best bonnets there are prizes, including lift tickets and gift certificates.

Later on, kids five and under can join the search for Easter candies in plastic bags, rather than actual eggs. Adults take to the slopes seeking to find two mammoth "eggs" which are really watermelons—one wrapped in silver, the other in gold. Okemo's lift operators hide them in between trails or behind tree trunks in the woods, and the lucky finders are awarded with gift certificates or multiple-day lift tickets. (802) 228–4041.

Killington, too, has a sunrise service. From 150 to 200 people commonly attend the Easter morning rites at the summit of Killington peak. A free continental breakfast is served up high afterwards. Dress warmly; it can get pretty chilly at 4,241-foot elevation, and the gondolas on the three-and-a-half-mile-long ride are enclosed but not heated. (802) 422–3333.

Depending on snow cover, **Smugglers' Notch** holds its sunrise service on either Mount Sterling or Mount Morse. It lasts about 30 minutes and is followed by a free continental breakfast of coffee, doughnuts, and Danish pastry. Real eggs are the goal in the annual Easter egg hunt, with chocolate rabbits and the like given as rewards. Yankee ingenuity is employed in concocting costumes for the ensuing Easter costume parade. A Smugglers' Notch spokesperson reports that Easter's festivities lure many local residents and non-skiers to their grounds. (802) 644–8851.

ONE MORE EASTER HUNT

IT IS APPLES, not eggs, that the Easter bunny hides at **Lyman Orchards' Apple Barrel** farm store in Middlefield, Connecticut. It was in 1986 that the holiday rabbit made his first appearance at the big, round produce and gift emporium, and he has since arrived annually to pose for photos and conceal apples on the store's lawn. Children from ages one to eight take part in the apple hunt while those aged eight and older can guess the total amount of jellybeans in a container. You might also find rabbits or other live animals on hand for demonstration or sale. Lyman Orchards, Route 127, Middlefield, CT; (203) 349–1793.

JEWISH HISTORY

THE SPRING PASSOVER season is an appropriate time to take **Uncommon Boston's Jewish Boston Tour**. If it isn't on their list of scheduled events, you can arrange one by appointment. Guides lead participants into neighborhoods with a Jewish connection, like Chelsea and the West End, one time haunts of Sophie Tucker, Bernard Berenson, and the grandparents of Barry Goldwater. Landmarks on this journey into history include East Boston's Temple Ohabei Shalom Cemetery, the city's first Jewish cemetery, and the Charles Street Playhouse in the theater district; the present-day theater was originally built as one of the city's first synagogues. Uncommon Boston, 437 Boylston Street, Boston, MA 02116; (617) 731–5854.

A similar tour is offered by **Urban Safaris**. Their **Jewish Boston** tour can last from four to six hours, and includes sights in the North End, the West End, and Brookline, as well as lunch. Urban Safaris, 9 Lewis Road, Swampscott, MA 01907; (617) 592–3284.

PATRIOTS' DAY: THE MIDNIGHT RIDE OF PAUL REVERE

Listen, my children, and you shall hear
Of the midnight ride of Paul Revere,
On the eighteenth of April, in Seventy-five;
Hardly a man is now alive
Who remembers that famous day and year.
Henry Wadsworth Longfellow

Thanks to the bard of Cambridge, more people know Paul Revere's name than the truth about his ride. The hard facts are that Revere was one of three riders, and that he and William Dawes, another messenger who rode out of Boston, were both captured. Only Dr. Samuel Prescott, who cut short a romantic interlude with a girlfriend in Lexington to join Revere and Dawes, managed to ride to Concord and alert the militiamen there about the advancement of British troops.

Today, Paul Revere's ride into fame is recreated every Patriots' Day, the third Monday in April in Massachusetts. Since 1976, a Natick veterinarian named Edward Zullo has portrayed Revere, hopping aboard a trusty Morgan at Paul Revere Mall in Boston at 10:00 on Patriots' Day morning, galloping through Charlestown, Somerville, Medford, and Arlington before arriving three hours later at Lexington Green.

Paul Revere's ride into fame is recreated every Patriots' Day.

Zullo dresses to the hilt for the part, garbed in colonial-style riding boots, tailored a bit to accommodate a lengthy ride along roads that are no longer dirt. Zullo's modified jodhpurs simulate Revere's knickers, which extended to just below his knees. And his frame is encased in a dark, wool cloak covering a vest and jabot, the better to camouflage a swiftly moving rider in the dark of night. No matter that Zullo recreates the ride in the light of day. Revere made the ride at night, and historical accuracy rules in dress if not time of day. Naturally, Zullo tops his pate with a tricorn hat.

Zullo stops briefly in each town he passes through, delivering to a mayor, selectman, or other designated recipient a scroll announcing the British advancement. Herein lies one concession to the twentieth century.

"Paul Revere passed on the message to all the people. Since there are so many people living in these towns today, I can't do that, so I give it to a selected person who accepts it for anyone," says Zullo.

Weather has never been a deterrent and April in New England is capricious. Zullo has ridden in the best and worst, even downpours with almost zero visibility. But in each community, Bay State residents and visitors stand and wait to catch a glimpse of Paul Revere.

"When I see the little children waving their small American flags saying, 'Hello, Paul Revere,' it's worth the long ride. That's where the true patriots are. I'll stop to let them touch the horse or my hand. I'll allow a parent to put a youngster on the horse with me. I might lose 120 seconds but it's enough to last the child a lifetime," offers Zullo.

He adds that photographers and other enthusiasts have the best chance of getting close to Revere in

Arlington, where there might be as few as 100 waiting twentieth-century residents, a dearth compared to the thousands that wait in Lexington. It is at Arlington where Revere/Zullo stops for about a half hour and indulges in tea and homemade biscuits offered by women in colonial hats and bonnets. (Interestingly, the modern town of Revere is bypassed.)

Simultaneously, a horseback rider in the less glamorous role of William Dawes leaves John Eliot Square in Roxbury at 10:00 and makes his way through Brookline, Cambridge, and Arlington before reaching Lexington a little over three hours later. The two meet once while en route, in Arlington, where they shake hands, ask each other if they encountered any conflicts along the way, and wish each other a good remaining ride.

In Boston and Lexington, festivities begin before the latter-day Revere and Dawes hop aboard their steeds. The Patriots' Day parade in Boston commences at Government Center just after 9 A.M. and winds its way through the neighborhood streets, ending at Paul Revere Mall. The parade, consisting of bands, color guards, and colonial and marching units, stops twice along the way for the placement of wreaths at the graves of William Dawes (at King's Chapel Burying Grounds at Tremont and School Streets) and Paul Revere (at Granary Burying Grounds at Tremont and Bromfield Streets).

Expect the parade to last from an hour and a half to two hours. One veteran parade participant says the best spot for watchers is at Government Center at the beginning of the route. There is usually no problem parking on this state holiday, although you can always take the T. Use the Government Center or State Street stops.

One veteran parade participant says the best spot for watchers is at Government Center at the beginning of the route.

PATRIOTS' DAY EVENTS AT THE OLD NORTH CHURCH

He said to his friend, "If the British march
By land or sea from the town to-night,
Hang a lantern aloft in the belfry arch
Of the North Church tower as a signal light,—
One, if by land, and two, if by sea;
And I on the opposite shore will be,
Ready to ride and spread the alarm
Through every Middlesex village and farm,
For the country folk to be up and to arm."
Henry Wadsworth Longfellow

THE OLD NORTH Church still stands guard like a silent sentinel at the foot of Hull Street, and every Patriots' Day eve, members of colonial militia march in full dress uniform into the church in commemoration of the hanging of the lanterns on April 18, 1775. In order to set a proper tone, the church is illuminated by candlelight and militia groups appear in colonial costume.

Traditionally, the opening procession is led by the color guard from the U.S.S. *Constitution*. They are usually followed by the Lexington Minutemen, the Ancient and Honorable Artillery Company, the Charlestown Militia Company, and other regiments in uniform. A selection of patriotic songs, such as the "Battle Hymn of the Republic" and "America the Beautiful", is led by the church's Old North Singers, and Paul Revere's account of his ride is read by a descendent. Near the end of the service, a descendent or namesake of Robert Newman, the sexton who displayed the lanterns on April 18, 1775, carries the church's lanterns into its steeple.

LEXINGTON EVENTS

THE EERY SOUND of tolling bells in the misty early morning air starts the activities in Lexington on Patriots' Day. At 5:30 A.M. the bell is sounded in a replica of the old belfry, followed by a rifle shot from the Buckman Tavern signalling the advance of British troops. Drum rolls echo through the center of town as a resident in the character of 16-year-old colonist drummer William Diamond sets the beat by which the minutemen assemble on the green.

Just before 6 A.M., the scene on Lexington Green is a moment from another era transported to the present. The British, in their striking red uniforms and holding their bayonets and muskets, face the farmer colonists in their homespun brown and black dress. The colonists' Captain John Parker is challenged to lay down his arms. He refuses, stating emphatically that the colonists will not retreat.

Though the identity of the firer of the first shot is lost to history, in the recreated skirmish the British shoot first. And the celebrated Battle of Lexington, just 15 minutes of time that have become legend, is fought once more before modern eyes.

Each member of today's Lexington Minutemen plays the role of an actual colonial minuteman in the battle. In January, each is assigned a part and in March, after two months of memorizing his character's actions, he is tested. Local women do their part as well. After the smoke clears, women in colonial dress cast as wives or other relatives rush to the green to aid the wounded or carry them to the near-by tavern. And the British march on, up present-day Route 2A, as if they were heading on to Concord.

Parade lovers get a double dose of entertainment. In the morning the youth of Lexington join local dignitaries stepping through town in the Sunrise Parade, a brief affair lasting about 20 minutes. The Afternoon Parade, over a mile long, takes significantly more

time to pass down Massachusetts Avenue. It is headed by the Lexington Minutemen, their color guard and float, and is followed by other color guards, floats, marching bands, Shriners groups, antique cars, and fire trucks. Most participants are local, but the parade has boasted bands from faraway states like Louisiana and Florida.

There is also a pancake breakfast, a road race, and various morning ceremonies, including a memorial service for those who served on the five Navy ships that have borne the name USS *Lexington*. In total, ceremonies centered around Lexington Green take the better part of ten hours.

ON PATRIOTS' DAY, LEXINGTON GREEN ONCE MORE BEARS WITNESS TO THE BATTLE OF LEXINGTON, RECREATED FOR MODERN EYES.

If you can't shake that patriotic feeling and have time on your hands, plan to visit any of the three nearby landmark buildings linked to the Battle of Lexington. The one that played the biggest role in the skirmish is the Buckman Tavern, across the street from the green.

The Buckman Tavern

THE TALE OF the battle, of 77 ragged colonists facing five times that many British, of bayonets glistening in the morning light, is recounted as you stand in the taproom. It was in this chamber with the cavernous fireplace and now reconstructed bar that the minutemen waited those tense early hours of April 19, 1775, for the British to come tramping into town.

This early American version of the corner bar had already been hosting local Lexingtonians and transients both for over six decades when it had its brush with immortality. In 1775, when John Buckman was the innkeeper, the tavern was bustling with activity. Area citizens gathered here for conversation ranging from gossip to news of the world; a literate man commonly read newspapers in the taproom to those unable to read, and all sat at the same tables on the same chairs you see today.

The scent and sight of burning tobacco was always in the air. A clay pipe on view is the type colonial men shared; each would break off a piece before putting it to his lips, and would continue to do so until just a remnant remained. When the tavern was restored in the 1920s, a hole filled with ends of clay pipes was discovered above the fireplace, obviously the dumping ground for pipe remains.

As you listen to your guide, you discover how many terms and expressions of language used today had their roots in colonial taverns like this one. A *loggerhead* was an iron rod heated in the fireplace and then used to warm alcoholic drinks. When men became abrasive, they were said to be "at loggerheads" with each other. You will hear also that "Mind your p's and q's," was another way of saying "Keep track of your pints and quarts." (However, at colonial print shops in New England we have also heard that the same expression evolved from eighteenth-century printers' devils, who confused the two letters on type pieces. You may believe whichever story sounds more credible.)

For lodging here, a man—women of that day would never have travelled alone—would part with

the equivalent of 25 cents. He also would have had the company of strangers. It was usual in colonial times to share not only your room, but your bed, with others whether you knew them or not. Beds were made of rope, and as your guide shows you how the ropes were tightened for support, you will hear how this practice was the derivation of the nighttime salutation, "Sleep tight."

While showing you the ropes, your guide will also point out an original linsey-woolsey quilt in the land-lord's bedroom. Buff in color and stitched exquisitely, the quilt radiates a glossy sheen, thanks to the egg whites that colonists brushed on it two centuries ago. Employing Yankee ingenuity to the fullest, they found additional uses for the versatile egg. Remnants of white paint made from egg shells, buttermilk, and clay are still visible on the kitchen ceiling beams.

The kitchen is the site of a free-standing cupboard, a symbol of the local resistance to taxes. Buildings were taxed according to total number of rooms, and closets were classified as rooms. The pewter dish-ware on the long, wooden table against the kitchen's back wall isn't typical, though. What we know now to be lead poisoning was a concern in colonial days, and residents and guests in the tavern would simply have eaten with their fingers.

And how did a traveller know if there was any

LEXINGTON'S BUCKMAN TAVERN WAS THE EARLY AMERICAN VERSION OF THE CORNER BAR.

room at the inn? Three lit candles in the lantern in the landlord's bedroom window stood for warmth and hospitality inside. Unlit candles meant there was no vacancy.

As busy as he was, innkeeper John Buckman found the time to sit for an artist. An oil painting of the dark-haired Buckman hangs in his bedroom, and he almost appears too young for the job.

Munroe Tavern and Hancock-Clarke House

THE MUNROE TAVERN was seized by returning British on the afternoon of April 19 and was used as a hospital for their wounded. In 1789, George Washington dined here while visiting the battle site. Preserved in the tavern's Washington Room is the arm chair and card table at which the first president supped, while the taproom shelters the tavern's original pine sign proclaiming, "Entertainment By Wm. Munroe, 1775."

It was at the clapboard Hancock-Clarke House where John Hancock and Samuel Adams were sleeping when Revere alerted them to the British troop advancement. In fact, when Revere arrived about midnight, minutemen guarding the house scolded Revere for making too much noise.

Hancock, awakened, urged Revere to enter the house. It was in the keeping room, like today's den or family room, where Hancock and Adams relaxed just hours earlier. The round table and the surrounding Queen Anne side chairs date from the early eighteenth century; also note the narrow, rectangular, indoor shutters. The kitchen where Revere and Dawes enjoyed a fast midnight meal (and you thought eating on the run was a late twentieth century custom) looks typically colonial with its high-backed settle, warm hearth, and tin kitchenware.

The three buildings are open annually from April 19 through October, and admission is charged. A combination ticket to all three is available. The Lexington Historical Society, Box 514, Lexington, MA 02173; (617) 861–0928.

To further inspect the historic locales that played paramount roles in that long ago April, plan a stop at **Minuteman National Historical Park**. The National Park Service property incorporates the battle road,

the North Bridge, two visitor centers, and **The Wayside**, home of the muster master of the Concord militia and a few generations earlier, the residence of authors the Alcotts, Nathaniel Hawthorne, and

THE MINUTEMAN MONUMENT STANDS SENTINEL AT LEXINGTON GREEN.

Margaret Sidney. Minuteman National Historical Park, Box 160, Concord, MA 01742; (508) 369–6993; (617) 862–7753.

PAUL REVERE HOUSE

IT WAS THE rare resident of Boston in the late eighteenth century who was unfamiliar with Paul Revere, a skilled silversmith and successful entrepreneur in the city's North End. By 1787, the year his 16th and last child was born, Revere was making a comfortable living selling looking glasses, scales, pewter, brass, copperware, and tools for jewellers and clock makers. At one time in his life he even practiced dentistry.

But he became prominent for notable reasons. In 1792 Revere cast the first church bell made in Boston; he would go on to cast over 100 more. Four years earlier he was instrumental in rallying his fellow Bostonians in support of the ratification of the new federal constitution.

A few years later Revere provided copper spikes and bolts for the USS *Constitution*, then designed one of his last silver tea sets for Edmund Hartt, *Old Ironsides*'s builder. When he died on May 10, 1818, at age 83, Paul Revere was eulogized as a craftsman, businessman, artisan, and patriot.

A total of 43 years later, Revere was immortalized by Longfellow in "Paul Revere's Ride," and a lifetime of accomplishments was reduced to one moment in the continuing thread of history.

At **Revere's home** in Boston's North End, visitors meet a man who lived a full life, as opposed to a rider who simply went out one night on horseback. They also get to see what stands as the only remaining seventeenth-century house in Boston.

The bulky, boxy, brown home was built about 1680, and today's visitors are shocked by the spaciousness of the rooms, a reflection not of Revere's wealth, but of that of the builder, Robert Howard. Said one interpreter: "When Paul Revere bought this home, he was middle class. If he was well to do, he never would have bought this building. It was almost 100 years old and very out of fashion." Revere did come into wealth, but after the revolution.

The tour is self-guided, but posted commentaries about the house and Revere's life, career, and children abound, and staff members are on both floors to answer questions. Of the four open rooms, only the hall, which at various times served as a parlor, a dining room, an office, a workshop, and a bedroom, is decorated to reflect the wealth and era of original owner Robert Howard. The maps on the wall are from seventeenth-century atlases, while covering a round table is a Turkish carpet, a common touch for the rich of that period. (Floor carpets would not be popular for another 100 years, and the wooden floor here is bare.) A text of seventeenth-century sermons joins a clay pipe and a twist of tobacco atop the table.

In Revere's kitchen, herbs dry over the fireplace and heavy, cast-iron pots used in cooking hang from an iron rod. A cradle sits comfortable and cozy by the hearth, a common sight in his family of 16 children.

A short, winding staircase takes you up to the best chamber and the children's room. Like the hall downstairs, the *best chamber* was a multi-purpose room, utilized both as an elegant parlor and a private bedroom. Such a practice was socially acceptable for middle-class homes lacking a separate parlor.

The bow-front dresser to the left of the canopied bed, the upholstered easy chair, and two black Windsor chairs are all original to the Revere family. A deck of cards has been dealt to four absent players. Take a close look at them; they are marked with

PAUL REVERE'S BOXY SEVENTEENTH-CENTURY HOME IS TUCKED AMONG THE MODERN BUILDINGS OF BOSTON'S NORTH END.

familiar suits but no numbers, as was the style in the late 1700s.

According to a staff member, most visitors' questions concern Revere's illustrious ride. Another favorite topic among the inquisitive is Revere's 16 children, and many modern-day homeowners wonder how he could find room for all in this house. Guides explain that because of the wide range in ages and the fact that five offspring died in childhood, it is unlikely there were more than five to seven youngsters in the house at any given time. The children's room, along with two rooms on the third floor, gave the Reveres ample space by the standards of his day.

Paul Revere may no longer be alive to teach his craft, but if you harbor a desire to learn silversmithing or other early American crafts such as leather working, weaving, or tailoring, plan a trip to the Revere House on Saturdays from May through October when special programs are scheduled.

Paul Revere bells are scattered throughout New England, although the best place to examine one is in the rear of the Revere House courtyard. This bronze bell was cast in 1804 for the East Parish Church in Bridgewater, Massachusetts. Paul Revere Memorial Association, 19 North Square, Boston, MA 02113; (617) 523–2338.

To set your eyes on Revere silver, head across town to Boston's **Museum of Fine Arts**, home to one of the largest public collections, (617) 267–9300. Other homes to Revere silver are:

the Fogg Art Museum of Harvard University, (617) 495–2387;

the Worcester Art Museum, (508) 799–4406;

the Henry Needham Flynt Silver and Metalware Collection at Historic Deerfield, (413) 774–5581;

the Bowdoin College Museum of Art in Brunswick, Maine (207) 725–3000.

EVERYDAY VISITS TO THE OLD NORTH CHURCH

THE BRICK FACADE of this sturdy, steeple-topped house of worship provides a touch of reverence to this residential downtown neighborhood. The church has welcomed Presidents James Monroe, Theodore Roosevelt, Franklin Roosevelt and Gerald Ford, and is home to a bust of George Washington, presented to the church in 1815 and believed to be the first memorial to our first president placed in a public building.

Inside the church worshippers and tourists sit in box pews, which from the rear resemble a massive maze. Hallmarks of the church's earliest days, the box pews, taller than those found in any other American church, were conceived to keep their occupants warm. During that time, congregants brought inside their own foot warmers, filled with hot coals or stones; such relics can be seen today on church window sills.

A pair of brass chandeliers hanging above the central aisle also date from Old North's primal days. They were first lit on Christmas Day, 1724. And although the original steeple was destroyed by Hurricane Carol in 1954, the present one supports the same weather vane that has sat atop the crest of the church since it was designed in 1740.

Next to the church is a small museum devoted to the church's history. On a far wall are the lanterns hung every April 18 (not original to 1775) and inside a glass case is the first prayer book in which prayers for the British crown were replaced by petitions for the President of the United States.

As an adolescent, Paul Revere was a member of the guild of bell ringers. But his most famous association with Old North is commemorated beside the entrance. It is a plaque that reads:

> The signal lanterns
> of
> Paul Revere
> displayed in the
> steeple of this church
> April 18, 1775
> warned the country
> of the march of
> the British troops to
> Lexington and Concord.

Old North Church, 193 Salem Street, Boston, MA 02113; (617) 523–6676.

MAY BREAKFASTS AND ARBOR DAY

IT TAKES A LONG TIME TO SET UP TABLES FOR 1,000 HUNGRY DINERS AT ONE OF RHODE ISLAND'S TYPICAL MAY BREAKFASTS.

When May arrives at Rhode Island's churches, diets across the Ocean State go to hell. To avoid the risk of sounding sacrilegious, we could instead say

they go awry. The point is, nobody gets thinner at Rhode Island's May breakfasts.

What's on the menus? Jonnycakes, clam cakes, biscuits, pancakes, ham, bacon, eggs, home fries, baked beans, doughnuts, sausage, grits, muffins, apple pie, hot and cold cereal, French toast, coffee, tea, orange juice, milk, and undoubtedly many other homemade samplings we've omitted can be found on the tables at the 50-odd breakfasts taking place in late April and May. And gluttons take note—most are open on an all-you-can-eat basis, and the prices are reasonable.

The raison d'être for these breakfast banquets is Rhode Island's singular claim for independence. It was on May 4, 1776, that Rhode Island foreshadowed what the other 12 colonies would do two months later, and declared itself independent of the mother country. As a result, May in Rhode Island is called

WHAT'S ON THE MENU AT MAY BREAKFASTS IN THE OCEAN STATE? HOW ABOUT JONNYCAKES, CLAM CAKES, BACON AND EGGS, HOME FRIES, MUFFINS, APPLE PIE, FRENCH TOAST, CORN BREAD, AND MORE?

Heritage Month, and is today commemorated by these examples of early morning epicurean sumptuousness.

The great-grandfather of all May breakfasts is held at the **Oak Lawn Baptist Church** in Cranston. The first took place in 1867, when the cannon fire on Civil War battlefields was barely a memory, and the President of the United States was Andrew Johnson. Clam cakes highlighted the 1867 menu and admission was 75 cents. Clam cakes are still the prominent selections, but the price has increased: in 1990 it was four dollars, still a bargain.

Reliability has been the hallmark of numerous May breakfasts. The Oak Lawn menu is the same yearly; in addition to clam cakes, hungry diners will find corn bread, ham, scrambled eggs, apple pie, baked beans, juice, coffee, and tea. Oak Lawn staff member Rick Sherman estimates the church serves 800 to 1,000 people per breakfast, and guesses that patrons imbibe upwards of a few hundred gallons of coffee.

No reservations are taken at Oak Lawn. On this special day, breakfast workers keep a schedule paralleling that of Bryant Gumble. Tickets are sold as early as 5:30, and waitresses dressed in colonial Quaker garb start serving a half hour later. No matter when you arrive, expect a wait at the door before you can be seated.

Bertha Crampton has been lending a hand at **Lime Rock Baptist Church**'s May breakfasts since the first jonnycake was cooked there in 1925. Bertha was ten at the time and recalls that her mother was on the Lincoln church's original breakfast committee. Her great-grandchildren attend now, making the Lime Rock breakfast a five generation family tradition. Her memories of the earliest breakfasts are of advancements in the grapefruit industry. "They didn't come seedless back then and by the time you cut all the seeds out there wasn't much grapefruit left to serve."

Lime Rock attracts as many as 500 diners to its feast. Bertha thinks the inclusion of jonnycakes made locally of cornmeal from Kenyon's 1886 Gristmill—as well as the usual offerings of scrambled eggs, ham, baked beans, pancakes, rolls, doughnuts, fruit, orange juice, coffee, tea, and milk—is cause for its popularity.

Jonnycakes, even more than clam cakes, are a Rhode Island institution and a staple of May breakfast menus. Introduced to settlers by native Indians, jonnycakes are small fried corn cakes, similar in size to a

Jonnycakes, even more than clam cakes, are a Rhode Island institution and a staple of May breakfast menus.

pancake but heavier in weight. A perfect jonnycake, say the experts, should be golden brown on the outside and fluffy inside.

Rhode Island chauvinists shun jonnycakes made elsewhere, claiming that only whitecap flint corn, grown and milled locally, should be used. Of course, it is said that real Rhode Islanders don't pour syrup over jonnycakes. Don't tell that to the many May breakfast aficionados who like them best with butter and syrup, both readily available.

And the name? It's probably a corruption of "journey cake", since cornmeal as well as fried corn cakes both were convenient to carry and were easily grilled or reheated by travellers.

Other churches with long-standing May breakfast customs are the **Park Place Congregational Church** in Pawtucket, which first hosted a May breakfast in 1882 and is the second oldest, and the **North Scituate Baptist Church**, which began its own trend in 1894. Although the greatest number of May breakfasts are held in greater Providence, you will find them served throughout the state. Indeed, Westerly's **Christ Church** hosted its first May breakfast in the days prior to World War I, and **St. James Episcopal Church** in Woonsocket debuted its initial May breakfast in 1920.

Nowadays you will also find civic and other non-religious organizations with their own May breakfast traditions. Rotary clubs like those in Jamestown and Warwick have been cooking ham, eggs, apple pie, and the like for their guests for a few decades, and even the Rhode Island Yacht Club and Providence's Federal Hill House Association have their breakfasts. The Norman Bird Sanctuary in Middletown, north of Newport, couples its May breakfast, an institution since 1982, with guided bird walks.

And at most breakfasts, it's not only Rhode Island's independence declaration that is commemorated. The fragrance of spring flowers floats through the air at many settings. You will find May baskets filled with cookies, flowers, or plants for sale at several; at Lime Rock Baptist Church they are handmade, decorated with crepe paper, and crammed with candies. Some breakfast hosts even post a color-packed maypole.

Although May breakfast season technically lasts from late April through late May, the majority of the filling feasts take place on the Saturday either before or following May 1. For a complete schedule of coming May breakfasts, contact the Rhode Island Tourism Division, Seven Jackson Walkway, Providence, RI 02903; (800) 556–2484 or (401) 277–2601.

ARBOR DAY CELEBRATIONS

AT THE SAME time that Rhode Islanders revel in their May banquets, people elsewhere cultivate trees. The last Friday in April is Arbor Day, a time of conservation and planting.

The Arnold Arboretum

The last Friday in April is Arbor Day, a time of conservation and planting.

WHILE ORGANIZATIONS and parks across New England honor the designated date, Arbor Day is especially feted at the **Arnold Arboretum** of Harvard University, located in the Jamaica Plain section of Boston. Their **Arbor Day Festival** takes place annually on the Sunday following Arbor Day.

An education-focused activity day for children, the fest is filled with undertakings that help sow in kids a friendship with nature. They might be taught to make birds' nests with grasses and the support of soft wire, thereby earning respect for birds that assemble their nests with grass only. Then it's time to test their degree of camouflage, as children scour the grounds searching for each others' nests.

Juvenile hands might also get a workout in other arts and crafts projects. Fabric painting using plant parts is a commonly scheduled activity.

Youngsters who would rather watch than do can enjoy the performances of puppets. "This is Your Life, Acer Maple," a take-off on the television program of the fifties, is the name of one puppet show that might be performed. All the maple tree's old friends, from furry animals to furniture, come and visit the tree of honor. Storytellers are usually on hand, too, imparting a tale or two with an ecological tone.

The winners of a poetry-writing contest conducted in Boston area schools are on hand to read their verses about trees; also-rans are posted on walls in the visitor center. Other in-person guests are furry and feathered as urban animals from the nearby Franklin Park Zoo are brought for show. Hedgehogs, ferrets, and owls can be seen making live appearances.

Late April weather has often been unkind to the Arbor Day fest, and activities have been forced indoors. In rain or shine, however, the day is always capped off with seed plantings. Young guests take seeds home in a pot with planting directions, and a tree is always planted on the arboretum grounds. Many children make return trips just to see how "their tree" is faring.

Other special annual days at Arnold Arboretum are **Lilac Sunday** (see page 44) in May, and a plant sale in September at the arboretum's Case Estates in Weston. But the arboretum's rolling grounds in Jamaica Plain tempt walkers and flower fanciers throughout the year.

While the general public might consider the arboretum a piece of country in the city, and home to 265 acres of trees and flowers to get lost among, the staff has a loftier purpose, calling the center "an international center for the scientific study and cultivation of trees."

"Our goal is to have a tree planted representative of any particular species that would grow in this climate anywhere in the world," says one spokesperson. "We're not that far from that goal but we're always learning of new species of trees growing somewhere in the world."

Trees are grouped according to type, making for convenient comparisons. The 137 kinds of maple trees are together so it's easy for a casual observer to compare an American maple to one from Japan and another from China, for example. In early spring, red maples display their flowers before their green leaves appear. Yet a most welcome spring sighting is the yellow-flowered forsythia, which blooms when New Englanders are just itching for warmer weather to arrive.

A STELLAR VIEW OF THE BOSTON SKYLINE IS YOURS FROM ARNOLD ARBORETUM.

Of course, you can even see color in winter, when the red berries of the Korean mountain ash stand out brightly compared to the snow blanketing the ground.

Arnold Arboretum has existed since 1872, making it the oldest in the country designed for both university and public use. Famous landscape designer Frederick Law Olmstead joined the arboretum's first director in arranging the property so it would resemble a New England woodland.

If you are driving, head up either Bussey or Peters Hill for a commanding view of the Boston skyline. A map of the grounds can be purchased for a nominal fee at the arboretum visitor center. Subway travelers can take the Orange Line to Forest Hills Station and walk two blocks west, or the Arborway bus from the Boston Public Library or at Copley Square to the Monument stop in Jamaica Plain, and walk three blocks south. The Arnold Arboretum of Harvard University, 125 Arborway, Jamaica Plain, MA 02130; (617) 524–1718.

The Bartlett Arboretum

CONNECTICUT RESIDENTS in search of a spring activity to celebrate the outdoors should take note that the **Bartlett Arboretum** of the University of Connecticut in Stamford hosts its **Rebirth of the Trees in Spring** nature walk in late April. Local trees that aren't often given special attention by area residents are the subject of discussion here, as they are seen springing to life. As you walk through the grounds, you might be shown the grey bark of the American beech, which one staff member says resembles an elephant's leg, or the bright, red flowers of the swamp maple as it begins to bloom. Processes that restart growth after dormancy, such as day length and temperature, are explained.

Like the Arnold Arboretum, the Bartlett Arboretum is also part of a university system with a mission to educate as well as offer a park-like facility in which people can relax and unwind. Self-guided trails with plant identification labels tempt those with extra time. If visitors admire the works of nature and learn a bit about area trees and shrubs, folks at the Bartlett will feel their mission has been accomplished.

Other special events at the Bartlett Arboretum are **Winterbloom** in February, where blossoming bulbs in the greenhouse are in the spotlight, and a trio of single topic walks later in spring (see page 47). Bartlett Arboretum, University of Connecticut, 151 Brookdale Road, Stamford, CT 06903; (203) 322–6971.

Dinosaur State Park

Hartford area residents aching to go outdoors can head to this park in Rocky Hill which almost always recognizes Arbor Day with special activities. Nature walks among the park's trees are typical. Call the park at (203) 529–8423 for specific details.

A HOT SUMMER DAY
IN VERMONT.

SUMMER

I f the changing seasons are nourishment for our
souls, summer is an ice cream cone. It's dessert
after eight months of vegetables, entrées, and
hors d'oeuvres. It's worth the long wait, it's purely
decadent, and it tastes so good. But it finishes too
soon, and the older one gets, the faster and faster it
seems to go.

Summer is likely New England's most old-fashioned
season, too. Just as dessert gourmets know that
upstarts like frozen yogurt and tofutti will never take
the place of rich, full, fattening ice cream, we too
know that modern pastimes that keep cocooners
busy in winter—video rentals and electronic games—
fall far behind when it comes to summer leisure.

This is the time for star-spangled fireworks and lazy
pop flies, for beach towels under the sun, and
Beethoven under the stars. Here in New England we
can boast both a Fourth of July celebration that's
been going on for two centuries, and an actual recreated nineteenth-century Independence Day celebration. Sand and water lure the tired and work-weary
not just to the coast, but inland as well; mountains

A CLASSIC NEW ENGLAND
SUMMER SCENE.

and forest-girding lakes equal eye-dazzling beachside vistas, while bathtub water temperatures tempt swimmers who could care less about the scenery. And if you like summer recreation, whether it be tennis or golf or just view-collecting, wait until you read what our ski areas offer when the snow melts.

Tanglewood draws the outdoor classical music crowd, but don't think for a moment that Lenox, Massachusetts, is the only site of alfresco concerts—all of our six states serve up music in the open air. Along the same line, friendly Fenway isn't a singular home to professional baseball. Many sports buffs frequent our minor league ballparks specifically to search for tomorrow's stars and see hard, gritty baseball played as it should be.

It is in the summer that we celebrate most of our natural food products, especially our seafood bounty, and what's more old-fashioned than digging into the fruits of a clambake—lobster and watermelon and clam chowder? New England's Native Americans, and there are more than you might think, meet in pow-wows and festivals, and these get-togethers—open to the public—are a perfect occasion to purchase authentic handcrafts, taste a slice of fry bread or an Indian taco, and learn the truth about a culture that's been ravaged over the years by Hollywood. As one Iroquois Indian told me: "People ask where's my horse. We live in the East in and around forests where horses wouldn't be of any use."

So there is some substance to the most decadent of seasons, after all.

SUMMERTIME IN SKI TOWNS

When President George Bush urged all to "prudently recreate" in the summer of 1990, he did so from his summer home in Kennebunkport, Maine. Coastal New England has called to recreation-minded folks for over a hundred years, and many, like the President's family, sought out their own piece of ocean-front property. In addition to Maine's Kennebunks, favorite summer sites included Bar Harbor, Newport, Cape Cod, and Old Saybrook, and the many waterside resorts in between.

Within a few decades, hotels, inns, motels, and resorts began hosting those seeking summer recreation who couldn't afford second homes or summer-long rentals. Day and weekend trips, as well as week-long vacations to the shore, became the rule for anyone in search of active diversions, from athletics to shopping to kid things like penny arcades or amusement rides.

Management at New England's ski areas watched enviously, noting that for all those who drove south or east, few headed north. But there was little reason to visit these places when ski lifts sat quietly, neglected like a school playground in July, and nothing seemed more sad than the green slopes of ski trails alone, empty, and unoccupied, incongruous with the sunny warmth, abandoned like last Christmas's tangle of electric lights.

Realizing that the far-reaching views from atop our mountain peaks are no less inspiring in summer than during ski season, ski area operators began operating lifts for warm-weather travelers. Gradually they added more amenities, like tennis courts or golf courses, and soon winter-only ski areas were turning into four season resorts.

Soon winter-only ski areas were turning into four season resorts.

Maine

The Rangeley Lakes Region of Maine is one that currently draws more daily visitors in summer than in ski season.

Actually, Rangeley began attracting tourists a hundred years ago, when Victorian-era Americans took a journey via railroad and steam ferry to any of six grand hotels in Maine's western mountains, for annual escapes from sweltering city heat. As it became commonplace for the American family to own, in Herbert Hoover's words, "a car in every garage," and as air conditioning progressed from novelty to necessity, the era of the grand hotel gradually faded. In 1958 the idea of Saddleback Ski Area was conceived, but the area has grown most substantially since the late 1970s.

Summer visitors nowadays employ the lakes for their fun. Boat tours are offered in old-fashioned Rangeley Boats (wooden square-sterned motorboats), and as part of three- to five-day trips in canoes. The Rangeley Sailboard Center gives lessons and has rentals, while fishing enthusiasts catch salmon and trout. Nearby is the 18-hole Mingo Springs golf course. Saddleback, Box 490, Rangeley, ME 04970; (207) 864–5671 for information and (207) 864–5364 for reservations.

New Hampshire

IN NEW HAMPSHIRE, **Loon Mountain** in Lincoln hosts summer visitors who wouldn't cross the street to reach a ski area in winter. But you don't even need to think about skiing to enjoy a warm-weather day or weekend in this White Mountain resort. The enclosed gondola lift that raises skiers to new heights in winter carries summer sightseers to the 3,050-foot summit of Loon Mountain. The cars hold four passengers each, and the ride covers 7,000 feet in ten minutes. After you reach the top your options are plentiful—you can climb the four-story sky tower to enjoy the majestic view, or explore Loon's glacial caves via the trails and boardwalks that constitute the Summit Cave Walk.

Then there is the chance to further stretch your legs on the half-mile-long hiking trail that leads to North Peak. Daily cookouts and Sunday morning pancake breakfasts are served at an outdoor barbecue area, and there is also a restaurant called The Dog Shop. To take advantage of all you can do on the summit of Loon, plan to spend 90 minutes to two hours up high.

The Mountain Club, Loon's own resort hotel, pampers guests with its full fitness center, swimming pools (indoor and outdoor), and tennis courts. Loon also maintains a mountain bike center, a riding stable, archery and target shooting ranges, and plenty of shops, selling antiques, pottery, leather, and children's toys, tailor-made to shrink the bulges in your purse.

A weekend-long arts and crafts fair attracts 40 to 50 dealers to Loon in mid-summer, while the mountain turns shades of tartan in mid-September when the **New Hampshire Highland Games** take place. Bagpipes are in abundance throughout the weekend, but there is also fiddling, drumming, and Scottish dancing, as well as sporting competitions like tug of war and tossing the *caber*, a bulky wooden pole. You might refrain from asking a fully outfitted participant whether anything is worn under his kilt, however, since the response may be: "No, nothing is worn under it. Everything is in great shape." Loon Mountain, Kancamagus Highway, Lincoln, NH 03251; (603) 745–8111.

Wildcat Mountain, near the entrance to the Mount Washington Auto Road in Pinkham Notch, also operates its gondola throughout the summer. Two-passenger cars travel about 12 minutes to reach the 3,960-foot summit. While on the 6,800-foot climb skyward, notice the gradual changes in vegetation as maples and birches at the base give way to spruce and fir trees farther up.

A stellar view of Mount Washington and other peaks greets you at the end of the ride. There are also hiking trails, an observation deck, picnic areas, and a snack bar. Don't be surprised to greet a few hardy hikers while on top of Wildcat; the summit sits on the famous Appalachian Trail.

Wildcat is the setting for two athletic competitions in late summer. The **Wildman Biathlon** consists of a ten-kilometer footrace, a 40-kilometer bike race into Pinkham Notch, and a five-kilometer footrace up the ski area's Polecat Trail, a climb of 2,100 feet. There is also a bicycle festival comprising various biking competitions, including a race up the Mount Washington Auto Road. Wildcat Mountain, Pinkham Notch, Route 16, Jackson, NH 03846; (603) 466–3326.

Still another tram takes summer passengers up **Cannon Mountain** in Franconia Notch, where one has existed since 1938. The present tram ascends 2,022 feet in about five minutes, and from the observation platform at the summit (elevation 4,180 feet) you can eyeball not only the peaks of neighboring mountains like Mount Lafayette, Mount Lincoln, and Mount Liberty, but also ranges in Maine and Vermont. Cannon Mountain, Franconia Notch State Park, Franconia, NH 03580; (603) 823–5563.

The only alpine slide in New Hampshire or Maine is found at **Attitash**, another White Mountains ski area. Those who ride the crawling chair lift up have a much speedier journey down. Sitting in a diminutive sled built for one, you scoot along a three-quarter-mile-long concrete track curving down a slope. Dare to look up and you can take in the commanding views. You are able to control your own speed, but most rides down take about ten minutes. Also on the grounds is a water slide. Attitash, Route 302, Bartlett, NH 03812; (603) 374–2368.

Tennis is king at **Mt. Cranmore** in North Conway. Special camps operate in July and August, and professional tournaments have been held at the Mt. Cranmore stadium. Four indoor and four outdoor tennis courts are included in the ski area's recreation center. When you are not raising a racket you can be climbing the walls—Mt. Cranmore boasts one of the largest indoor climbing walls in the Northeast, an

THE CANNON MOUNTAIN AERIAL TRAM TAKES VISITORS OVER 2,000 FEET UPWARDS IN ABOUT FIVE MINUTES. A VIEW OF MOUNTAINS IN THREE STATES IS YOURS FROM THE SUMMIT.

adequate place to try your skill at this new sport before taking on the White Mountains. The community of North Conway entices visitors with both its three golf courses and shopping opportunities. Don't look for Mt. Cranmore's well-known Skimobile; it has been dismantled. Mount Cranmore, P.O. Box 1640, North Conway, NH 03860; (603) 356–5543.

Like much of the White Mountains, **Waterville Valley** has been a target of summer recreation seekers for over a century, but it wasn't until the 1930s that the Waterville Inn stayed open in winter to house adventurous skiers schussing down old logging roads on Mount Tecumseh. However, Waterville Valley became a giant of a recreation center only after Olympic skier Tom Corcoran purchased the inn in 1966.

The panorama of the 4,000-foot-high peaks surrounding Waterville Valley was the draw in the

1800s, and might to this day still be the biggest lure. Over 60 miles of marked and maintained trails are available for your use, whether you are searching for an easy amble or a challenging uphill hike. Mountain bikes can be rented at the dining and shopping center called Town Square. There are also riding stables, 18 outdoor red-clay and two indoor tennis courts, a substantial fitness center, and nine holes of golf, all on the grounds. And shoppers can delight in the boutiques, where everything from sterling silver jewelry to cookware and active wear is sold. Waterville Valley, Inc., Waterville Valley, NH 03215; (800) 468–2553 or (603) 236–8311.

You don't need to visit the White Mountains for a mountain view. The triple chair lift at **Mount Sunapee State Park** hauls sightseers a mile and a quarter to the summit of Mount Sunapee, 2,743 feet high. (The chair lift is not enclosed, and though you are never more than about 30 feet above the ground, a park spokesman says that the openness might make some prospective riders anxious.)

About halfway up the mountain the view widens, and you are awarded with a spacious tableau of New Hampshire's White and Vermont's Green Mountains. On especially clear days you can see south into Massachusetts and west into New York State. Hiking trails criss-cross the summit and there is a cafeteria at the top, too. Mount Sunapee Ski Area, Sunapee, NH 03772; (603) 763–2356.

Vermont

VERMONT'S BIG SKI areas are no less enterprising in summer than New Hampshire's. Winter ski giant **Killington** in the middle of the state is a virtually self-contained bastion of culture and recreation from June to Labor Day. The Killington Music Festival brings classical chamber music to the Snowshed Base Lodge on a weekly basis for about half the summer, while the Killington Playhouse takes to the stage throughout the season with musicals in repertory.

The theater for much of the sporting action is the 18-hole, par 72 golf course, designed by Geoffrey Cornish. Located at the base of Killington Mountain, the course sits at a cool elevation of 2,000 feet, and includes four ponds and a few tributaries of the Roaring Brook, making up the water hazards. Killington also offers a five-day-long tennis school on

The Killington Playhouse takes to the stage throughout the season with musicals in repertory.

its eight clay and cushion courts built expressly for instruction.

Killington gives its visitors two methods of reaching its 4,241-foot summit. The gondola departs from Route 4 near its junction with Route 100 and climbs three and a half miles to reach the peak. The chair lift travels a mile and a quarter to the summit and leaves from Killington Road, five miles north of the junction of Routes 4 and 100. On radiant, sunny days you can see into five states and Canada. A restaurant, observation deck, and a nature trail are additional peak attractions. Summer Events, 402 Killington Road, Killington, VT 05751; (802) 422–3333 or (800) 343–0762 for golf and tennis information.

When Gerald Ford was in the White House and disco was in vogue, the folks at **Bromley Mountain** in Peru introduced a European institution to North America by constructing the first alpine slide on this side of the Atlantic. The slide's original two tracks were complimented by a third built in 1978, and today's visitors have a choice of sledding down any of the three 4,000-foot-long tracks. The 700-foot vertical descent takes you through the woods and meadows of Bromley Mountain. For another vantage point, hop aboard the chair lift to the summit of Bromley Mountain, site of a lookout tower. Bromley Mountain, P.O. Box 1130, Manchester Center, VT 05255; (802) 824–5522.

Pico Ski Resort, near Killington, has its own alpine slide as well as a miniature golf course. And there's an extensive fitness center, too, with a 75-foot lap swimming pool. Pico Ski Resort, 2 Sherburne Pass, Rutland, VT 05702; (800) 225–7426, (802) 775–4345 for the alpine slide, or (802) 773–1786 for the fitness center.

At one time, folks in **Stowe** like to point out, visitors to this part of northern Vermont were outnumbered by cows. But the Stowe Area Association comments that in 1988, summer revenues first surpassed those of winter. Drawing tourists when the grass is green and the mountain peaks are not capped in white powder is a menu full of appetizing sightseeing and recreational selections.

The majority of your options are based at **Mount Mansfield Resort**, where area boosters flaunt three ways of ascending Vermont's highest peak: the gondola, the auto road, and, of course, on foot. And there is a fourth way to get back down: Stowe's own alpine slide, covering 2,300 feet.

From the 4,393-foot-high summit, views of Lake Champlain, New York's Adirondacks, and New Hampshire's Presidential Range in the White Mountains are all possible. Closer at hand are alpine flowers such as the mountain cranberry and mountain sandwort, which are found in few other settings in Vermont. Rangers staffing the summit will impart what they know about these chilly environs which, climatically speaking, are closer to that of Canada's Hudson Bay than the village of Stowe beneath you.

The gondola seats four passengers who disembark at the Cliff House, a restaurant 3,650 feet above sea level. If you would rather take your car, allow 20 minutes for the drive, and stay in first gear the entire way. When we last drove the auto road, it took half an hour, although we made several stops to rest our car and inspect the area flora. The road ends at 3,850 feet, but you can hike to a higher level.

Or you can stay at ground level and spend your time exercising for fun at Mount Mansfield Resort, with the clubs on an 18-hole, par 72 golf course, or the rackets on any of six clay courts. In addition, the resort contains three outdoor pools and a full fitness center. You'd be advised not to set foot in Stowe Village without your credit cards and without plenty of leisure time for browsing or buying. Mount Mansfield Resort, P.O. Box 1310, Stowe, VT 05672; (802) 253–7311.

Another northern Vermont resort attracting more and more summer travelers is **Smugglers' Notch** in Jeffersonville. Water is the key that breathes life into this ski center every summer as it turns into a water playground with six pools (including two wading pools for toddlers) and three water slides (one just for kids). The longest water slide, called Giant Rapid River Ride, is nearly 30 feet tall and over 300 feet long; guests navigate this cascading water flume on specially crafted inner tubes.

Indeed, visitors to Smugglers' Notch find time to explore the natural waters surrounding the resort, too, like the Brewster River, Smugglers' Stream, and the Lamoille River, just right for fishing, canoeing, and wading. Smugglers' facilities also include a huge day care center with ten rooms of activities—toys, video equipment, fish tanks—and a playground with ramparts, forts, and a pirate ship to keep youngsters intrigued. For adults, there are also tennis, horseback riding, and a fitness center. The Village at Smugglers' Notch, Smugglers' Notch, VT 05464; (802) 644–8851.

Barbecues, tennis, and nature hikes are on the agenda at **Bolton Valley**, about 25 minutes from Burlington. This resort claims its own nature center, many trails including a portion of the Long Trail, and over 150 different wild flowers; both guided and self-guided walks are available. Barbecues and clambakes are scheduled weekly, and there are eight outdoor and two indoor tennis courts. Within a 15-minute drive are two 18-hole golf courses. Bolton Valley Resort, Bolton Valley, VT 05477; (800) 451–3220 or (802) 434–2131.

Jay Peak, at Vermont's rooftop, keeps its 60-passenger tram to Jay Peak in operation all summer long. From the 3,984-foot-high summit, you can see into Maine, three other states, and Canada on clear days. There is also a heated outdoor swimming pool and three Har-Tru tennis courts, and plans are underway for the construction of a golf course. Jay Peak Ski Area, Route 242, Jay, VT 05859; (800) 451–4449 or (802) 988–2611.

At the opposite end of the Green Mountain State is **Mount Snow**. Because of its proximity to heavily populated areas further south, Mount Snow has always attracted skiers from Connecticut, New York, and New Jersey. The area has managed to parlay its popularity into a thriving summer center, too. The golf school opened in 1978, the mountain bike school in 1988. All mountain bike teaching takes place on a 140-mile trail network, serving all levels of ability, that winds its way through the Green Mountain National Forest.

Other country diversions for city dwellers include the **Summerfest** performing arts series, which brings jazz, comedy, classical music, ballet, and other entertainment to southern Vermont. Mount Snow Resort, Mount Snow, VT 05356; (800) 451–4211 or (802) 464–3333.

Stratton Mountain, another self-contained recreational community in southern Vermont, has hosted everything from professional golf and tennis tournaments to a jazz festival and folk music concerts in summer. For those who would rather participate than observe, Stratton is the home of a 27-hole golf course designed by Geoffrey Cornish, and a sports center comprising a fitness room, indoor swimming, and 15 tennis courts.

Equestrians will find Stratton a tempting place to horse around—Stratton Stables offers escorted rides

MOUNTAIN BIKE RIDERS AT MOUNT SNOW SKI AREA CAN RAMBLE
OVER 140 MILES OF DIRT ROADS AND WOODED PATHS.

A RELAXING AFTERNOON WITH THE CLUBS IS PAR FOR
THE COURSE AT STRATTON MOUNTAIN'S LINKS.

along the wooded trails at the foot of the mountain; pony rides and carriage rides are available, too. Additional activities? You will find wind surfing on Stratton Lake, mountain biking along the adjoining back roads, and gondola rides to the top of Stratton Mountain. The Stratton Corporation, Stratton Mountain, VT 05155; (802) 297–2200.

Massachusetts

SOUTHERN NEW ENGLANDERS shouldn't think summer thrills are limited to the north country. In the shadow of Interstate 91 in Holyoke, Massachusetts, is the **Mount Tom Ski Area** and some fancy water works. The 9,000-square-foot wave pool simulates an ocean beach with everything but the sand crabs. Rafts can be rented or you can body surf in the deep end. There are also a 400-foot water slide and a 4,000-foot alpine slide slithering down a hillside. Mount Tom, Route 5, Holyoke, MA 01040; (413) 536–0416.

Jiminy Peak in Hancock near the New York State line bursts with recreational opportunities. Tennis camps offer an opportunity to raise many a racket, while an alpine slide lets you wind up your visit by winding your way downhill. There is a championship putting course with fairways, roughs, bunkers, and water traps, and a pond stocked with rainbow and brown trout ready to give you a vigorous tussle. The school of fish is joined by a school of fishermen: an Orvis fly fishing school is on the premises. Jiminy Peak, Hancock, MA 01237; (413) 738–5500.

MUSIC IN THE GREAT OUTDOORS

In summer there is only one way to listen to music—outside, under the stars or lazing in the sunshine, with an overflowing picnic basket by your side and a blanket or lawn chair as your seat. Whether it be pops, rock, the great classics, a Sousa march, or an anthem from the Broadway stage, sounds that would be sufficiently enjoyable inside a hall are more energizing in the open air. Classics are livelier, rock more animated, pops more effervescent, and marches more commanding.

Tanglewood

TANGLEWOOD: SETTING FOR THE CLASSICS UNDER THE STARS.

THE BEST KNOWN venue for music in the great outdoors in New England is **Tanglewood** in Lenox, Massachusetts. The summer home of the Boston Symphony Orchestra is snuggled among the Berkshire hills near the New York State border; it is

actually a shorter drive to Tanglewood from New York City than from Boston. Anyone who has ever attended a concert on a balmy summer afternoon or evening is certainly familiar with the elaborate picnic settings—candelabra and fancy tables—set up by music gourmets. You might be just as happy with a worn out old blanket and a bucket of Kentucky Fried chicken. But one must admit that the audience is always part of the show.

One segment of Tanglewood's 210 acres is under cover. Buy a ticket for a seat in the Music Shed and you sit under a roof, safe from the elements. Buy a ticket for the lawn and you are out in the open, but also unprotected from rain. Many feel the outdoor atmosphere is worth the risk, but that's up to you.

How did Tanglewood come to be? Its story begins during the days of rumble seats, Franklin Roosevelt, and Paul Whiteman. It was in 1934 when a group of summer residents of the Berkshires—obviously not bothered by, or perhaps in spite of, the woes of the Great Depression—organized a series of three outdoor concerts by members of the New York Philharmonic under the direction of celebrated composer and conductor Henry Hadley. A smashing success, the series was offered the next year, and the Berkshire Symphony Festival was incorporated.

For 1936 the festival committee invited the Boston Symphony Orchestra to take part, under the leadership of another noted conductor, Serge Koussevitzky. The BSO's debut concert in the Berkshires took place on August 13, 1936, under a large tent at a former Vanderbilt estate called Holmwood. Later that year members of the wealthy Tappan family offered their estate, Tanglewood, as a gift to Koussevitzky and the orchestra, and the following year an all-Beethoven program became the first Tanglewood concert.

Little did anyone suspect that the second concert, the following week, would be a total disaster. The concert was to be devoted entirely to the music of Richard Wagner, but it would become near legendary due to the weather. Thunder and torrential rains twice interrupted the *Rienzi Overture* and forced the cancellation of the *Siegfried Forest Murmurs*, a piece too soft to be heard through the noisy downpour. During the concert intermission, a festival founder took to the stage and made an impassioned plea for donations for the building of a permanent pavilion to house the symphony. Within a brief period of time, $100,000 had been raised.

Koussevitzky chose renowned architect Eliel Saarinen to design a new home for the orchestra, but his initial plans far exceeded the budget. Told to trim down the elaborateness of his design, Saarinen offered a simplified version which was rejected once more for being far beyond the limit of the budget. Throwing up his arms in disgust, Saarinen wrote that to stay within the budget the festival trustees would have to limit themselves to "just a shed" that "any builder could accomplish without the aid of an architect."

So the trustees turned to a local Stockbridge engineer, Joseph Franz, to further simplify Saarinen's design in order that it be affordable. Franz succeeded, and the new building was inaugurated on August 4, 1938, with the first concert of that season. The building, with a few alterations, stands today, and except for the years of World War II has been the summer home of the Boston Symphony Orchestra ever since. In 1988, its fiftieth anniversary, the pavilion was renamed the Serge Koussevitzky Music Shed.

Today, Tanglewood draws over 300,000 music aficionados annually for concerts by the BSO, as well as chamber music concerts, prelude concerts and open rehearsals, the annual Festival of Contemporary Music, and almost daily performances by the members of the Tanglewood Music Center, which is a learning center for young music students from around the world.

For a schedule or other information on Tanglewood, contact Symphony Hall, Boston, MA 02115; in summer, call (413) 637–1600; during the rest of the year, call (617) 266–1492.

OTHER OUTDOOR CONCERTS

YOU NEED NOT travel to the far reaches of western Massachusetts, however, to savor music in the great outdoors. Chances are there are similar settings near your home, where you are encouraged to break open the picnic basket and relax as you are serenaded by man's most melodic sounds in nature's choicest settings.

Connecticut

CONNECTICUT HAS ITS own Tanglewood, the **Charles Ives Center For the Arts**, on the Westside Campus of Western Connecticut State University in Danbury. Musicians perform in a pavilion shaped like

a gazebo—with a steep, sloping, shingled roof—that appears to be floating atop a tree-lined pond. The octagonal pavilion hosts about a dozen concerts per season and has witnessed an ample variety of head-liners.

The most frequent occupant of the pavilion is the Ives Symphony Orchestra, conducted by Skitch Henderson, who, you might recall, fronted the Tonight Show band in the 1960s, and James DePreist, former musical director of the Oregon Symphony. Other performers have included jazz saxophonist Gerry Mulligan, country music diva Tammy Wynette, Louisiana Creole king Buckwheat Zydeco, and key-board legend Ray Charles. Charles Ives Center for the Arts, P.O. Box 2957, Danbury, CT 06813; (203) 797–4002.

Sounds on the Sound is a fitting name for the summer music series at **Harkness Memorial State Park** in Waterford. For six weeks you can hear the classics or jazz performed against a backdrop of sail-boats and ferries cruising Long Island Sound. Patrons sit inside a tent (capacity 850) or on the lawn, and picnicking is encouraged; prizes are awarded for

IN CONNECTICUT, MUSIC LOVERS CAN HEAR A VARIED MENU OF POPS, CLASSICS, COUNTRY, ZYDECO, BLUES, AND MORE AT THE CHARLES IVES CENTER FOR THE ARTS.

most elegant picnic, or you can have one prepared for you by advance reservation. Performers have included pianist Peter Serkin, flutist Jean-Pierre Rampal, and jazz kingpin Chick Corea. Pops and family concerts with puppets or guest narrators are also scheduled. Summer Music, Inc., 300 Captain's Walk, Suite 503, New London, CT 06320; (203) 442–9199.

Hartford residents have a couple of outdoor concert series from which to choose. The **Evelyn Preston Memorial Fund Concert Series**, named for the daughter of a Travelers Insurance executive and benefactor, brings a musical mulligan stew to a variety of locations. Jazz performers have included Mel Hinton and the Illinois Jacquet Orchestra. Other concerts have been devoted to bluegrass, salsa, mariachi, rock, chamber music, and the classics, in settings like Elizabeth Park, Keney Park, Goodwin Park, Charter Oak Landing on the riverfront, and Trinity College. Evelyn Preston Memorial Fund Concert Series, Yvonne Harris, 25 Stonington Street, Hartford, CT 06106; (203) 722–6488.

Meanwhile **Trinity College** is the site of weekly outdoor carillon concerts following indoor chamber music performances on Wednesday evenings, mid-June through mid-August. It is common for patrons to attend the 45-minute-long chamber concert, then chow down on picnic dinners to the accompaniment of show music, classics, hymns, and original compositions performed on the carillon. The carillon concerts last an hour and each draws around 1,500 listeners. Admission is free. Trinity College Chapel, 300 Summit Street, Hartford, CT 06106; (203) 297–2000.

New Haven offers a series of concerts similar to Hartford's Evelyn Preston Series. **Picnic Performances** are informal music shows generally attracting 200 to 500 people and taking place in various city parks. A spokesperson for series sponsor Park Friends and City Spirit Artists says: "Our mission is to encourage park use. A lot of people are afraid of their parks. But they shouldn't be. We usually try to match musical style with specific neighborhood parks." Concerts have focused on Scottish, gospel, reggae, folk rock, salsa, and classical styles. Park Friends and City Spirit Artists, 720 Edgewood Avenue, New Haven, CT 06515; (203) 787–8023.

Jazz New Haven on the Green can attract 20,000 to 30,000 persons per concert to hear name artists like Max Roach, Tony Williams, and Tito Puente, as well as regional jazz-oriented musicians. There are usually four to six a year on July or August weekends in the heart of downtown, in what coordinator Allen Lowe calls, "as nice of a downtown setting as you will find in any city." You can bring your own dinner, but concert-goers are encouraged to patronize venders specializing in international cuisines. Mayor's Office, 95 Orange Street, New Haven, CT 06510; (203) 787–8228.

Maine

Picnic & Pops is a trio of concerts presented by the highly regarded Portland Symphony Orchestra at Fort Williams Park (home of the famous Portland Head Lighthouse) in suburban Cape Elizabeth. Sousa marches, ballads, and jigs, and the works of Tchaikovsky supplemented by fireworks over Casco Bay are typical concert highlights. You can order gourmet box suppers or bring your own picnic. Portland Symphony Orchestra, 30 Myrtle Street, Portland, ME 04101; (207) 773–8191.

The Portland Symphony also travels to Damariscotta annually in mid-summer for an outdoor concert at **Round Top Center for the Arts**. Patrons sit on a hillside overlooking a natural amphitheater and the Damariscotta River. The Round Top Center has additionally hosted outdoor music by the Portland Brass Quintet and other performers. Round Top Center for the Arts, Box 1316, Damariscotta, ME 04543; (207) 563–1507.

The respected **Kneisle Hall Music School** holds its festival from late June into late August, with chamber music on Friday evenings and Sunday afternoons. Up to 280 listeners sit on a screened-in veranda outside the main concert hall. The school was founded in the 1920s and continues to attract students from around the world. Kneisle Hall, P.O. Box 648, Blue Hill, ME 04614; (207) 374–2811.

Maine is a haven for town bands.

Maine is a haven for town bands. The communities of Waterville, Hallowell, Lincolnville, Machias, and Farmington are just a few that support their own town bands that perform outdoors. But the most highly regarded are likely the Casco Bay Community Band and the Bangor Band.

Based in South Portland, the **Casco Bay Community Band** plays outdoors at least twice per summer—at Mill Creek Park in South Portland in mid-June, and on the River Green in Kennebunkport on July 3. You might hear everything from P. D. Q. Bach to highlights from *Fiddler on the Roof.* (207) 799–0912.

You can hear the sounds of the **Bangor Band**, which has existed since 1859, by the Paul Bunyan statue in Bangor's Lower Bass Park on Tuesday evenings throughout the summer. Marches, overtures, patriotic tunes, and Dixieland jazz offerings make up most of their concerts. The band is purposely limited to 36 members in order to form a perfect fit in the park bandstand. Some of the average of 450 to 500 fans at each concert bring picnics; others listen in their cars and honk their horns after each number. Music by Maine composers like R. B. Hall and Harvey J. Woods is often featured. (207) 942–1917.

In late June, Maine celebrates **R. B. Hall Day**, honoring the state's homegrown composer. Held outdoors in a different city each year, the day consists of music performed by favorite town bands from morning until late at night. Call the Maine Publicity Bureau for exact date and location. (207) 289–2423.

Massachusetts

IS THERE SUMMER outdoor music beyond Tanglewood? Certainly, and even in western Massachusetts. The **Springfield Symphony Orchestra** delights fans of show and big band music with its quartet of pops concerts at Stanley Park in Westfield. Guest artists have included Judy Collins, Doc Severinsen, and Cleo Laine, and most performances draw 3,000 to 4,000 followers. Venders sell picnic dinners or you can bring your own. As at Harkness Park, there is a picnic contest, and previous winners have designed their picnics to resemble a Hawaiian luau and the set from Phantom of the Opera. Springfield Symphony, 1391 Main Street, Springfield, MA 01103; (413) 733–2291.

An eclectic program is on tap for **Wednesday Folk Traditions**, another western Bay State outdoor music series, taking place evenings in the sunken garden at the **Porter-Phelps-Huntington House Museum** in Hadley. Picnickers are welcome and will hear a wide gamut of tunes, from Sephardic Jewish canticles to pre-colonial West African song and dance to Irish and Scottish folk music. A limited number of chairs are provided, or you can assure yourself of a seat by bringing your own chair or blanket. Concert audiences can be as large as 450.

A limited number of chairs are provided, or you can assure yourself of a seat by bringing your own chair or blanket.

The Porter-Phelps-Huntington House Museum also serves up **A Perfect Spot of Tea**, a revival of the colonial custom of afternoon tea, pastries, and music, on the museum veranda. Linger over a cup while admiring the view of the Connecticut River Valley's lush corn fields backed by the rolling river, and savor the sounds of baroque chamber music. There are two seatings, each limited to 50 or 60 people. The house, built in 1752, is home to furniture and collectibles gathered by ten generations of one family, and is open for afternoon tours Saturday through Wednesday. Porter-Phelps-Huntington Foundation, Inc., 130 River Drive, Hadley, MA 01035; (413) 584–4699 or (413) 586–7870.

New Bedford has a series of **Heritage Concerts**, a half dozen musical events talking place on the back terrace of the **Rotch-Jones-Duff House & Garden Museum**, a Greek Revival masterpiece built by a whaling merchant in 1834. A few hundred generally show up Friday evenings to hear music relating to the people of this southeastern Massachusetts city;

Irish music will dominate each concert. Rotch-Jones-Duff House & Garden Museum, 396 County Street, New Bedford, MA 02740; (508) 997–1401.

The heart of Roslindale bursts with live music Thursday evenings when **Concerts à la Carte** take place in Adams Park. You might hear Irish music one week, fifties rock and roll the next, and perhaps a Greek or Brazilian concert the following week at these concerts sponsored by Roslindale Village Main Street in conjunction with the Mayor's Office of Business and Cultural Development. The small triangular park usually fills with 300 to 500 people per show, with impromptu dancing occurring on the tiled mosaic walkway. The park's benches are occupied early so plan to bring a blanket or lawn chair. Katie Pinchin, Roslindale Village Main Street, 4258 Washington Street, Roslindale, MA 02131; (617) 327–4065.

If **Henry Wadsworth Longfellow** were to come back to his Cambridge home today, he'd likely be surprised by the size of the surrounding city but not by the music performed on the east lawn. Every other Sunday starting in mid-June, period music is offered, all in keeping with the poet's preferences. There might be nineteenth-century folk balladeers or brass bands, or possibly the works of Mozart or Schubert, Longfellow's favorite classical composers. About 400 to 500 attend each event, with seating provided for about half of them. The National Park Service tries to utilize local talent, including musicians attending the prestigious Berklee or Longy Schools. Longfellow National Historic Site, 105 Brattle Street, Cambridge, MA 02138; (617) 876–4491.

New Hampshire

The Saint-Gaudens National Historic Site, caressing the Vermont border in Cornish, comprises the home, studios, and gravesite of Augustus Saint-Gaudens, perhaps America's most illustrious sculptor. The site also holds about eight concerts per summer, with musicians sheltered comfortably in the Little Studio and the listeners either inside the studio or outside on the grass or porch; bands have performed outside on occasion. About 500 to 600 regularly show up to hear a brass band, ethnic music, or perhaps classical romantic pieces rendered by a cello and piano duet. Picnicking is permitted and admission to

the concerts is free. Saint-Gaudens National Historic Site, RR 3, Box 73, Cornish, NH 03745; (603) 675–2175.

A concert locale oozing small town Americana is the green in **Walpole** in the bucolic Monadnock Region of the state, site of Sunday evening musical performances lasting from Independence Day weekend through Labor Day weekend. Around 500 usually come to partake in a potpourri of big band music, Sousa marches, jazz, or bluegrass, mostly interpreted by local town or other bands. Light snacks may be purchased or you can bring a picnic from home. Admission is free. (603) 756–4771.

One group that regularly plays Walpole is Temple, New Hampshire's **Temple Town Band**, claimed to be the oldest in the country. The band was formed in 1799 and was revived around 1980. Today's approximately 45 members bring live music to area villages like New Ipswich, Milford, Wilton, and Jaffrey, as well as their own home, Temple. They practice throughout the winter, performing works by Sousa, Leroy Anderson, Andrew Lloyd Weber, and many

IN THE SHADOW OF SCULPTOR SUPREME AUGUSTUS SAINT-GAUDENS'S *DIANA*, YOU CAN BE SERENADED ON SUMMER AFTERNOONS.

others. For a schedule or information, contact Band Manager Lucille Longo, (603) 878–2829.

Rhode Island

Summer Concerts by the Bay is a succession of seven concerts at Blithewold mansion in Bristol, with two held outside on the grounds. One, usually featuring a brass quintet interpreting classics, theater music, and patriotic songs, takes place around July 4. The other, in August, varies each year and might consist of folk, big band, or jazz. Usually about 300 concertgoers attend and bring lawn chairs and picnic lunches. Blithewold Gardens and Arboretum, 101 Ferry Road, Bristol, RI 02809; (401) 253–2707.

Vermont

The **Vermont Symphony Orchestra** takes to the road with its **Picnicking and Pops** series, presenting light classics and popular favorites at settings like the Trapp Family Meadow in Stowe, Shelburne Farms in Shelburne, Hildene (Robert Todd Lincoln's mansion) in Manchester, Sugarbush Ski Resort in Warren, and Giorgetti Park in Rutland. The approximately 60-piece orchestra serves up everything from Mozart's *Magic Flute* to the works of Sousa and Copland to the *1812 Overture*, complete with fireworks and cannons. Patrons are invited to bring a family picnic and stretch out on the grounds. Vermont Symphony Orchestra, 2 Church Street, Burlington, VT; 05401 (802) 864–5741.

The **Vermont Mozart Festival**, three weeks in mid-summer, also travels, but limits their concert settings to northern Vermont such as the Trapp Family Meadow and Shelburne Farms. Expect to hear the Austrian composer's most haunting chamber music, performed by a single recitalist or a 40-piece orchestra. Picnicking music lovers have been known to set up elaborate spreads for alfresco dining. Also slated are workshops for music students and Mozart Odysseys for anyone; the odysseys are multi-media events involving lectures, private concerts, and interviews exploring single topics regarding Mozart's life and music. Vermont Mozart Festival, P.O. Box 512, Burlington, VT 05402; (802) 862–7352.

The **Trapp Family Meadow** is the scene of other

melodious offerings, as well. **Music in the Meadow** on the Trapp Family Lodge property has hosted jazz and brass bands, and pop singers like Livingston Taylor. Enjoy music amid the mountains in the pastoral Stowe setting, and bring a picnic for these concerts sponsored jointly by Stowe Performing Arts and Stowe Area Association. Stowe Performing Arts also joins with the **Helen Day Art Center** in sponsoring music—marches and the like—a few times a year at the art center gazebo. Admission is free but donations are welcome. Stowe Area Association, Box 1320A, Stowe, VT 05672; (802) 253–7321.

In addition to the Vermont Symphony Orchestra, **Hildene** hosts two concerts by the **Washington County (New York) Concert Band** on the grounds of this majestic mansion in Manchester. They take place in July and August with gates opening at 5:30 P.M. for picnickers, and concerts starting at 7 o'clock. You can anticipate hearing patriotic numbers, show tunes, and other traditional music just right for a balmy summertime evening. Hildene, Box 377, Manchester Village, VT 05254; (802) 362–1788.

Vermont's oldest regularly playing town band is in the southern Vermont village of **Grafton**, home of the historic Old Tavern and referred to by some as the most photographed village in the Green Mountain State. The all-volunteer Grafton Band, formed in 1867 to perform at the first Memorial Day observance, plays throughout the area, but mostly on Sunday evenings on the town green in this luscious little burg. Their schedule is posted on town bulletin boards, but you can also receive information by calling the Grafton town clerk, (802) 843–2419.

THE MOST FESTIVE FOURTHS

M any are the places in New England to celebrate the Fourth of July with more than just a bang (to say nothing of a whimper). Every village and town bigger than a shopping mall toasts the Fourth with the usual rites—fireworks, a rock band, and a hot dog on a bun. However, you can celebrate Independence Day in a distinctly traditional or festive manner by attending any of these events.

The Fourth of July at Old Sturbridge Village

THE FIRST PEOPLE you might notice are the children in long gowns standing on the town common, legs bent, arms poised, tossing hoops back and forth, trying to catch them on two sticks in a game they call "the graces."

Their parents are nearby, enjoying an outdoor version of some primeval ancestor of bowling. One pin is missing but nobody cares. They keep rolling, trying to knock down all nine. You may have the urge to tell them their game should be disqualified since they are lacking a tenth pin.

But it's easy to forget that one can't think in twentieth-century terms at Old Sturbridge Village in Sturbridge, Massachusetts, especially on the Fourth of July.

You can celebrate Independence Day in a distinctly traditional or festive manner by attending any of these events.

Walk into the sturdy, steeple-topped meetinghouse that borders the common. You might hear a hearty male voice boom: "Fellow citizens: more than a half a century has fled since the sons of Columbia fanned the sacred fire of liberty upon the altar of American independence.

"There has been no revolution known in the history of mankind so memorable in its consequences."

A Massachusetts patriot named Josiah Snow wrote those words to celebrate the Fourth of July over 150 years ago. At Old Sturbridge Village, a leading "citizen" from the nineteenth century reads them.

His contemporaries in the meetinghouse wear black coats or gowns and bonnets. Onlookers from the twentieth century wearing jeans and T-shirts or sport shirts or summer dresses listen intently, absorbing the feel of this man's impassioned tribute to liberty.

In many ways, the Fourth of July in the 1830s was celebrated as ours is, with speeches, celebrations, and recreation. But the nineteenth-century versions of those activities were far different.

For example, when Old Sturbridge Village opens its doors at 9 A.M., the costumed inhabitants ring in Independence Day with the chiming of the meetinghouse bell. Then the day's activities start with a blast from the past, as stalwart young men in militia uniforms fire their muskets on the common.

The common, in the nineteenth century, was the social center of most New England villages; this is where the Fourth of July fun takes place.

But the spiritual and governmental center was the meetinghouse. Church and state hadn't yet separated in the time depicted here, so this building hosted most of the serious holiday observances like the traditional Independence Day service and assembly. Orations are changed every year at Sturbridge, so while you might hear Josiah Snow's words in eloquent discourse, visitors a different year can hear others, including an oration on the Constitution and slavery, followed by anthems and prayers. "Anacreon in Heaven" is the name of one such anthem. A stanza from "Anacreon" goes:

> To the sages who spoke, to the heroes who bled,
> to the day and the deed strike the harp strings of glory,
> Let the song of the ransom'd remember the dead,
> and the tongue of the eloquent hallow the story.

For the benefit of modern-day visitors, the service, which would have lasted two hours in the nineteenth-century, is trimmed down to 30 minutes. Similarly, another nineteenth-century tradition is altered for the sake of modern-day visitors.

It was customary in the 1830s to read the Declaration of Independence in the meetinghouse. But since seating indoors is limited, at 2 P.M. a leading Old Sturbridge Village citizen recites the words from a

A LEADING CITIZEN OF THE NINETEENTH CENTURY READS THE DECLARATION OF INDEPENDENCE FROM A FLAG-BEDECKED PODIUM AT OLD STURBRIDGE VILLAGE EVERY FOURTH OF JULY.

podium in front of the meetinghouse, enabling all those within earshot to hear.

Routine life goes on, too, just as in real life. Not everyone is on the common celebrating. On the Freeman Farm chores have to be tackled, and a holiday is no exception. When you visit the farm, you'll see hired hands feeding chickens or pitching hay. In the residential Fitch house the housekeeper is busy baking a tomato pie for the evening's meal. She's pleased to share with visitors the ingredients: tomatoes, eggs, sugar, cream, and a dash of nutmeg.

But she's not pleased that she's missing the fun on the common. Head there in the afternoon and you will see nineteenth-century games like hoop rolling and nine-pin bowling. (Anyone care to join and try for a perfect 270?) And weather and wind permitting, a staff member will raise his toy hot-air balloon.

Those not partial to such elementary pastimes are welcome to watch the parade of militiamen, farmers, tradesmen, and leading Sturbridge citizens, or the afternoon demonstrations of lively nineteenth-century dances like the cotillion or the galop to the accompaniment of fiddles.

MUSKETS, DRUMS, AND AUTHENTIC COSTUMES MARK THE HOLIDAY PARADE AT OLD STURBRIDGE VILLAGE.

Visitors can also listen to the martial band who, dressed in authentic costumes, play fifes and drums to tunes like, "Go to the Devil and Shake Yourself," "Jefferson and Liberty," and "Captain Money's March."

Never heard these songs? That's not surprising. They are very popular at Old Sturbridge Village. But then, news can travel slowly in the 1830s. Old Sturbridge Village, Sturbridge, MA 01566; (617) 347–3362.

The Oldest July 4 Celebration in the Country

IN 1785, THE Reverend Henry Wight gathered with a small group of his fellow citizens in Bristol, Rhode Island, most likely at the Congregational Church, on the Fourth of July, where they listened to a series of recitations and orations commemorating the anniversary of the signing of the Declaration of Independence.

Every year since then, the people of Bristol have marked Independence Day with an official celebration. In the early 1800s the observances were similar to those held at Old Sturbridge Village today, with speeches, bonfires, the sounds of rifle fire and cannon blasts, and official toasts. In 1865, Civil War veterans were welcomed home with a prominent place

THE UNIFORMS ARE DIFFERENT BUT THE SPIRIT IS THE SAME AT THIS JULY 4 PARADE, PART OF THE OLDEST INDEPENDENCE DAY CELEBRATION IN THE COUNTRY, IN BRISTOL, RHODE ISLAND.

in Bristol's parade. In 1943, women in the military appeared in the parade for the first time and in 1948, the first Miss Fourth of July was selected.

Presently Bristolians mark the day with a two-hour-long parade. Walk along Hope Street in the wee hours of July 4 morning, long before the rest of world has awoke, and you will see a spectacle of lawn chairs and coolers and blankets, marking parade-watching spots, staked out well in advance. The most prized seats are near the center of Bristol, around Hope and Church or Hope and State Streets, or around the viewing stand at the town common on Church and High Streets.

By 10:30, when the procession starts at Hope and Chestnut Streets, the parade route, two and a half miles along Hope Street and on High Street south of the common, is one massive sea of humanity. About 175,000 observers show up annually, including countless spectators from all of southern New England. Since traffic into the city can jam up by 8:30 A.M., out-of-town parade viewers should plan to arrive as early as 8 o'clock.

For several years in the mid-1980s, there was an acknowledged problem of rowdiness, and in 1988 nine bands sent letters stating their refusal to participate unless the crowds were better controlled. The parade route was subsequently declared an "alcohol free zone" and the problem has diminished. Today those acting like clowns are probably covered in make-up and are paid to act that way.

Annual favorites vary according to one's tastes, but it's not a stretch to say that the Mummers bands from Philadelphia, decked out in their gaudiest rhinestones, feathers, and silk, are perhaps the most awaited. Horses and antique fire engines also claim their devotees. There are also fife and drum corps, marching bands from close by and as far away as the Midwest, mounted police color guards, and floats, floats, floats. You can commonly expect to see over three dozen floats coast by. And speaking of floats, Navy ships have made guest appearances here since the USS *Juniata*, sloop of war, arrived in 1876. There will likely be a Navy ship that you can board anchored in Bristol Harbor when you visit.

Following the parade, all's fair at the carnival on the town common, often followed by a pops concert. The Rhode Island Philharmonic takes their turn with a pops concert in the evening at Colt State Park, before giving way to the booms and glares of fireworks. (401) 253–7739.

OTHER FESTIVE FOURTHS

Massachusetts

Boston Harborfest is a big city bash lasting several days, incorporating the Fourth. Concerts and cruises are just a couple of the nearly 100 events scheduled annually for this behemoth of a festival. The tastiest is the Boston Chowderfest, in which visitors sample clam chowder cooked up by the chefs from a dozen-odd city restaurants and cast ballots for "The Best Chowder in Boston". In one recent year, nearly 11,000 chowder-heads emptied more than 65,000 cups of chowder. Admission is charged.

Other happenings include the Constitution Cup Regatta, tours of U.S. Coast Guard and Navy ships, cruises to the neighboring pastoral Harbor Islands, and the Party on the Plaza, a family-oriented blowout at City Hall, featuring music usually from the fifties or sixties. And of course, there's the 21-cannon salute fired from *Old Ironsides* (a.k.a. the USS *Constitution*) and the Boston Pops Concert at the Hatch Shell, in which Tchaikovsky's *1812 Overture* is accompanied by fireworks high in the sky over the Charles River. Boston Harborfest, 45 School Street, Boston, MA 02108; (617) 227–1528.

Connecticut

WHILE BOSTON PAYS tribute to its harbor, Connecticut's capital does the same with its Connecticut River. Hartford and East Hartford celebrate **Riverfest** for one day on the closest weekend to July 4. Head to Great River Park or Charter Oak Landing to spy on the colonial battle re-enactment on the river, or to watch hydroplane racing or a water-ski show. Or sail down the Connecticut on a river-boat cruise. Additional usual features are a juggling jamboree at the Old State House, an arts and crafts show, and much music, provided by a fife and drum corps, a Dixieland band, and the Hartford Symphony Orchestra. Fireworks cap the 14 hours of festivities. Hartford Downtown Council, 250 Constitution Plaza, Hartford, CT 06103; (203) 728–3089.

At **Mystic Seaport** in Mystic the costumes and cus-

THE SKIES OVER DOWNTOWN HARTFORD ARE DECORATED EVERY JULY 4 BY FIREWORKS DURING RIVERFEST.

toms on view date from 1877. Step onto the village green for a lively game of croquet with historically dressed nineteenth-century residents. Gather at the bandstand for speeches and songs, including the national anthem, "America." (In 1877, "America," not "The Star-Spangled Banner," was the national anthem.) Watch demonstrations of sail handling and whaling. Youngsters can don paper hats and noise-makers and fall in step in the children's parade, following a Fourth of July parade headlined by Uncle Sam, a paragon of patriotism wrapped in red, white, and blue. Then they can refresh themselves with ice cream or lemonade squeezed from fresh lemons on the waterfront, both sold by costumed venders. Mystic Seaport, 50 Greenmanville Avenue, P.O. Box 6000, Mystic, CT 06355; (203) 572–0711.

Maine

WHAT DOES IT mean to be first? In Eastport, Maine, where locals say the sun hits mainland America first (though we'd advise you not to say that to anyone from neighboring Lubec), it means you can be the first in the country to celebrate the Fourth, coinciding with its **Old Home Week**.

The usual four-day fiesta is noted for an all-American array of entertainment: a parade, a firemen's

muster, the presence of American and/or Canadian Navy ships in the harbor waiting to be toured, a barbershop quartet, a pancake breakfast, mud wrestling (G-rated, we might add), and a fireworks spectacular. Arrive three days earlier and you can celebrate Canada Day, July 1, with Eastport's Canadian neighbors, a proverbial stone's throw from downtown. (207) 853–4644.

AT MYSTIC SEAPORT, THE FRIVOLITY OF PAPER HATS AND THE CACOPHONY OF NOISEMAKERS ADD A TOUCH OF LEVITY TO THE SERENE MARITIME LOCALE DURING JULY 4 FESTIVITIES.

New Hampshire

SHOULD A SUMMER vacation take you into New Hampshire's White Mountains on Independence Day, you can attend an **Old-Fashioned Fourth of July** in the twin towns of Lincoln and Woodstock. Residents gather in the afternoon for the gala parade with trophies awarded to floats in the categories of most original, most humorous, and most patriotic, among others. In the evening, concerts are presented from the bandstands in Lincoln and North Woodstock followed by a fireworks display in the night air above the mountains. (603) 745–6621.

Rhode Island

If the nickname "Ocean State" ever wears thin, Rhode Islanders might want to call their home the "Parade State."

IF THE NICKNAME "Ocean State" ever wears thin, Rhode Islanders might want to call their home the "Parade State." The big Bristol event isn't the only long-standing July 4 procession in the state. What began as an Ancient and Horribles parade in 1925 is today the **Arnold Mills Parade**—four divisions of antique and vintage cars, tractors, fire engines, bands, clowns, and assembled "horribles" proceeding down the Nate Whipple Highway (Route 120) in the Arnold Mills section of Cumberland. The "horribles" are usually in costumes satirizing recent events, having hauled a wagon marked "Tammy Faye Bakker's Make-up", and marched as part of the "Save Donald Trump" brigade. The parade is preceded by a road race, and is followed by a concert on the green. Arnold Mills Parade Association, P.O. Box 7473, Cumberland, RI 02864; (401) 658–1502.

Vermont

IN PLYMOUTH NOTCH, Vermont, there is a dual celebration on the Fourth of July, commemorating not only Independence Day but the birth of favorite son Calvin Coolidge. The 30th president of the United States, the epitome of stern austerity, and a Yankee Doodle Dandy if there ever was one, is the only president literally born on the Fourth of July.

President Coolidge's birthday is observed—appropriately some might say—in a solemn manner with a guided walk from the center of Plymouth Notch where he was born, to the Notch Cemetery, where he is buried among six generations of his family. The president's grave is simple, distinguished from those of the other Coolidges only by the presidential seal and four stars.

The walk takes about 20 minutes, is usually led by a Vermont National Guard color guard, and draws about 500 visitors. Different Coolidge quotes on related topics, such as the holiday, Yankee independence, or the American character are offered briefly at the gravesite. In the village, a commemorative envelope honoring Coolidge's birth is sold. The village's museum buildings—Calvin's boyhood home, his birthplace, the visitor center and museum, among others—are open as usual, and you should allow one to two hours to tour them. There is no nighttime fireworks presentation in Plymouth Notch, but there is one in nearby Killington. The Calvin Coolidge Memorial Foundation, Plymouth, VT 05056; (802) 672–3389.

Life in Vermont when Calvin Coolidge was in rompers is the focus of **Old Time Farm Day**, held annually on July 4 at Shelburne Museum in northwestern Vermont. Living history is the rule as a road-weary Yankee peddler regales the assembled multitude with tales of his travels, or musicians with Vermont's fastest fingers play homegrown fiddle and banjo tunes. Children can try their luck in the pea-shucking contest, cooks of all ages can submit entries in the pie-baking contest, and baseball fans can take part or watch others play a nineteenth-century version of America's pastime. Don't adjust your glasses; the baseball diamond is supposed to be square, and who ever heard of a foul ball? Admission is charged. Shelburne Museum, Shelburne, VT 05482; (802) 985–3346.

NATIVE AMERICAN POWWOWS AND FESTIVALS

The story goes that a blueblood trying to impress guests at a party was boring all with the details of her ancestor who had arrived on the *Mayflower*. Finally, she asked a man if his roots were as pure as hers. The man, part American Indian, responded, "No, my ancestors didn't come over on the *Mayflower*. They met the boat."

You needn't journey to Arizona or New Mexico to get a taste of Indian culture. You can step inside a wickiup or wigwam, watch centuries-old moccasin or war dances to the hypnotic beat of drums, or chow down on a buffalo burger much closer to home. The American Indian has an extensive heritage in New England, and you will find it celebrated in annual powwows and Native American gatherings throughout the summer.

For Indians the powwow is both a chance to celebrate their heritage and a reunion of sorts. Carolyn Norback, a Blackfoot who lives in New Hampshire, has been attending New England's powwows for a quarter of a century. She says: "The powwow is where you meet your friends. Native Americans who live in an urban setting don't have contact with each other as do those who live on reservations. The powwow provides that contact. After the commercial part is over, that's when we gather around the drum for storytelling and socializing."

Visitors are welcome at any of the following authentic and traditional events, to observe and learn from Native Americans. The dances are real and the handcrafts are genuine; you won't find tomahawks with Day-Glo feathers on display at these fetes.

Quinnehtukqut Rendezvous and Native American Festival

EXAMINE THE WORD "Quinnehtukqut" carefully and you can see how "Connecticut" evolved from this Algonquian word, meaning "the land of the long tidal river." Appropriately it is along the banks of the Connecticut River, in Haddam Meadows State Park, where the three-day **Quinnehtukqut Rendezvous** get-together transpires in August.

One could easily spend an hour or two browsing through arts and crafts tents. While the majority of sellers are eastern Indians, this affair does bring in craftspeople and traders from throughout this country and Canada. When we visited, one woman had come from the faraway Acoma Pueblo in New Mexico to sell her traditional pottery—brown bowls and jars marked with their distinctive geometrical designs.

Thanks to the wide range of tribes on hand, visitors can expect to find a huge variety in crafts. We were

REALISTIC NATIVE AMERICAN HOUSING IS RECREATED AT THE QUINNEHTUKQUT
RENDEZVOUS AND NATIVE AMERICAN FESTIVAL IN CONNECTICUT.

told that the turtle plays a sacred role in the Mohawk creation myth—it is believed that a giant turtle supports the earth on its back—and we saw a wide selection of turtles for sale, made of corn husks or incorporated into jewelry, for example. And there were purses and other accessories made from entire turtle shells.

Contrasting with the Acoma pottery and the Mohawk turtles were *dreamcatchers* from the Ojibwa tribe. These circles of willow or grapevine reeds are filled with a network of feather webs and are spotted with a few dabs of turquoise, then suspended over the cribs of Ojibwa children to catch their bad dreams; a hole in the center of the dreamcatcher allows good dreams to pass through.

Bracelets, earrings, and other jewelry, weavings, rugs, purses, and sweetgrass baskets were in abundance. Kids seemed to gravitate towards the handmade drums, and novelties like the Apache *skullcracker*, a wrapped rock dangling from a carved stick, or the detailed eagles carved from moose antlers. Medicine wheels, somewhat like zodiacs for earth worshippers and based on the cyclical nature of life, fascinated the astrology buffs.

Perhaps most intriguing were the Iroquois *no-face dolls*. An Iroquois legend about their origin says that the Corn Spirit asked the Great Spirit what she could do for her people. She was told to make a doll from her husk. She did so, giving it a beautiful face. The doll went from village to village, where Indian children repeatedly complimented her on her beauty. It wasn't long before she became conceited, and would stop to admire her reflection in a pool of water.

The Great Spirit warned her that a terrible punishment would befall her if she kept thinking she was better than others.

The Great Spirit warned her that a terrible punishment would befall her if she kept thinking she was better than others. But the doll didn't listen. After being called to the Great Spirit's lodge, she looked once more into the pool of water and was greeted with a reflection of herself without a face. So the Iroquois don't put a face on the corn husk doll, as a reminder to children never to think they are better than others. Haunting corn husk dolls with blank faces populated the festival craft tents.

As you talk with the craftspeople, watch the dancers, and listen to their stories, you will find that Hollywood images fade away and are replaced by truisms. An Iroquois man told us: "People hear I'm an Indian and they ask me, 'Where's your horse?' I explain that I'm an Iroquois and we don't have horses. We didn't live on the plains of the West. We live in the East in and around forests where horses wouldn't be of any use."

As a quartet of Iroquois dancers from the Allegany Reservation near Salamanca in western New York State took to the center stage, spokesperson Kyle Dowdy pointed out: "You will notice we don't wear long headdresses like the Indians out West. All we wear on our hats is a single feather."

After the Iroquois performed their welcome dance, fish dance, rabbit dance, and war dance, Dowdy offered: "This is why we Iroquois got beat. We danced all night and were too pooped to fight back."

Apache dancers from Arizona performed in their extensive head gear and black hoods, totally covering their faces and contrasting sharply with the eastern Indians. Though dance competitions between Indians of specific age groups are scheduled regularly, the best times to note the variations in dress and style are during the intertribal dance exhibitions.

An Anakabi woman from Connecticut wearing an antelope skin told us: "In many ways the different tribes are like people from different countries. Our languages and lore vary quite a bit from one another."

Her costume, she added, was truly Native American, but at home she would wear jeans and a T-shirt. The authentic garb was for the sake of the visitors, who expect to see Indians in their traditional clothing. "I'm sure people would be disappointed seeing me in what I wear at home."

BY THE BANKS OF THE CONNECTICUT RIVER, NATIVE AMERICANS SERVE UP A LOOK AT LIFE IN THESE ENVIRONS A FEW HUNDRED YEARS AGO.

In that vein, observers in Haddam are also afforded the chance to examine a simulation of an archetypal Indian village. A couple sat outside of a recreated eastern wigwam, a conical shelter made of white poplar bark, while we stepped inside a wickiup, a pyramidal hut of cattail reeds, and stood on the floor of hard-packed dirt. Eastern Indians, we heard, would have covered the floor with cattail mats while those residing in the West, with its drier soil, used mats made of animal hides.

Another method of getting a taste of Indian culture is by patronizing the food booths. While you can purchase your basic hot dog at the fest, why not treat yourself to the exotic and Native American, like venison sausage or barbecued buffalo burger, tasting not much different from grilled hamburger meat? Buffalo boosters on hand proudly pointed out how their chosen victual is lower in calories and cholesterol than other red meats.

Another sampling fresh from the West was the Indian taco, topped with chili meat, cheese, onions, lettuce, and tomato, and different from the Mexican variety since fry bread replaces the traditional corn or flour tortilla. Meanwhile, vegetarians could have opted for the side dishes of combined corn, beans, and rice.

New England Native American cuisine was represented by clam cakes, deep fried breading stuffed with clams and resembling a fritter in texture and taste. The Mohawks sold buffalo burgers, hot dogs, and cold cuts on their puffy, chewy scon bread, and also served up Mohawk-style corn soup made with Indian corn, beans, and pork.

At this particular festival, the Native American gathering is supplemented by the Rendezvous, three groups of craftspersons recreating encampments that occurred during three early American periods: the French and Indian War, the American Revolution, and the Rocky Mountain fur trade era. Frontier events like the woman's frying pan throw competition and black powder shooting matches are scheduled daily, while craftspersons in early American garb—knickers, vests, cotton shirts, simulated beaver hats, and the like—sell handmade wares appropriate to the period they represent. We saw everything from rocking chairs to jewelry, lanterns to freshly milled and packaged grains. Quinnehtukqut Rendezvous, 290 Roberts Street, 203C, East Hartford, CT 06108; (203) 282-1404.

OTHER FESTIVALS

BUT THIS HARDLY is the only Native American gathering in New England. Others take place elsewhere in Connecticut, and in Massachusetts and Rhode Island.

Connecticut

THE CONNECTICUT RIVER Powwow Society, Inc., sponsors three events. Mid-June's **Strawberry Moon Powwow** at Ferry Park in Rocky Hill is held to commemorate the spring moon associated with the season of strawberries. The **Mohegan Homecoming & Powwow** at Fort Shantok State Park in Montville was for many years a homecoming just for the Mohegan people. In order to increase awareness of their tribe, however, in 1989 the intertribal powwow was added.

The Connecticut River Powwow and Rendezvous, which has taken place in Portland and Southington, began as part of the statewide celebration for Connecticut's 350th anniversary in 1985, and evolved into an annual gathering. Elaine Alson, spokesperson for the society, says that it was developed by Native Americans in response to the perceived commercialism of the Quinnehtukqut Festival. But, Alson adds, the historic old ways are not necessarily the rule at the society's powwows.

She says: "Some Native Americans show up in traditional regalia, while some go into the circle wearing sneakers, jeans, and jackets. Some of the storytellers may not follow age-old traditions. We have featured a Mohawk ventriloquist and singers who do country western and folk. We insist that all crafts are made by Native Americans but some, like a silversmith we know, are coming out with modern designs.

"We want people to know," Alson adds, "that Native Americans are working in factories, or in entertainment, or have office jobs. Native Americans are doctors and lawyers. They are no different than anyone else."

For more information on any of the three powwows, call (203) 684–5407.

Another American Indian powwow brings Indian traders, storytellers, dancers, and musicians to Black Rock State Park in Watertown in September. It is intertribal and is sponsored by two Connecticut-based Native American groups, American Indians for

Development and Eagle Wing Press. For more information, call (203) 238–4010.

Massachusetts

CAPE COD IS the setting for the annual three-day Mashpee Wampanoag Powwow, held early in the summer. Mashpee resident Nosapocket (Ramona Peters), who has served as powwow master of ceremonies, says: "There are many powwows, but for Mashpee, this is like a homecoming. Many tribes and nations come here."

You can expect to find Native American foods like succotash with corn, rice, beans, buffalo meat, and venison stew alongside handcrafts for sale.

You can expect to find Native American foods like succotash with corn, rice, beans, buffalo meat, and venison stew alongside handcrafts for sale. Likely events include drum and dance contests and the purification of the circle (focal point at the contest) by the Supreme Medicine Man using smoke and feathers. Mashpee Wampanoag Indian Tribal Council, P.O. Box 1048, Mashpee, MA 02649; (508) 477–0208.

An appropriate place to hold a powwow is the Mohawk Trail in western Massachusetts. In Charlemont there's a weekend-long affair every August with dancing, singing, storytelling, food, and crafts. A spokesperson reports: "You never know who's going to be here. One year the Navajos were here; another time Indians from Bolivia came." (413) 339–4096.

Rhode Island

THE NARRAGANSETT INDIAN Tribe entered the 1990s with their 314th Annual August Meeting. But Tribal War Chief Mosqua (John Thomas) cautions: "That is only since the meeting has been recorded by the Europeans. The tradition goes back much further to the thirteenth or fourteenth centuries."

The Charlestown Indian Grounds in Charlestown, off Route 2, is the place where this six-century-old tradition endures every August. Says John Brown, tribal medicine man understudy: "This is the continuation of living history that predates any colonial contact."

Like other Native American gatherings, this two-day event is open to members of other tribes and their guests. It also begins with the cleansing of the circle by the tribal medicine man and includes other ceremonies, singing, dancing, handmade crafts, and traditional foods, many with a Rhode Island flair. For sale are jonnycakes and other foods made with quahogs, clams, crabs, Jerusalem artichoke roots, wild onions, squash, and pumpkin. For information, contact Chief and Council, Narragansett Indian Tribe, P.O. Box 268, Charlestown, RI 02813; (401) 364–1100 or (401) 364–9832.

An additional powwow is sponsored by Rhode Island's Algonquian Indian School in Providence's Roger Williams Park on the second weekend of July. Scheduled for the two-day gathering are traditional chanting and dancing, arts and crafts demonstrations, and Native American foods.

Says school spokesperson Little Crow: "The human and spiritual resources of Native Americans swept aside and forgotten through progress are being renewed by the Native people at the Algonquian Indian School. The school's powwow is fundamental to the sharing of those resources with others, and has helped to discourage stereotyping and to some degree has lessened prejudice towards the American Indian."

Admission is free. (401) 785-9450.

The Dovecrest Trading Post in Exeter hosts its day-long **Strawberry Festival** in June, and a **String Bean Festival** in mid-summer. In addition to dancing and crafts, foods made from the honored items are sold. In October the cranberry is celebrated, while in spring it's maple sugar. (401) 539–7795.

Food, Glorious Food

Summer is the time to pay gustatory honors to—as they say in France, as well as Quebec—the fruits of the sea. At various oceanside locations New Englanders can be found offering tributes to lobsters, clams, oysters, scallops, chowders, and quahogs. Our culinary kudos aren't limited to seafood though, as anyone digging into a plate of souvlakia, kielbasa, or jambalaya at one of New England's ubiquitous summer food festivals will tell you. Our motto could be, "If it tastes good, indulge."

The Maine Lobster Festival

WHEN KING NEPTUNE arrives in Rockland, Maine, from the salty brine via a Coast Guard cutter with siren blaring all the while, you know the **Maine Lobster Festival** is about to begin in earnest. The full-bearded Neptune, Roman god of the sea, is just one of the characters you can expect to encounter during four days of maritime mayhem in this mid-Maine coastal seaport.

EXPECT TO ENCOUNTER SEA GODS AND GODDESSES, PIRATES, AND A HOST OF SCALAWAGS AT ROCKLAND'S MAINE LOBSTER FESTIVAL.

Neptune is always accompanied by seafaring celebrities including the locally chosen Sea Goddess, her Crown Princess, Bluebeard the pirate, and a host of scalawags. There is also a local fellow nicknamed Popeye, who looks and dresses the part of the grizzled cartoon sailor, and frequents the festival grounds during this tribute to Maine's most famous product.

The fest actually commences on the day before Neptune makes his first official appearance, since food and commercial venders begin selling their wares Thursday afternoon, and there is a children's parade and a pancake breakfast Friday morning. Pancakes and Neptune aside, however, this is an event where seafood is the real god that's honored

GUESTS OF HONOR AT THE MAINE LOBSTER FESTIVAL
ARE WAITING TO BE SERVED IN SUNDRY WAYS.

and the aromas of cooking waft through the seaside air.

In the late 1970s, in fact, the title of the gala was changed to the Maine Seafood Festival. But while there are all types of seafood, "lobster dinners are what we do best," says one festival spokesperson, and the name was changed back in 1985.

No one goes hungry here. Booths selling lobster in a plenitude of forms, in addition to every other variety of seafood, are abundant. And visitors get to sample the goods dished out by entrants in the seafood cooking contest. Recipes containing any fish caught in Maine waters are eligible, and while you are sure to have your fill of lobster Newburgh, pie, and quiche, as well as scallops and other shellfish, you should also be able to taste-test some of the less usual, such as a squid pasta casserole or a crab meat dip served flat and round and resembling a pizza.

Other seafood morsels can be yours at the many showcase tents where exhibitors, such as the Maine Sardine Council, will demonstrate how the lilliputian herrings are caught as you sample one or two. Sardines are also the center of attention in the periodic sardine packing contest, where sardine packers vie for cash prizes and the title of "Fastest Packer in the East."

You might not see the sardine struggle when you visit, but other competitions will certainly be scheduled. One annual event is the Great International William Atwood Lobster Crate Race, named in honor of the supplier of the lobster crates.

A total of 50 crates are stuffed with seaweed and made buoyant, then tied together, with the end crates tied to floats. Contestants in different weight classes then run from crate to crate, back and forth. He or she who runs over the most crates without falling is the winner. One veteran observer advises: "You have to get off one and run onto the next one pretty darn fast or you end up in the cold, wet harbor. Most people last until the third crate and then fall off."

The all-time champion is a local girl of 17 who, in a feat that would have exhausted any out-of-shape combatant, hopped, skipped, and ran across 3,007 crates before falling in the water.

Musical performances and puppet shows take place on the main stage or at various tents, and Saturday evening usually is highlighted by name performers (though not necessarily famous household names). Other features? There are crafts demonstrations and sales; you might see a glass blower one year, a weaver the next. There's a parade through the center of town with a different theme annually. And there are some serious presentations, like a boating safety booth sponsored by the Maine Marine Patrol.

Finally, Sunday afternoon, the festival officially closes when the God of Honor, Neptune, returns to the far reaches of the sea.

The Maine Lobster Festival, an annual event since 1947, is held in early August. Maine Lobster Festival, P.O. Box 552, Rockland, ME 04841, or Rockland Area Chamber of Commerce, Harbor Park, P.O. Box 508D, Rockland, ME 04841; (207) 596–0376.

OTHER SEASIDE FOODFESTS

Maine

DON'T EXPECT TO see many revelers in clamdiggers but do count on many who dig clams at Yarmouth, Maine's annual **Clam Festival**, held in mid-July. Similar in many ways to Rockland's Lobster Festival, this three-day tribute to all things clammy features a parade down Main Street, a lot of music (some performers appear at both Maine fests), and crafts—jewelry, furniture, stained glass, baskets, and the like—for sale. And similarly, there is a cornucopia of food, transcending the festival honoree. Soft-shelled clams may be supplemented by fish chowder, scallop rolls, lobster stew, and oysters, not to mention generic fair foods like pizza, doughboys, ice cream, and hot dogs. The clam festival has been a Yarmouth institution since 1965. Yarmouth Chamber of Commerce, 16 U.S.1, P.O. Box 416, Yarmouth, ME 04096; (207) 846–3984.

Connecticut

WHILE THE CITIZENS of Maine fete lobsters and clams, in Connecticut they honor oysters. Norwalk has a pearl of an **Oyster Festival** annually in early September. The two-day, three-night event is one of the Constitution State's largest events, drawing over 200,000.

Since 1978, oyster lovers have been paying gustatory homage to this mollusk by dining, shopping, and letting themselves be entertained by name musicians, commonly big band survivalists or golden oldies groups from the fifties through the seventies—the

HOW MANY OYSTERS CAN AN
OYSTER SHUCKER SHUCK? IN
THE OYSTER SHUCKING
CONTEST AT THE NORWALK
OYSTER FESTIVAL, ENTRANTS
VIE FOR TOP HONORS.

Grass Roots, the Turtles, and Blood, Sweat, and Tears appeared at a recent fest.

At a couple dozen food booths you will find oysters on the half shell, fried oysters, and everything from steamers and shrimp to ethnic foods like souvlakia and tacos. Over 200 craft booths are there to tempt your purse strings, and a small contingent of tall ships usually makes an appearance in the harbor. And shucks, you might even win the oyster shucking contest. Norwalk Seaport Association, 92 Washington Street, South Norwalk, CT 06854; (203) 838–9444.

A smaller but no less tasty **Oyster Festival** lures about 20,000 to Milford's historic town green one day every August. Those who gather here relish the taste of oysters, shrimp, clams, kielbasa, grinders, hot dogs, and hamburgers among other goodies, as well as listen to similar musical offerings. There are also events like a canoe race, a health fair, and fitness demonstrations. An annual happening since the early 1970s, this festival features the singularity of Milford's town green and its surrounding nineteenth-century houses and shops. Milford Oyster Festival, P.O. Box 3090, Milford, CT 06460; (203) 877–1569 or (203) 874–1518.

Mystic Seaport serves up seaside foodfests with

atmosphere. Memorial Day weekend (call it Decoration Day weekend and you will fit perfectly in the nineteenth century), is the time for the recreated village's **Lobster Festival**, three days of boiled lobster dinners, sea chanteys, sail setting, and lobstering demonstrations. Decoration Day's high points are a procession by nineteenth-century villagers in period clothing and a wreath-laying ceremony.

INDULGENCE EN MASSE AT MYSTIC SEAPORT'S LOBSTER FESTIVAL.

Sandwiched into summer along with the lobster festival is Labor Day weekend's **Fish Fry Weekend**. Dine on traditional New England fish dinners of Yankee flatfish (filet of sole), broth-style clam chowder, and frankfurter platters, as Mystic's chanteymen offer renditions of authentic seafarers' songs. The seaport hosts a third seafood celebration, their **Chowderfest**, on Columbus Day weekend. Regular admission is charged to all special events. Mystic Seaport, 50 Greenmanville Avenue, P.O. Box 6000, Mystic, CT 06355; (203) 572–0711.

Massachusetts

MASSACHUSETTS CAN CLAIM both a long heritage and a coastline to match as well as two much-visited capes. On Cape Ann in the town of Essex—where locals proudly declare the fried clam was invented— is the one-day-long annual **Clamfest** in early September. Clam chowder tasting, thanks to the efforts of about a dozen area restaurants, is the major draw, although there are also clam shucking demonstrations, music, and crafts. Cape Ann Chamber of Commerce, 33 Commercial Street, Gloucester, MA 01930; (508) 283–1601.

For over 20 years in the canal area of Cape Cod, tribute has been paid to the clam's cousin at the **Bourne Scallop Fest** during three days in early September. Several dozen booths offer food and crafts and there are ongoing musical presentations. Cape Cod Canal Region Chamber of Commerce, 70 Main Street, Buzzards Bay, MA 02532; (508) 759–3122.

Rhode Island

HOGS IN ARKANSAS might be razorbacks but in Rhode Island they are quahogs, ocean-dwelling mollusks about as un-porcine as anything you will eat off a plate. These hogs are glorified during North Kingstown's **International Quahog Festival** in late August. Quahog connoisseurs can sample the end results of the Stuffie Cook-off (a "stuffie" is the local tag for a stuffed quahog), or can have their fill of quahog chili, cakes, and chowders. Also offered are other types of seafood like lobster and steamers. Culinary pleasures aside, there are shucking contests, crab races, and live music performances. International Quahog Festival, P.O. Box 1437, North Kingstown, RI 02852; (401) 885–6061.

Sushi, calamari, mako shark, and snail salad are among the delectable tidbits that have been offered for visitors' consumption at the **Charlestown Seafood Festival** in the coastal Rhode Island town of Charlestown. Naturally, you can also sample more traditional fare like quahogs and clam chowder. The early August one-day bash has been around since 1985. You will find about 50 food booths and 50 craft booths on the grounds, and you can take part in events like the crab race and the amateur cooking competition. Corn on the cob and hot dogs are also sold for your dining pleasure, and live music is scheduled all day long. Charlestown Chamber of Commerce, P.O. Box 633, Charlestown, RI 02813; (401) 364–3878.

OTHER FOOD FESTIVALS

LEAVE THE SEACOAST behind and you will find innumerable food festivals across New England. Some are under the guise of ethnic fests, while others come intertwined with music and folk art. Following are just a few of the many favorite inland fairs where our best known edibles are toasted and roasted.

Kielbasa

"KING KIELBASA" TAKES center stage at the **World Kielbasa Festival** in Chicopee, Massachusetts. The "king" is a mammoth sausage prepared annually to be the largest ever stuffed. In the last few years, the king has measured over 26 feet long and weighed in at over 430 pounds, and often has worn a protective three-ply casing to prevent breakage. There are kielbasa cooking and eating contests, though hungry visitors can treat themselves to other Polish dishes like *kupusta, pierogi, golombki,* and generic consumables like hot dogs and popcorn. Polka bands vie with golden oldies groups for music fanciers during the four-day September blast, a Chicopee red-letter day since 1974. The Fireball Club, 93 Church Street, Chicopee, MA 01020; (413) 594–2101.

Souvlakia

THREE DAYS TO fill yourself with *souvlakia, gyros, baklava, diples,* and other traditional Greek foods make up **Glendi**, the annual September celebration of Greek Heritage Week in Springfield, Massachusetts. This ethnic extravaganza, held since 1978, also offers festivalgoers the chance to dance the *sirto*, examine the fine points of worry beads and other Greek arts and crafts, and work off any newfound calories in a road race. Saint George Greek Orthodox Cathedral, 8 Plainfield Street, Springfield, MA 01104; (413) 737–1496.

Potatoes

WHERE ELSE IN New England can you find the likes of mashed potato wrestling and a sit-down dinner served inside a potato storage house (with burlap

ONLY AT THE MAINE POTATO BLOSSOM FESTIVAL CAN YOU FIND THE POTATO PACKING CONTEST.

tablecloths and potato sacks hanging from the rafters)? Head to the northern reaches of Maine for this paean to the potato that also includes a likely visit from the governor, the Little Miss Potato Blossom Pageant, and everything but a Mr. Potato Head Look-Alike Contest. There has been a **Maine Potato Blossom Festival** since 1936, when one Irene Griffith was chosen Miss Potato Blossom Queen and, but for the years of World War II, it has continued unabated since. The week-long fest held in mid-July is filled with athletic contests—basketball, softball, bicycling, home run hitting, golf, and potato picking, as well as potato wrestling. Potatoes are eaten as well as wrestled in, but partakers can also chow down on barbecued chicken and blueberry pie. Crafts are sold, a parade marches down Main Street, and a fireworks display caps off the event the last night. Fort Fairfield Chamber of Commerce, P.O. Box 607, Fort Fairfield, ME 04742; (207) 472–3802.

Pasta

REVELERS TAKING PART in the **Pasta Challenge** in Providence, Rhode Island, consume more than five tons of cooked pasta in this one-day jubilee held annually in September. You can plan on finding perhaps sixty pasta specialties being served from two or three dozen regional restaurants. And you judge for yourself and vote for the best. Keep Providence Beautiful, Inc., The Foundry, Suite 226, 235 Promenade Street, Providence, RI 02908; (401) 351–6440.

Jambalaya

THE ONLY ALLIGATORS you can see adorn festivalgoers' shirts but otherwise the **Cajun Festival** in Escoheag, Rhode Island, could just as easily be taking place in south-central Louisiana. Sizzling Cajun music fills the air as sizzling Cajun food fills stomachs. In addition to jambalaya, there are other Cajun and Louisiana favorites to be tasted including *etouffees*, blackened seafoods, alligator (no—that's not a typo), red beans and rice, and *beignets*. Kids can make jewelry that would fit perfectly in any Mardi Gras parade, and anyone can participate in dance and music workshops. The three-day Labor Day weekend *fais do-do* (a party, to the non-Cajun) has been a regular thing since 1980. Cajun Music/Franklin Zawacki, 151 Althea Street, Providence, RI 02907; (401) 351–6312.

Assorted Ethnic Treats

A VIRTUAL SMORGASBORD of edible ethnicity is yours at the annual Lowell Folk Festival. While music of all types, ranging from blues and jazz to bluegrass and Native American, might be the biggest draw, visitors to this Massachusetts town can help themselves to a mosaic of culinary delights. Lowell National Historical Park, 169 Merrimack Street, Lowell, MA 01852; (508) 459–1000.

SWIMMING INLAND

For a fresh approach to beaches, consider the freshwater beach, the under-promoted and less publicized alternative to the miles of strand where the salt water laps harshly on the sand.

If you are no Mark Spitz or Donna De Varona and feel less than confident at the ocean, you can relax knowing that daunting waves are non-existent at freshwater beaches. In addition, the water temperatures are much warmer. Try finding any stretch of ocean in New England where the water reaches 78 degrees. And the words "fresh water" alone bring welcome relief to sunbathers less than fond of the heavy salt content of the ocean.

The facilities at freshwater beaches are not lacking. Most have picnic areas and grills, and several have playgrounds. Many areas, especially state parks, are laced with walking and hiking trails and are abundant in lakeside and mountain vistas. (Most also charge an admission for use of the beach.) And unlike ocean beaches, many inland locales offer sun venerators a choice of sandy or grassy areas where they can stretch out with a trashy paperback and a tube of suntan lotion.

Connecticut

A TYPICAL SUMMER experience for Constitution State residents is the pilgrimage to the shore—an agonizingly long traffic jam on Route 9 heading south to Rocky Neck and Hammonasset State Park. The alternatives are to head north, east, and west to some of Connecticut's enticing land-locked beaches.

Joe Hickey, a planner for the Connecticut state park system, named his own choices for the beachfront gems in the state. Foremost is **Bigelow Hollow State Park** on Mashapaug Pond, hugging the Massachusetts border near Interstate 84. Bigelow Hollow is one of the more undeveloped inland beaches, but in Hickey's estimation the most beautiful in the state. "It's crystal clear, with a sandy, gravelly beach," he

reports. "There are a few cottages along the lake but mostly it's wooded, hilly countryside." Bigelow Hollow can be filled to capacity—about 800 people—on hot weekends, and might tend to attract a younger crowd than some of the other lake beaches.

If Bigelow Hollow is a bit out of the way, consider other Hickey favorites. Two in western Connecticut are **Lake Waramaug** and **Mount Tom** State Parks, a short drive from each other near New Preston.

A REFRESHING SWIM UNDER A NINETEENTH-CENTURY COVERED BRIDGE — A SETTING YOU WON'T FIND AT A BUSY OCEAN BEACH.

On Mount Tom Pond, **Mount Tom State Park** offers the triple bonus of sparkling clear water, warm temperatures, and little company. You can expect water temperatures to reach as high as 80 degrees on hot, summer days, and with a small, sandy beach, no more than a few hundred people on hand. An extra nugget is the view from the lookout tower high atop 1,291-foot Mount Tom, reached by a hiking trail.

Lake Waramaug State Park, with a campground and a grass and sand beach, can draw up to 1,000 sunbathers on a single day.

Along the eastern border with Rhode Island is **Pachaug State Forest**, with a small, welcoming beach on Green Fall Pond. An easy walking trail circuits the pond.

In southern Connecticut, along Route 9 about 15 miles north of Old Saybrook is **Cockaponset State Forest**, which boasts a tidy beach on the shores of Pataconk Reservoir. The beach, which rarely lures more than 300 to 500 people, is surrounded by woods and includes a hiking trail.

City dwellers looking for quick escapes can find beaches at the following handy though not necessarily picturesque locales. Hartford residents can cruise up Route 44 to Route 202 and **Stratton Brook State Park.** New Haven citizens often head east along Route 80 to **Chatfield Hollow State Park**, to such an extent that there can be crowds of up to eighteen hundred there on torrid summer days. North of Waterbury is **Black Rock State Park.** Rough crowds in the eighties made it a place to avoid, though an alcohol ban has led to a better family atmosphere. **Squantz Pond State Park**, north of Danbury and hugging the New York border, can attract a hearty crowd of 4,000 people escaping city heat.

Two other hospitable beaches aren't part of the state park system. The recreation area on **Lake McDonough**, three miles from the junction of Routes 219 and 44 near New Hartford, has been a teen-age magnet for decades. Many Hartfordites recall the urge to skip school and head out to what was then referred to as Barkhamsted. The sandy beach still attracts young people (especially on "Skip Day" near the end of the school year), although on weekends you will find a substantial number of families fleeing Hartford and New Britain and their suburbs for a picnic and swim. The water temperature can reach the mid-70s by August, and there are hiking paths that are part of Connecticut's Blue Trail System.

Sandy Beach on the grounds of the White Memorial Foundation in Morris near Litchfield sits on

Bantam Lake, the largest freshwater lake in the state. The expansive beach is 800 feet long, and the water is warm, between 75 and 80 degrees in the summer. Visitors can break from sunbathing by joining a game of volleyball·or lunching in the picnic area.

Maine

HUMAN POLAR BEARS might brave the water at Maine's ocean beaches, but those in search of a more pleasant place to swim head to the state's interior. The busiest freshwater beach is likely at **Sebago Lake State Park** on the lake's north shore, about a half hour from Portland.

Says Ron Hunt of the Maine state park system: "The beach is a unique attraction. It lies at the mouth of the Songo River on a natural delta and is three quarters of a mile long with extremely fine granular sand. It's a quality beach and would remind you of the type you'd find at the ocean. You could mistake it for Casco Bay and not know the difference."

Sebago is a deep lake and therefore is cool at the start of the season, but the water can warm to the high 60s by August. It can also fill to capacity on sweltering summer weekends, drawing well over 2,000 visitors. There is a slew of diversions at the park, too, including a campground and a playground.

Not far from Lake Sebago is the site of likely the warmest water at a Maine inland beach. **Range Ponds State Park** in Poland Spring, adjacent to the famous Poland Spring bottling plant, contains a series of shallow ponds. The sand is very fine, there is also a grassy mall area, and the water warms to the low 70s early and stays warm. You can bring the bat and glove, too; a ball field is on the grounds. Close as it is to heavily populated southwestern Maine, Range Ponds is also one of the busiest state parks.

For a beach with a view, head north. To name the beaches with the best vistas, Ron Hunt picks those near mountains: Rangeley Lake and Mount Blue State Parks in northwestern Maine, Lily Bay State Park on Moosehead Lake, and Peaks-Kenny State Park near Dover-Foxcroft.

The beach at **Rangeley Lake State Park** consists of a grassy mall with a rocky shoreline. Because of the depth of Rangeley Lake, the water is very cold, topping out in the low 60s. The same holds true for the water at **Lily Bay State Park**, although the beach there is coarse gravel. Sebec Lake, home of **Peaks-Kenny State Park**, is also chilly, while the beach is a combination of fine sand and grassy. However, Webb Lake, site of **Mount Blue State Park**, is fairly shallow and therefore warmer than the other mountain lakes. The beach is 200 yards long and is composed of very fine glacial till sand. All four of these scenic jewels have playgrounds to keep young ones occupied.

Between Belfast and Augusta lies **Lake St. George State Park** with another of the state's busier beaches. It's mostly grass with split stone steps to the water, the temperature of which usually peaks in the mid-60s.

The least visited are likely Lily Bay and **Aroostook State Park**. Aroostook, near Presque Isle in the northern reaches of the state, has a fairly coarse gravel beach a quarter of a mile long.

Massachusetts

ONE WOULD THINK Cape Cod would need little publicity when it comes to drawing beach lovers, but Cape Cod Chamber of Commerce Executive Director Michael J. Frucci says the Cape's freshwater beaches, where summer water temperatures often reach into the mid-70s, are relatively unrecognized. As an alternative to the heavily frequented Craigville, Sea Gull, West Dennis, and national park beaches, consider **Hamblin's Pond**, one of the Cape's largest ponds, off Route 149 in the Marstons Mills section of Barnstable. Like most freshwater ponds on the Cape, Hamblin's is fairly shallow, ensuring warm water for swimmers. It also has a picnic area.

Similar inland Cape beaches are **Scargo Lake** and **Princess Beach** off Route 6A in Dennis, **Sheep Pond** and **Long Pond** off Route 124 in Brewster, and **Great Pond** and **Wiley's Park Beach** in Eastham. There is also a beach on **Pilgrim Lake** in Orleans, although it is spring fed and tends to be cooler.

Another Cape Cod freshwater beach, though not undiscovered, is at Flax Pond at **Nickerson State Park** in Brewster. Its small sandy area is a favorite of tourists, although it rarely fills to capacity, and the clear, deep water makes it a visual gem. Camping and picnicking facilities are available.

At **Miles Standish State Forest**, south of Plymouth, locals head to the beach on College Pond, while people in the Taunton-Fall River area visit the sand and grass beach at **Massasoit State Park**'s Middle Pond. Both have been known to fill to capacity on weekends, though College Pond has the bigger of the two beaches, with parking for about 200 cars.

College Pond also features picnicking, camping, and concessions, while Massasoit State Park has a camping area.

South of Winchendon in north central Massachusetts is spacious **Lake Denison State Park** with a sizable grassy and sandy beachfront area. With room for 400 cars, the park rarely fills, and since there are no deep drop-offs, it is a preferred beach for families with small children. The water is warm, too, with summer temperatures reaching into the low 70s.

Chilly but clear Wallum Lake, straddling the Rhode Island border as part of **Douglas State Forest**, has a small beach with very fine sand and usually an abundance of sunbathers out for an escape from their homes in Worcester or the Ocean State; it is usually packed on Sundays.

Midway between Worcester and Springfield is **Streeter Point Recreation Area**, with a usually crowded beach on the shores of East Brimfield Reservoir. In 1989, it was made totally handicapped accessible, with easy access for the physically challenged to the picnic tables and other facilities on the grounds. The water is shallow and fairly warm, and fishing enthusiasts often come home bearing a pike or muskie fresh from its waters.

Combine a refreshing swim with a bit of history at world famous **Walden Pond** in Concord (yes, that Walden Pond). Inspect the sparsely furnished replica of Henry David Thoreau's cabin, or walk one of the nature trails around the lake to the site of the nineteenth-century essayist's actual residence. The pond, a natural sinkhole, gets fairly warm and the beach is very busy in summer.

The two beaches at **Hopkinton State Park** off Route 85 in Hopkinton are also swarmed in hot weather. Both can fill up by 10 A.M. on a sizzling Sunday or holiday. The first beach, on the shore of a warm and relatively shallow man-made pond near Hopkinton Reservoir, consists of a desirable grade of fine sand. The sand at the second beach, located directly on the reservoir, is coarser and more gravelly, and the water doesn't get quite as warm. Picnic and barbecue facilities are at the park, and motorized boats are banned from the water.

Cochituate State Park offers swimming and a beach by an abandoned reservoir near Framingham; boaters also share the water there. At **Willard Brook State Forest** in Ashby near the New Hampshire border is a beach on another man-made pond. The water is usually a bit cooler than that at Walden Pond or Hopkinton State Park, but is still comfortable, and there are camping, picnicking facilities, and a maze of hiking trails.

Those looking for sheer esthetics should visit the sandy beach at North Pond in **Savoy Mountain State Forest** in the hilly Berkshires. Assistant Regional Forests and Parks Supervisor Mike Terrell says the cool, spring-fed pond has "probably the clearest water you'll ever swim in and, since no motorboats are allowed, the water is always calm." A second choice for placid water is Benedict Pond in **Beartown State Forest** with both large, grassy and small, sandy beach areas.

In **Tolland State Forest** in the southern Berkshires is Otis Reservoir, site of both a large campground and a public access boat ramp. The beach is mostly sand, with a small grassy area. There is also a man-made beach at Lulu Cascade in **Pittsfield State Forest**, though the water rarely warms higher than the frigid 50s. But Mike Terrell says, "It gets swimmers, especially on very hot days in the nineties or around 100 degrees." All four Berkshire area beaches are heavily used, and all but Pittsfield State Forest have designated swimming areas for small young ones.

New Hampshire

WITH ITS ABBREVIATED coastline, New Hampshire has never been a seductress of ready and willing beachcombers. But beauty is only skin deep, and the Granite State will satisfy sun and sand seekers if they only venture inland from the state's lilliputian littoral. Indeed, they will find the water is warmer and the scenery more satisfying inland, too.

The high profile and heavily visited White Mountains are home to probably the state's most sought-after settings. Visit the town of Conway's compact beach on **Conway Lake** and you have a chance to combine mild water temperatures with spectacular mountain scenery. The lake is shallow—only about 40 feet at its deepest point—with a slow drop-off and the beach is mostly filled with coarse sand. There are no picnic areas or other facilities, however.

Miles of mountains surround you in **Franconia Notch State Park**, too, and stretching out on the beach at Echo Lake with its commanding views has soothed many a weary working person's rattled nerves. This vista is one to be savored. The water is a bit cool, rarely climbing above the mid-60s, and the beach is a combination of sand and grass.

There is another Echo Lake to the east in Pinkham Notch, home of **Echo Lake State Park**. Because of its lower elevation, the waters of this Echo Lake will reach the low 70s in August. A full fledged park, this facility contains hiking trails and picnic areas as well as a stellar view from Cathedral Ledge, reached by an auto road. Neither of the Echo Lake beaches have had to turn people away due to lack of parking.

The sight of Mount Sunapee poking up past rows of forest, coupled with water temperatures that can reach 77 degrees, have made **Mount Sunapee State Park** one of the heaviest used rural refuges in New Hampshire. Admission is limited to 2,500 persons per day, though the park is usually filled to capacity only eight to ten days during a normal summer. The beach, on the southwest end of the lake in Newbury, draws users from a wide area, as far as Keene to the south, Hanover to the north, Concord to the east and Springfield, Vermont, to the west.

Mount Sunapee State Park is one of New England's paramount recreation areas. Summer visitors can ride the chair lift to the mountain's summit (see page 87) and can partake in a buffet dinner cruise on the MV *Kearsarge*, (603) 763-5477, or in an excursion ride on

THE WATER IS USUALLY PRETTY WARM AT NEW ENGLAND'S INLAND BEACHES. THIS INVITING SETTING IS AT BEAR BROOK STATE PARK IN NEW HAMPSHIRE.

the MV *Mount Sunapee II*, (603) 763-4030. You will also find at the park a concession stand, a small playground, and a cookout area at the back end of the parking lot, separated from the beach for safety reasons. ("Hot coals and bare feet do not mix," says one park spokesperson.)

If Mount Sunapee State Park has a rival for pulling crowds, it would be **Pawtuckaway State Park** in Raymond, between Portsmouth and Manchester. Pawtuckaway has a sand and grass beach that sits at the shore of a deep lake that warms to the upper 60s. There are also a concession stand, picnic tables, camping, and walking trails.

A bit to the west is **Bear Brook State Park** with two beaches, one public, the other reserved for campers. The public beach is sandy but small. Park Guide Rachel Mailhot says the water is pretty warm, but "you need a couple of minutes to get used to it." There is also swimming at **Hopkinton-Everett Lake**, an Army Corps of Engineers project west of Manchester.

ABUNDANT EVERGREENS SHELTER BEACHGOERS AT GREENFIELD STATE PARK.

The beach at **Silver Lake State Park** near Nashua is also immensely popular and will fill on hot weekends. The water is comfortable too, reaching the low

70s. The water at **Greenfield State Park** in the Monadnock Region will also reach the same level of warmth, but rarely sells out. Because all the lakefront property is owned by the state, your line of vision is filled only with trees and hills—no houses or other man-made structures.

The view looking down might be superior at **Wellington State Park** on Newfound Lake south of Plymouth. "You can be out in forty feet of water and see bottom," marvels a state park service staffer. Looking up affords some splendid sights, too. The lake is fringed by mountains. Across the street, for the energetic, are trails leading up Big Sugarloaf and Little Sugarloaf Mountains. The water will reach about 70 degrees in mid-August, and the park may be filled to capacity on a hot Sunday.

At aquatic colossus Lake Winnipesaukee you will discover **Ellacoya State Park**, but you will find that numerous others have discovered it before you. Its sand and grass beach is very popular, but is also roomy. The quiet setting of **Wentworth State Park** at nearby Lake Wentworth is commonly less crowded but can fill to capacity on a particularly grueling humid day. The lake is shallow and rocky with peak water temperatures in the upper 60s. Further north is the sandy beach at **White Lake State Park** south of Tamworth, which can also get crowded, but seldom turns people away. Like Greenfield State Park, White Lake is enclosed by state-owned property and is free of buildings.

Rhode Island

SUGGESTING INLAND BEACHES to residents of Rhode Island, a state with 400 miles of coastline, might seem akin to selling Connecticut's ski areas to residents of Colorado. But the calmer and warmer inland water does draw its share of sunbathers and swimmers away from the dozens of saltwater beaches in the Ocean State.

The beach at little **Browning Mill Pond**, part of Arcadia Management Area north of Hope Valley, is generally a find for those seeking an escape from oceanside crowds. The pond is shallow and good for parents with small children, and many take advantage of the ample picnic area.

Beach Pond State Park Beach, in the western sector of Arcadia Management Area and partly in Connecticut, is the preferred beach for those seeking esthetics and, says a park spokesperson, is almost always packed, especially on weekends, with a mixture of families and teens. However, according to one observer, most teens head to the saltwater beaches with surf and crashing waves, leaving the freshwater beaches to families.

One of the most popular rural inland settings is **Burlingame State Park**, with two beaches on Watchaug Pond in Charlestown. The water temperature here can reach the upper 60s. **Pulaski State Park Beach** is in the hilly and wooded northwestern corner of the state, in the George Washington Management Area. When not stretching out on the sand, visitors there take hikes along the cross-country trails.

John Faltus, director of environmental management for the state, says that **Frank Moody State Beach** in Lincoln Woods State Park outside Providence is the busiest freshwater beach in Rhode Island, drawing as many as 7,000 mostly city residents a day. Many of them also take advantage of the plenitude of facilities like the hiking and horse trails, ball fields, and concession stands. The two **Twin Rivers** beaches, east and west, and **Sand Pond**, **Posneganset Lake**, and **Gorton's Pond** in nearby Warwick also serve mainly as urban refuges. Woonsocket folks take full advantage of **World War II Memorial State Park Beach** which, says Faltus, can attract a daily total of 2,000 visitors, in spite of the fact that it's a small area with few facilities.

Vermont

For a state with no coastline, Vermont has a hefty share of beaches.

FOR A STATE with no coastline, Vermont has a hefty share of beaches. Actually, state boosters insist that Vermont does have a coastline, and they are prone to calling **Lake Champlain** New England's West Coast. Carrot-shaped Lake Champlain is home to at least 15 beaches, as well as its own version of the Loch Ness Monster, known as Champ. Does Champ exist? According to one area resident who rents boats for lake users, "Champ only goes to people who believe in him."

The city of Burlington, largest in the state, maintains three Lake Champlain beaches. **North Beach** is the busiest and often hosts 2,000 visitors per summer day. Get set to hear strains of Guns 'n' Roses and Madonna; North Beach has long been the favorite haunt of local teenagers. More family-oriented are the beaches at **Leddy Park** and **Oakledge Park**. Leddy

Park boasts wooded walking trails and sports fields, while Oakledge Park Beach, probably the least bustling, sports playground equipment sure to entice energetic young ones.

For a taste of quiet and tranquility, bring your towels and blankets to the isolated sand and grass beach at **Knight Point State Park** in North Hero on Grand Isle, an island in the center of the lake reached by bridges. On one typical July Sunday, Knight Point logged in only 588 visitors while **Sand Bar State Park** on the mainland north of Burlington teemed with 3,400 sun searchers.

And then there is sheer solitude, the aloneness you can share with just the trees and the water and sand and perhaps the company of a handful of other seekers of seclusion. For this type of desolation, you need to head to the sparsely settled Northeast Kingdom. Spring-fed Maidstone Lake in **Maidstone State Park** dazzles observers with its beauty. Near Guildhall close to the New Hampshire border, the park is located five miles up a dirt road, and is one of the least busy in Vermont.

Another tranquil spot in the Northeast Kingdom is **Brighton State Park** in Island Pond, with two beaches. Swimming sans suit is an option on the south shore of **Lake Willoughby** in Westmore, but be forewarned; the lake is spring fed and the water is cold. There are also family beaches on the lake's north and south shores, and one local resident says the view of Mount Pisgah rising up above the lake is one for the camera.

In the Green Mountain State's busy southwestern corner, **Lake Shaftsbury State Park** stands out as one of Vermont's most used. Man-made and shallow, Lake Shaftsbury is also one of the warmest; one park ranger reports the water temperature has reached 83 degrees. There are fewer people at **Lake Paran**, not far away, at a beach operated by the Lake Paran Recreation Association, but the water is spring fed and therefore colder, rarely climbing over 70 degrees. A playground is on the grounds.

Tennis, horseshoes, miniature golf, basketball, and volleyball are some of the alternatives to swimming at the municipally-run beach at **Prouty Park** on Lake Memphremagog at Vermont's rooftop in Newport. You will find water temperatures in the low 70s at this much-visited beach.

Regarded as one of the state's cleanest is **Lake Fairlee** about 20 miles north of White River Junction. It's also warm, with the water reaching the mid-70s.

The beach at **Treasure Island Recreation Area** on the lake is supplemented by tennis, volleyball, and horseshoes, and can get crowded.

Across the state at **Bomoseen State Park** north of Fair Haven on the New York border, an abundance of weeds growing in the swimming area had long kept attendance down. But in 1989 polyurethane mats were distributed across the lake bottom to block weed growth. And the results? Thumbs up.

Additionally, southern Vermont can claim one of the state's newest parks. Once a Boy Scout camp, **Camp Plymouth State Park** was established on little Echo Lake in the mid-1980s. Because of its relative newness, the park's large, sandy beach is still moderately undiscovered.

CLAMBAKES

BAKE MASTERS TEST THEIR CULINARY EFFORTS AT THIS RHODE ISLAND CLAMBAKE, WHERE FOOD IS COOKED BY THE HEAT DEVELOPED IN PILES OF ROCK.

The origins of the clambake are shrouded in history. There is documentation that explorer Samuel de Champlain witnessed eastern Indians preparing bakes in the late 1500s, but who was responsible for the first and when it took place is lost in oblivion.

Culinary historian Lou Greenstein of North Reading,

Massachusetts, says that long before Indians acquired metal containers in trade, they would boil a stretch of rawhide to use as a vessel, placing it inside an earthen pit and filling it with water, before dropping in hot rocks. (Some were known to bypass the rawhide and the water, building fires in the pit and placing rocks inside it.)

These early New Englanders would rake away the embers and place rockweed, a type of seaweed containing little chambers of sea water, on top of the rocks. Then the day's catch of lobster, fish, or clams, in addition to vegetables like corn or squash, would be placed on top of the rockweed. The heat would cause the little chambers in the rockweed to burst, creating steam, and soil and sand would be placed over the bake to keep the steam in.

Greenstein says that similar cooking methods exist elsewhere, such as Hawaii, where luaus involve the same kind of steam cooking process, causing one to ponder whether or not luaus and clambakes share a common ancestor. It is believed that European settlers stole the idea from the Indians and later made their own changes, to the point where today there are regional differences in clambakes. Maine clambakes are primarily lobster bakes, while in Rhode Island bottomless stave barrels are soaked in sea water, placed over the pit, and covered to hold in steam. Connecticut and Rhode Island engineered the concept of the bakemaster, who would oversee the whole baking operation from the raking of the pit to the starting of the fire.

What is there to know about eating at a clambake? Plan to start a diet the next day.

Because of increasing costs and intensive labor, many enterprises have limited their clambakes to large groups like bus tours, business outings, or organizations. For example, Woodman's, a Cape Ann legend in Essex, Massachusetts, halted their public clambakes in the late 1980s. Others limit their public bakes to one or two a year.

What is there to know about eating at a clambake? Plan to start a diet the next day. Other than that, keep in mind that the broth served alongside your steamed clams is for dipping, not drinking. Clams burrow down into the mud and need a bit of cleaning before they are eaten (not so for mussels, which attach themselves to rocks and don't get as dirty). The broth can also be used to keep your steamers warm.

How do you eat a lobster? Any clambake veteran will be glad to help out if you are at your first. But here is a little help if you are on your own. Holding the body of the lobster with one hand, use your other hand to twist off the claws. Using a nutcracker or stone, break open the claws and pull out the meat with your fork or fingers. Break off the tail and end flippers and with your fork push the tail meat out the bigger end. Then break off the small claws and suck the meat out of them. Don't forget to eat the lobster liver, technically called the *tomalley*, which is considered by connoisseurs to be an epicurean treat. Above all, feel free to make a mess; that's why you are given bibs.

Following is a quartet of public clambakes where seafood fanciers in search of lobster, chowder, hot dogs, corn on the cob, and watermelon will find exquisite success.

Connecticut

IN A SEASIDE setting that would warm the heart of any salty mariner, **Mystic Seaport** in Mystic, Connecticut, is host to nightly clambakes at 6:30 from May into October. Jim Farrell, the museum village's restaurant manager, notes that while the bakes are cooked in rectangular pots rather than smoldered in seaweed, they are still considered traditional. Says Farrell: "They are traditional because the bake is cooked over an open fire. And in the late nineteenth century when (area residents) got into smithing, pots like this were used."

The Mystic Seaport clambake menu includes chowder; steamers and mussels served with hot broth and butter; a choice of a pound and a half of lobster, steak, or chicken; corn on the cob; sausage; cole slaw; boiled red potatoes; *anadama bread* (an old New England molasses-based bread); and for dessert, watermelon.

Farrell says that due to the prevalence of red tide and pollutants in Connecticut's waters, the seaport uses steamers from Maine, Maryland, and Canada. Mussels and lobsters, however, are local. The lobsters are served with tails split and claws cracked so diners need not struggle to find the meat. The whole dinner takes about 90 minutes. Mystic Seaport Museum, 50 Greenmanville Avenue, P.O. Box 6000, Mystic, CT 06355; (203) 572–0711.

Maine

FOR FOUR DECADES the summertime sea air around York Harbor has been permeated with an alluring scent of pine needles, smoked wood, and seething seaweed. It has been that long that **Bill Foster's Downeast Lobster and Clambakes** have filled the stomachs of visitors and residents alike in this historic community 11 miles across the New Hampshire border.

The clam kingpin Bill Foster sold the family-run enterprise to two area businessmen, Kevin Tacy and Paul Murphy, in 1984, and the new owners have retained the founder's name. Unlike the Mystic clambakes, Tacy and Murphy use steel plates for cooking, with a layer of seaweed spread over the plates and the food atop that. Says Tacy: "We cook over a wood fire and the food is steamed in its own juice. We use just enough seaweed to add flavor. We don't drench it in seaweed since too much gives it a smoky flavor that dominates all the foods."

Patrons at Foster's sit at large tables in a screened-in pavilion (which can be made weather-tight and heated in spring and fall) and eat family style, chowing down on clam chowder; steamers with melted butter; a choice of lobster, steak, or chicken; corn on the cob; roasted red potatoes; roasted onions; hot dogs; rolls; and coffee, tea, and watermelon. And there is always a side order of music, usually sing-alongs with nautical themes.

Clambake season at Foster's extends from late April through October, and each bake lasts about two hours. About 250 can be seated per bake and there are often three or four bakes a day. Reservations are required. Bill Foster's Clambakes, P.O. Box 486, York Harbor, ME 03911; (207) 363–3255.

Rhode Island

THE TWO MAJOR summer holidays serve as ready excuses for annual public clambakes in different locales. **Kempenaar's Clambake Club** in Newport caters bakes for large groups throughout the summer, but hosts one special bake for the general public every Fourth of July.

Actually, Independence Day and clambakes go back a long time in Rhode Island. One of William Henry Harrison's most successful political rallies during his 1840 presidential campaign was a July 4 Rhode Island clambake that drew 10,000 supporters. (Four months later Harrison would win in a landslide.)

The tradition continues. Today's Ocean State residents might spend the day's early hours at the beach or along Hope Street watching Bristol's famous parade, then head to Kempenaar's grounds in the late afternoon or evening to play horseshoes, badminton, volleyball, or lawn bowling, passing time before the bake bell tolls to tell all it's time for eating. Kempenaar's clambakes have a Rhode Island flair. A spicy Portuguese sausage called *chourico* is an integral part of the bake, along with New England clam chowder, steamed clams, mussels, lobster or steak, fish in a bag, chicken drumstick, potato and onion, brown bread, and a fruit platter for dessert. Country dance music is provided. Tickets must be purchased in advance. Kempenaar's Clambake Club, 37 Malbone Road, Newport, RI 02840; (401) 847–1441.

On Labor Day, **Moosup Valley Grange Number 26** in Foster holds its annual bake, a pastime that has only been interrupted twice since the first took place in 1928. (World War II and Hurricane Carol in 1954 were cause for the only two cancellations.) Preparation for the bake starts the day before with a laundry list of chores, fun things like washing clams, grinding quahogs and onions for chowder, washing and bagging potatoes, cutting fish, and setting up tables and benches.

The wood fire is started about 6 A.M. on Labor Day for noon and 2 P.M. sittings, and the bake is prepared the old-fashioned way, with heated rocks topped by seaweed, which in turn is covered with the food to be baked. The whole bake is then enveloped with canvas and left to cook. The bounty usually includes chowder, clam cakes, clams with melted butter, fish stuffed with sausage, white and sweet potatoes, corn, tomatoes, cucumbers, brown bread, lemonade, coffee, and watermelon. Reservations are a must. For information, call Paul Rush, 6502 Flat River Road, Greene, RI 02827; (401) 397–7069.

BASEBALL OUTSIDE FENWAY

THE BALLPARKS ARE cozy and billboards along the outfield walls carry advertisements for hardware stores or radio stations, and the atmosphere is one of days long past. This is the setting for minor league baseball, still thriving in New England as it has been since the days when Lou Gehrig made putouts at first base for the long-ago disbanded Hartford Chiefs.

RED SOX SUPERSTARS ROGER CLEMENS AND WADE BOGGS, IN THEIR YOUNGER DAYS AS STANDOUTS FOR PAWTUCKET'S RHODE ISLAND RED SOX.

If you don't wish to fight crowds and traffic in Boston's Kenmore Square but you have the desire to see a live professional baseball game, head to any of New England's minor league ballparks. Currently we have three teams: the Rhode Island Red Sox in Pawtucket, the New Britain Red Sox in Connecticut, and the Pittsfield Mets in the hills of western Massachusetts.

Over the years, we have had dozens more. At one time or another the following teams, among others, have played professional baseball in a stadium somewhere within the borders of our six states: the Springfield Ponies, the Worcester Coal Heavers, the West Haven White Caps, the Lynn Cornets, the New Haven Profs, and the Lawrence Millionaires.

The professional minor league baseball system is organized in four divisions, or classes. Most players begin their careers in either Rookie or Class A leagues. Improved players are advanced to Class AA and Class AAA ball; Class AAA is the last stop up the minor league ladder before the major leagues.

Two professional sportswriters, Steve Gilbert of *The Keene Sentinel* and Gary Fitz of the *Nashua Telegraph*, are both major league fans of the minor leagues, and each highly recommends a day at a minor league ballpark as an enjoyable family outing. For one thing, advises Fitz, it's affordable.

Offers Fitz: "The average price per person at Fenway, if you include seating, parking, and refreshments, is about $25 a person. For the same thing at a minor league game, you'll spend about $5 a person."
And there is no such thing as a bad seat at compact minor league parks. Even the worst seats bring spectators close to the action.

Steve Gilbert adds: "The players are friendlier and more accessible. They are more willing to give their time to kids. It's a whole different world from baseball card shows where major league players sign autographs only in exchange for money."

Gilbert is, like many minor league fans who play their own game at the ballpark, trying to surmise which players have a future in the major leagues. Actually, statistics show that 65 percent of the players who reach AAA level play at least one game in the major leagues, but a significantly smaller number become full-fledged stars.

Steve Gilbert recalls: "The first time I saw Wade Boggs was in Pawtucket and I knew he was a 'can't miss' player. When I first saw Ken Griffey, Jr., he struck out three times and I thought 'this kid is going nowhere,' " proving that even experts can be fooled.

Says Gary Fitz: "Triple A ball is pretty close to the major leagues in terms of ability, but there are differences. A minor leaguer might do certain things, but not everything, as well as a major leaguer. The center fielder might be able to field or hit but might be a little slow for his position. Or you might see a talented player not playing the right position for his abilities."

Rhode Island Red Sox

THE FACT IS that headline makers like Boggs, Roger Clemens, Mike Greenwell, Ellis Burks, Bruce Hurst, Fred Lynn, and Jim Rice all played minor league ball in Pawtucket before they advanced to the Red Sox.

The season for the **Rhode Island Red Sox** extends from the first week of April to early September, for a total of 146 games. In a season that long, one is bound to see some standout games. Those lucky fans who attended the April 18, 1981, game at Pawtucket's McCoy Stadium (seating capacity, 6,010) saw history being made; of course, only 27 fans were there for the entire first act.

On that day, the Pawtucket Red Sox and the Rochester Red Wings played the longest game in professional baseball history. The match, which started 30 minutes late due to a power failure, went 32 innings that evening and was finally suspended at 4:08 the next morning with the score tied 2–2. The game was resumed on June 23 and lasted one more inning, with the Red Sox's Dave Koza singling to drive in Marty Barrett with the winning run in the bottom of the 33rd.

Two men who would find fame in the major leagues years later played integral roles in that marathon. Future Boston manager Joe Morgan was Pawtucket's manager at the time (and early on was tossed out of the game), and the winning pitcher was Bob Ojeda, who would later hurl for the Red Sox and Mets. In total, there were 50 strikeouts, 35 hits, and 49 men left on base in that one game.

You may not be lucky enough to watch such a history-making spectacle, but you will see true professionalism. Steve Gilbert says: "It's major-league-type ball. There is a subtle difference between the majors and minors once you get to that level."

Pawtucket has been the home of the AAA Red Sox affiliate since 1973, although the Rhode Island city has hosted minor league baseball since the mid-1940s. Rhode Island Red Sox, P.O. Box 2365, Pawtucket, RI 02861; (401) 724–7300.

Pittsfield Mets

A CITY WITH an even longer legacy in minor league baseball is Pittsfield, whose Wahconah Park has witnessed minor league baseball since 1919 when the Pittsfield Hillies of the Eastern League swung for the fences there. (The Hillies played in Pittsfield until 1930. The park was then vacant for ten years, a period in which much of the grandstand served as kindling wood.)

Other occupants of Wahconah Park have included the Pittsfield Electrics from 1940 to 1951, the Pittsfield Red Sox from 1965 to 1969, the Pittsfield Rangers (née Senators), the Berkshire Brewers, and in the mid-1980s, the Pittsfield Cubs. The Pittsfield Mets, in the Class A New York–Penn League (Pittsfield is just a pop fly from the New York border) started playing in western Massachusetts in 1989. Pittsfield Mets, P.O. Box 328, Pittsfield, MA 01202; (413) 499–METS.

New Britain Red Sox

THE EASTERN LEAGUE, in which the **New Britain Red Sox** play, also has a storied history. It's been an entity since 1923, and a AA class division since 1963. New Britain has had a team since 1983 when it replaced Bristol, Connecticut, as the Red Sox affiliate. The New Britain Red Sox play in Beehive Field, capacity 4,000. Eastern League graduates who have made it to the majors include Boggs, Clemens, Ryne Sandberg, Eric Davis, and Nolan Ryan. New Britain Red Sox, P.O. Box 1718, New Britain, CT 06050; (203) 224–8383.

AUTUMN

Autumn is real New England. Its mention conjures up images of stereotypical New England: a craft fair surrounding a bandstand on a town green, entertainment provided by the color works of nature's foliage factory.

VISITORS FROM THROUGHOUT AMERICA COME TO NEW ENGLAND IN FALL JUST TO SEE SCENES LIKE THIS ONE.

But autumn has a split personality. Through mid-October we see the warm side of fall, when the scenery is exquisite and the temperatures are ideal, and no one needs to tell you to leave the house. After mid-October we encounter the less agreeable side of autumn's disposition, when the trees are as naked as a newborn baby and the skies are melancholy. Thank God, one might sigh, for holidays and football.

Actually, one doesn't need to be a football fan to take advantage of the cultural opportunities on our college campuses and along the streets of our college towns. It's just that football brings people to campuses who wouldn't otherwise set foot near the halls of ivy. With or without the opening kickoff, this is the optimal time of year to explore Cambridge, Hanover, and the rest of our centers of academia.

Halloween and Thanksgiving supply their own diversions. A nighttime stroll through Boston's graveyards led by a masked and caped wizard, a spooky ride on a haunted trolley, and a personal audience with Nathaniel Hawthorne in Salem, Massachusetts, the original Witch City, prove there is more to Halloween than ringing doorbells. And Thanksgiving offers opportunities in our recreated villages and historic houses to dine on mince pie and oyster bisque served by waitresses in gingham dresses and bonnets.

During peak leaf season, you can just hop in your car and drive. We offer five geographically diverse foliage tours in this chapter. Then again, you might trade your car for an alternative viewing method; the autumn custom of scanning the trees can be less distracting when the driver trades the highway for the rails, the rivers, or the sky.

Consider planning a leaf-scanning trip around one of our many fall and harvest festivals, as commonplace as red, plump Macs ripe for the picking. Grab a plate of homemade ice cream and apple pie, stare at pumpkins the size of Idaho, learn the skill of making a corn husk doll, or try your best to devour a doughnut hanging by a string. And shop, shop, and shop.

In autumn, you will find New England to be just as you pictured it.

HARVEST AND FALL FOLIAGE FAIRS

The dazzling fall colors compete for your attention with the alluring aromas of baked goods and fresh apples throughout New England in the autumn. It's the time for fall harvest, which means the perfect excuse for a country fair. Bring an empty stomach and a full purse as you will find the choicest of foods and crafts for sale beneath the sprawling maples of the Yankee heartland.

Vermont

DUMMERSTON APPLE PIE FESTIVAL About 1,500 pies are concocted for the annual affair at the Dummerston Congregational Church on the common in this village north of Brattleboro. Buy an entire pie or just a slice, and top a piece with a scoop of homemade ice cream or Vermont cheddar cheese. Then grab a seat on the foliage-filled common for a literal taste of autumn in Vermont. Doughnuts and cider are also vended, while across the street the local grange usually sells handcrafts. The fest begins at noon on the Sunday of Columbus Day weekend, and continues until all pies are sold. On a beautiful day that can be as early as 2 or 3 P.M. The ice cream often goes much faster. Gladys Miller, Route 2, Box 835, Putney, VT 05346; (802) 254-9158.

VERMONT APPLE FESTIVAL Here is another happening with apple appeal. Vermonters head to Springfield in the southeastern part of the state in early October, where they proceed to eat apples, bob for apples, identify apples, and bake apples in countless pies. Those who do the best or the most are usually given awards. There has even been a contest to find the longest apple peel. Visitors might also get the chance to help press cider, watch sheep shearing, do a bit of early Christmas shopping, and listen to the folksy renderings of the state's best pickers (guitar, not apples). Vermont Apple Festival, 55 Clinton Street, Springfield, VT 05156.

NORTHEAST KINGDOM FALL FOLIAGE FESTIVAL

Buy some stock in Kodak before journeying to Vermont's alluring Northeast Kingdom to attend the six-day paean to the region's natural and man-made beauty. Each of six small towns—Walden, Cabot, Plainfield, Peacham, Barnet, and Groton—has its own day in the spotlight, hosting a flurry of activities such as a tour of llama or dairy farms, art shows, glass blowing demonstrations, band concerts, and lots of breakfasts, dinners, and lunches. Expect to chow down on home-cooked Vermont Yankee fare, like pancakes with Vermont maple syrup, chicken pie, beef stew, and sugar on snow. Fall Festival Committee, Box 38, West Danville, VT 05873.

BILLINGS FARM & MUSEUM'S

HARVEST CELEBRATION Kids and even some adults

standing up to their knees in corn husks are common sights during the combination farm and museum's day-long tribute to 1890s harvest time. Stripping husks from corn as fast as humanly possible is the object of the husking bee, and all are welcome to lend a hand. As was common 100 years ago, a barn dance with a live caller and band follows the husking bee and fills about 90 minutes of the October afternoon. You can swing your partner or just watch others or, if you would rather, try your hand at making corn husk dolls.

Says Billings Farm spokesperson Darlyne Franzen: "Today we throw away corn husks, but they kept everything. Nothing was worthless and everything had a use back then. Luxuries were few and far between, so they invented their own."

You might also watch others stooking cornstalks, which might sound obscene but simply means cutting and tieing stalks together for the purpose of strengthening the plants, as one step in the harvest-

ing process. You could also witness corn being *traced* (braided for decorating purposes) and shelled (stripped of its kernels) in a mechanical sheller. In our high-tech world, says Franzen, "people are amazed that something can be done so simply."

There is more than corn at Billings Farm's **Harvest Fest**. Food preservation techniques, including canning, may be offered, or you might see cider being pressed, butter being made, or woolen clothing knitted the nineteenth-century way. At midday what might seem like the biggest pumpkins in Vermont are brought in on a stone boat, and you might be asked to try to guess how many pies could be made from them.

About a month earlier, the farm and museum complex presents **Wool Day**, where the many steps of the old-fashioned wool-making process "from sheep to shawl" are demonstrated. Knitted garments of the 1890s are displayed, and you can take part in carding or drop-spindle spinning. Billings Farm & Museum, P.O. Box 489, Woodstock, VT 05091; (802) 457–2355.

SHELBURNE FARMS HARVEST FESTIVAL
Lively cloggers, long-eared rabbits, and log-splitting lumberjacks are some of the in-person guests at the annual family event celebrating harvest season at this non-profit

YOUNGSTERS STANDING KNEE-DEEP IN CORN HUSKS IS A COMMON SIGHT AT BILLINGS FARM & MUSEUM'S HARVEST CELEBRATION.

farm outside of Burlington. Hands-on experiences, garden tours, and demonstrations comprise the bulk of the activities for visitors on this late September day. You might be led through an organic garden that produces tomatoes well into November, or be given a close-up look at the neighboring woodlands. Green Mountain draft horses may be in attendance to pull you around on a wagon, and you can indulge in Vermont produced foods such as Ben & Jerry's ice cream, Vermont lamb, Indian pancakes, and fresh-roasted corn on the cob, while listening to the strains of bluegrass music. Shelburne Farms, Shelburne, VT 05482; (802) 985–8686.

New Hampshire

LOON MOUNTAIN FALL FOLIAGE FESTIVAL For over a quarter century this ski area has brought upwards of 75 exhibitors to the White Mountains. Potters, jewelers, weavers, woodworkers, and photographers present their wares while others sell homegrown produce, over the course of three days during the heart of foliage season. Loon's gondola brings leaf scanners to its summit where an observation tower allows for a 360-degree view of the area's color-sheathed peaks and valleys; a short wait might be necessary to get to the top. Loon Mountain, Kancamagus Highway, Lincoln, NH 03251; (603) 745–8111.

WARNER FALL FOLIAGE FESTIVAL About 18 miles west of Concord is Warner, a quiet town of 2,000 in the shadow of Mt. Kearsarge that swells to eight to ten times its normal size for two days in early October. From 15,000 to 20,000 visitors come to get a slice of small town Americana, as well as one of apple or pumpkin or some other home-baked pie.

Says former Festival President Debbie Cantrell: "The people in Warner want you to have the best time possible. I think many of the people we get are from bigger towns that don't have the real sense of community you get up here."

The fall colors are always the biggest draw, but there is always entertainment—bagpipers, jugglers, or vocal groups—as well as a small midway, a woodsmen's contest, a half-hour-long parade, crafts for sale, and lots of food. The fest was first organized in 1947, but Warner's hospitality has been legend in the Granite State for some time. The town hosted its first street fair back in 1871. Warner Fall Foliage Festival, P.O. Box 152, Warner, NH 03278; (603) 456–2117.

New Hampshire Farm Museum's

Harvest Weekend

HARVEST WEEKEND The scents of fresh produce and mulled cider surround you as you dig potatoes or learn the art of splint basket making during the two-day ode to harvest season at this museum on the New Hampshire–Maine border. You have a choice of putting your muscles to work by grinding corn or using a winnower or fanning mill, or just taking a seat and relaxing as an expert explains all you want to know about herbal roots. Natural seasonal ornaments like dried flowers or gourds are sold, too, on this October weekend.

In September, the museum holds **Apple Day**, when you can learn the secrets of making apple butter or press your own apples into cider. New Hampshire Farm Museum, P.O. Box 644, Milton, NH 03851; (603) 652–7840.

Strawbery Banke's Annual Fall Festival

While some attractions offer demonstrations of harvesting techniques from one era, the preserved seaside historic neighborhood Strawbery Banke in Portsmouth, New Hampshire, commonly presents harvesting methods from different centuries. For example, the eighteenth-century Wheelwright House might be the site of a colonial-era interpreter drying fruits or salting meats as was done 200 years ago. Meanwhile, over at the 1950s Drisco House, a guide garbed in poodle skirt and glasses with pointed rims is canning beans or making pickles as was done when we were a lot younger.

Victorian-era games like hoop rolling or marbles can lure 1990s kids who are used to Nintendo and video arcades, while craftpersons like a cooper or boat builder, important tradesmen in this coastal location, may also be offering demonstrations. The festival takes place in mid-October. Strawbery Banke, P.O. Box 300, Portsmouth, NH 03801; (603) 433–1100.

Harvest Day in Shaker Village

HARVEST DAY IN SHAKER VILLAGE The Shakers might be gone but their buildings still stand and their methods thrive in Canterbury, New Hampshire. On this mid-October day visitors can witness old-time craft making and harvesting techniques like plowing, harrowing, and planting with draft horses and field equipment. You might be able to lend a hand in activities like pressing cider, whittling a whistle, or making an herbal wreath, or examine obsolete but once irreplaceable appliances like a clothes wringer or potato grater. Most of the craftpersons relate their trades in some way to the Shakers. Canterbury Shaker Village, 288 Shaker Road, Canterbury, NH 03224; (603) 783–9511.

Maine

OLD LEDGE SCHOOL FAMILY DAY AND APPLE FESTIVAL
Apples are celebrated, toasted, and tasted in this Yarmouth, Maine, benefit for the local historical society. You can bob for apples on a string or bring the longest apple peel to win a contest, or simply taste the many varieties exhibited, whether raw or cooked in a pie or bread.

And after you are appled out? Get a taste of education from the pre-NEA days by taking a lesson with Mistress Swan in the nineteenth-century one-room brick schoolhouse. Or learn traditional skills like basket making, quilting, stenciling, and rug making, while your kids try writing with a quill pen or decorating paper with potato stamping. Yarmouth Historical Society, P.O. Box 107, Yarmouth, ME 04096; (207) 846–6259.

Massachusetts

EDAVILLE RAILROAD CRANBERRY FESTIVAL
The most famous color of fall in southeastern Massachusetts is not gold or orange but a vibrant crimson, thanks to the cranberry bogs found in this corner of the state. While the first cool nights of autumn are turning the leaves of New England their many colors, they are also transforming the cranberries into their special shade of red. This turn-of-the-century railroad theme park in South Carver celebrates the season with a festival on three consecutive weekends. Antique steam trains carry visitors for five and a half miles past bogs where they can see harvesting take place. The bogs are flooded and the berries are dislodged by mechanical reels, forcing them to float to the surface and giving the bogs their vivid red color. Once on the surface the berries are scooped into trucks.

Other festival events include entertainment such as puppet shows or Dixieland music. And the rest of the village attractions are open as usual. Edaville Railroad, Route 58, South Carver, MA 02366; (508) 866–4526.

Thornton Burgess Society Farmer's Market and Fall Festival

A personal appearance by the Briar Patch's Peter Rabbit in his farmer's overalls occupies children at the Burgess Society's fall festival, while their parents pore over crafts, baked goods, herbs, and plants. Also entertaining young ones are games based on author Burgess's famous fictional characters like Peter, Reddy Fox, Hooty the Owl, and Paddy Beaver. They can also help their parents pick a pumpkin for Halloween or taste a sample of apple cider, all to the tune of live country music. Thornton W. Burgess Society, 6 Discovery Hill Road, East Sandwich, MA 02537; (508) 888–6870.

Northern Berkshires Fall Foliage Festival

"Pop a wheelie!" yell pockets of spectators as Shriners on mini-bikes happily oblige in the fall festival's annual parade. The crowd also roars their approval as a dozen floats, marching bands, and some 20-foot-tall puppets file by. The parade, which normally draws 50,000 to 75,000 onlookers, is the climax of the week-long fall festival, held in North Adams, a former railroad center in the color-filled northwestern corner of Massachusetts. Arts and crafts shows, dances, dinners, and road races round out the happenings, but the trip along the Mohawk Trail (Route 2) from Greenfield to North Adams is worth the drive in fall, parade or no parade. Northern Berkshire Chamber of Commerce, 69 Main Street, North Adams, MA 01247; (413) 663–3735.

Autumn Weekend at Hancock Shaker Village

Another of New England's Shaker museums also allows the inquisitive to explore the world of the Shakers during harvest season. During **Autumn Weekend** at this restored Shaker village in the western Berkshires, demonstrations of nineteenth-century chores like candle dipping, flax breaking, and grain threshing are scheduled. In addition, you might also be lucky enough to hear Shaker hymns from the Victorian era, or taste some of the offbeat in the village cafe, like Shaker onion pie, green tomato pie, rosewater apple pie, or ginger soup. Kids might enjoy meeting the resident animals; the village farm replicates as much as possible the livestock kept by the Shakers in the mid to late nineteenth century. Hancock Shaker Village, P.O. Box 898, Pittsfield, MA 01201; (413) 443–0188.

NEWBURYPORT FALL HARVEST FESTIVAL "One of
the things we really want to do is make this festival
more than a craft show and a farmer's market," says
Shirley Magnanti of the Newburyport Chamber of
Commerce. That in mind, feel free to have your
hands tied behind your back while you try your best
to consume a doughnut hanging by a string in the
annual doughnut-eating contest.

Of course, there is a farmer's market with pumpkins, corn, and antique farming equipment brought
by area farms, along with craft exhibitors. But past
fairs have also highlighted live music, whether it be
jazz, country, or classical; pet shows; fashion shows;
and the infamous doughnut-eating contests. Newburyport Chamber of Commerce, 29 State Street,
Newburyport, MA 01950; (508) 462–6680.

NASHOBA VALLEY WINERY HARVEST FESTIVAL
Press your own cider and taste apples in a plenitude
of forms at the winery's fall event. You also have the
chance to taste the wine, tour the orchard, listen to
the bluegrass, and add a few new recipes to your
culinary collection. Nashoba Valley Winery,
100 Wattaquadoc Hill Road, Bolton, MA 01740; (508)
779–5521.

HARVEST DAYS AT DRUMLIN FARM This farmstead
in Lincoln, Massachusetts, a sanctuary of the
Massachusetts Audubon Society, becomes the proverbial hive of activity during this three-day event. At
past fairs, demonstrations have included beekeeping,
cheese making, chair caning, weaving, cow milking,
blacksmithing, and, as is appropriate for the season,
cider pressing. There are usually plenty of hands-on
opportunities to learn new skills with bluegrass or
folk music accompaniment. Morris dancers have also
been known to put on a show while fair-goers tired
of being on their feet have had ample chances in the
past to hop aboard a horse-drawn hay ride.
Massachusetts Audubon Society, (508) 259–9807.

DAY IN THE COUNTRY Similar to the Audubon
occurrence is this pastoral pastime at Smolak Farms
in North Andover. Open-fire cooking demonstrations,
hay rides, blacksmithing, cider pressing, and beekeeping are a few of the activities that have taken
place on this special day. Folk or other musicians will
serenade you while desserts and apple treats will
give you good reason to open your belt a notch or
two. North Andover Historical Society, 153 Academy
Road, North Andover, MA 01845; (617) 686–4035.

Rhode Island

HARVEST FESTIVAL AND APPLE PIE CONTEST
This fund raiser for the South County Museum in Narragansett, Rhode Island, is a one-day, mid-October showcase for handmade crafts, which have ranged from Victorian birdhouses to corn husk dolls, and tons of food. At one fest you could lunch on clam cakes and jonnycakes and a multitude of sandwiches, feasting on "college inn pie" (are you ready for a combination of mincemeat and pumpkin?) for dessert. And there is always the search for the perfect apple pie. South County Museum, P.O. Box 709, Narragansett, RI 02802; (401) 783–5400.

Connecticut

APPLE HARVEST FESTIVAL
What began as an excuse to sell apple pie in Glastonbury, Connecticut, has become a weekend-long varied event. Of course, 3,000 pies might be sold over the course of the weekend, along with numerous arts and crafts, vend-

CATCH AN APPLE WITH YOUR TEETH, THEN DIG IN. FLANDERS NATURE CENTER FALL FESTIVAL IN CONNECTICUT IS THE LOCALE FOR THIS OLD-FASHIONED AUTUMN GAME.

ed by around 130 exhibitors. In one past fest, one was able to buy everything from wreaths made from corn husks to sweatshirts adorned with scenes of Connecticut beauty spots. There is also a bed race and a parade, with storytelling, face painting, and clowns to keep children enthused. Glastonbury Chamber of Commerce, 2400 Main Street, Glastonbury, CT 06033; (203) 659–3587.

FLANDERS NATURE CENTER FALL FESTIVAL A tribute to nature and all things natural in Woodbury, Connecticut, this one-day affair provides a chance for youngsters to make leaf prints on paper with non-toxic paints, to lend a hand making apple cider, or to bob for apples hanging by yarn from trees. Their parents can watch artists and craftspersons demonstrating their trades; past festivals have included a Chinese watercolorist, an artisan who transformed cumbersome logs into handy baskets, an expert in the Scandinavian tradition of *rosemaling* (decorative painting on wood), and a man who employs herbs and other natural elements to dye wool. Hay rides, guitar and fiddle players, and foods like lamb chili and harvest soup are also part of the outing. Flanders Nature Center, P.O. Box 702, Woodbury, CT 06798; (203) 263–3711.

FALL FOLIAGE DRIVES

The following routes are included to offer some guidelines to finding prime fall colors among classic New England settings. But by no means limit yourself to these treks. Half the fun of fall is shunpiking—rambling along back roads just for the sake of doing it.

Trip #1: Western Maine

WELCOME TO THE breadth of nature's masterworks in western Maine. Thick woodlands and languid lakes are entertainment for the eyes in any season, but during peak foliage, they merit long, leisurely trips that might otherwise seem extravagant.

This 115-mile-long loop begins in Fryeburg on Route 302, hugging the New Hampshire border, about seven miles east of the resort center of Conway. Initially an Indian settlement named Pequawket,

this town of white, clapboard buildings is today best known for the **Fryeburg Fair**, (207) 935–3268, an agricultural bonanza taking place the first week of October. The archetypal Congregational Church, white with green shutters and black clock, is perfectly in place in this country town. You can also take a little detour to see one of Maine's eight remaining covered bridges. To reach the 100-foot-long Hemlock Bridge, take Route 302 in East Fryeburg to Hemlock Bridge Road; follow this mostly dirt road for three miles to the bridge.

Then head east on Route 302 past the brick Fryeburg Academy, a prep school dating from 1791. Cruise up and down a few hills, passing stone fences on your left and right, until you reach the Bridgton town line about seven miles from the academy. Within two miles, Highland Lake and Moose Pond will surround you, while Pleasant Mountain behind you keeps a close watch over the valley. There is a small picnic area along the shore of Highland Lake on your left.

Take a left at the Civil War Memorial in the center of Bridgton, then continue south on Route 302 toward the popular resort town of Naples. Approaching Naples, you will start to see glimmers of Long Lake through colorful trees on your left. Should you crave an ice cream cone or a jaunt inside an antiques store, consider stopping for a while in Naples. The *Songo River Queen II*, (207) 693–6861,

VENTURE INLAND FROM MAINE'S COASTLINE AND BUCOLIC FALL VISTAS LIKE THIS AWAIT YOU.

cruises the length of the lake for some on-the-water views through September, but the vista of the water backed by layers and layers of hills in the distance can be yours just by walking along Route 302 in the center of town.

Travel north once again by taking two-lane Route 35 along the eastern shore of Long Lake toward Harrison, passing through a glut of leaf-laden trees along the way. The old cemetery beside Harrison's Seventh Day Adventist Church, built in 1835, is worth a photo stop. In the center of Harrison, take Route 117 heading toward Norway. Crystal Lake on the left will keep you company for about a mile and a half, and if you have a picnic lunch with you, consider taking advantage of the picnic tables on the right past the junction with Plains Road.

Take a left onto Route 118—there is a picnic area on your right at the junction—and admire the stellar views of Lake Pennesseewassee. A mile later take a right at Lake Pennesseewassee Park, site of another picnic area, onto Lake Pennesseewassee Shore Road, a rambling, narrow thoroughfare on which you might spot some classic scenes of bucolic Maine—a farm, a horse or two, and some heavy woods. Bear right at the fork three miles from the junction. Four miles later, take a moment to savor the sight of the multicolored hillside reflected in the water on your left.

At Route 219, take a left, then an immediate right towards West Paris, home of Perham's, a well-known jewelry and rock shop where Maine tourmaline is the specialty. Take a left onto Route 26 and pass through the villages of South Woodstock, Bryant Pond, and Locke Mills, before reaching the resort town of Bethel, an appetizing place to stretch your legs and take out the camera. Sunday River and Mount Abram ski areas are nearby, but the most prominent feature in the village is the mostly brick Gould Academy campus, founded in 1836. If you have time, take a walk through the Broad Street Historic District, where you will find the Moses Mason House, oldest structure in town, dating from 1813. It's now a historic museum, open by appointment in fall. (207) 824–2908.

From Bethel, continue west along Route 2, which parallels the Androscoggin River and soon enters the White Mountain National Forest, affording some beauteous sights of water, fall color, and mountains. At Gilead, take a left onto Route 113 for an 11-mile-long jaunt into the thick of the national forest and the most commanding scenery on the trip. There are a few turnouts where you can park and take a closer look at nature.

Take a moment to savor the sight of the multi-colored hillside reflected in the water.

Stay on Route 113, which will take you into a snippet of New Hampshire, until you reach the junction of Route 302 in Fryeburg. Allow three hours to drive this loop with no stops, and an extra hour if you plan to do a little exploration.

Trip #2: Quiet Massachusetts

YOU'RE IN MASSACHUSETTS. The two-lane roads meander and wind through thick woods. Every now and then your view of the foliage-filled forests is punctuated by glimpses of blue-tinted hills in the distance or a murmuring brook by your side. White colonial churches with spiky steeples introduce you to inert villages. But you are not trapped in a line of cars as long as the Mississippi, nor is there a circus of tour buses choking the air with diesel exhaust fumes. This is not the Berkshires.

The setting for this 100-odd-mile loop is the quiet portion of Massachusetts, the often ignored central part of the state, encompassing Wachusett Mountain and the Quabbin Reservoir. This route offers a look at small towns and countryside without the congestion, foliage without the frenzy.

You might want to preface the foliage drive with a

chair-lift ride to the 2,006-foot-high summit of Wachusett Mountain, (508) 464–5731. The drive itself begins in earnest about six miles south of the Wachusett Mountain Ski Area, at the junction of Routes 31 and 62 in Princeton. Follow Route 62 for a little over 13 miles west, past stone walls shielding forest thick with foliage, until you reach Barre, a masterpiece of a small village with a giant-sized green. Separated by roads into three spacious segments, the green supports a war memorial and a bandstand, while across the street there is the First Parish Church, with a Paul Revere bell dating from 1814.

The most captivating view is from the south end of the common looking towards the Barre Congregational Church topped with its traditional steeple. The local historical society, housed in a Federal-style building dating from 1834, contains mostly old photos and documents related to Barre. If you wish to visit, call (508) 355–2298 or (508) 355–2810.

Continue north on Routes 32 and 122 for eight miles to Petersham, then south on Route 32A heading to Hardwick, ten miles away. A narrow, two-lane road, Route 32A crosses the Swift and Muddy Rivers, and takes you close to the woods. It also parallels the Quabbin Reservoir, although you can't see it from the road. Little Hardwick consists of a common, a general store, a town hall, and a historical society, among other buildings, as well as a historical marker devoted to colonial statesman and fierce Loyalist Brigadier General Timothy Ruggles. The general was a French and Indian War veteran who served Massachusetts as Chief Justice, then fled to Nova Scotia in deference to the Crown, to live out his remaining years.

Continue on Route 32A, passing woods and a pasture where you might see horses at play, into Gilbertville. Less than a mile out of town is Bridge Street, scene of the narrow, two-lane Gilbertville Covered Bridge, dating from 1886 and spanning the Ware River.

Continue south on Route 32A, then west on Route 9 toward Belchertown through the industrial center of Ware, which could understatedly be called one of the less scenic portions of the trip. Between Ware and Belchertown are three entrances to the park section of the Quabbin Reservoir, a perfect place for picnicking with a view. (Quabbin is an Indian word meaning "the meeting of the waters.")

Quabbin is an Indian word meaning "the meeting of the waters."

About six miles past the reservoir, head north on Route 202, also known as the Daniel Shays Highway, named for the Revolutionary era insurrectionist. There is nothing revolting about the scenery, however, along this relatively wide two-lane road paralleling the western shore of the Quabbin. Once you embark on this avenue you will encounter nature's best esthetic efforts—miles of color-filled woods fronting ranges of blue hills in the distance with few houses or other man-made structures to interfere, forming probably the most beautiful settings on the loop drive.

Pass through New Salem and North New Salem, then head east on Route 122 for nine miles to Petersham. Take Route 32 north, then 101 north toward Templeton. The waters of Queen Lake add an aquatic touch to your foliage viewing, while the town center of Templeton affords you another chance to inspect an archetypal small New England village with spacious common and steepled church.

Continue to Route 2 to Route 140, which will take you back to Route 31 to Wachusett Mountain. Or you can continue on Route 101 to Route 119, through the Willard Brook State Forest into Ashby and Townsend. Allow three and a half to four hours to drive this loop.

Trip #3:
New Hampshire's Upper Valley

QUINTESSENTIAL NEW HAMPSHIRE is yours by following this approximately 100-mile-long loop through the Granite State. You will find a major lake, a major river, small towns, a covered bridge, a bit of history, and a bumper crop of hills and mountains. And, of course, trees with variegated leaves of sundry shades.

Commence on Routes 11 and 103 heading east in Newport, a little industrial town of 6,500 that is best known as the home of Sarah Josepha Hale. Though that name might be as alien to you as your mother-in-law's hairdresser, Hale was a writer and editor who authored the famous rhyme, "Mary Had a Little Lamb," and was instrumental in lobbying for a national Thanksgiving holiday. (See page 222)

A little over three miles later, the routes split; take Route 103 toward 2,743-foot Mount Sunapee, which you can see ahead. The sight of Mountain View Lake, on your left 3.4 miles later, will whet your appetite for the setting of Lake Sunapee a bit further. A half mile later you will pass Route 103B and the entrance to Mount Sunapee State Park, with hiking, picnic tables, and a chair lift. And a half mile beyond the park entrance you will see on the left a vision of the lake with the misty blue hills in the background. The excursion boat *Mount Sunapee* offers rides in the fall. See page 186 for more information.

At the junction of Routes 103 and 103A in Newbury is the Center Meeting House, designed by Charles Bulfinch and regarded as a museum piece of the 1820s; in another four miles you will scoot past the shores of Lake Todd.

In Bradford, nine miles past the park entrance, take a left onto Route 114 and within a half mile you will see a choice view of mountains to your left. The road narrows as you enter South Sutton, ancestral home of the Pillsbury flour milling magnates and home to at least one Minnesota politician. For a little detour, bear right past the Joseph Pillsbury historic marker and follow the little dirt road to the right of the church. Your drive will be accompanied by thick woods and a stone fence before reaching a cemetery with numerous old tombstones on your right. There are several Pillsburys buried here, including Micajah Pillsbury, who died just after the turn of the nineteenth century.

Retrace your steps and follow Route 114 under Interstate 89 to the junction with Route 11. Instead of turning, consider driving two miles ahead to the center of New London, a college town majoring in colonial architecture. The brick buildings of Colby-Sawyer College contrast sharply with the white frame New London Inn and the many craft shops. The oldest college building is the Old Academy, built in 1838. The town is also home to the Barn Playhouse where you can find the smell of greasepaint in summer.

Backtrack on Route 114, then follow Route 11 east into Andover. When you see the covered bridge (closed to cars) on your right, take a left onto Route 4A, where Kimpton Brook will keep you company on the right, and you will enter the wildwood of the John F. Gile Memorial Forest. At the Gardner Memorial Wayside Park, just past the historical marker for Mason's Patent, are picnic tables in the thick of the woods.

Continue on Route 4A to Enfield Center, where a Shaker community thrived in the nineteenth century on the shores of Lake Mascoma. In the 1920s, the last surviving handful of Shakers moved to the community at Canterbury, north of Concord. But the Shaker presence is felt today in the Shaker store, restaurant, and museum, (603) 632–4346. On a portion of the remnants of the Shaker village on the left is the LaSalette Shrine, a replica of a similar shrine in France, which is best known in the state for its spectacular display of Christmas lights.

At the end of Route 4A, take a left onto Route 4 and follow it for just under two miles to the intersection with Interstate 89. Take the interstate for 6.2 miles to exit 20, then head south on Route 12A. The fast-food strip will end in less than a mile, and soon your traveling partner on the right will be the Connecticut River, seen through trees and barns and country houses. The two-lane road takes you to Plainfield, about eight miles south of the interstate.

If you had lived in Plainfield or Cornish, about five miles south, at the turn of the century you would have had some of the country's most renowned writers, sculptors, poets, and artists as your neighbors. The Cornish Colony thrived for about 50 years. The best-known residents were artist Maxfield Parrish and sculptor Augustus Saint-Gaudens. Though an attempt at a Parrish museum failed in the early 1980s, the home and galleries of Saint-Gaudens, well marked by signs, are run today as a National Park Service historic site. (603) 675–2175.

There's another must-see in Cornish. The nation's

largest covered bridge crosses the Connecticut River between Route 12A and Windsor, Vermont. You will find that the panorama of the bridge and the river under sheltering Mount Ascutney serves as a stoplight.

About 5.3 miles past the bridge is the junction with Route 103; a left turn and a drive of about 13 miles will bring you back to Newport. Allow two and a half to three hours to drive the route, more if you stop for sightseeing.

Trip #4: Vermont's Back Roads

PEOPLE FROM MANCHESTER, New Hampshire, to Manchester, England, venture to Vermont solely to surround themselves with fall colors in a setting dripping with Americana. And there is no reason why you shouldn't join them in their search for autumn in New England.

As you ramble along Vermont's autumn byways, you might spot license plates from all 50 states and the District of Columbia over the course of a weekend; then again, you might witness 50 Winnebagos

AN AUTUMN SCENE ALONG A COUNTRY ROAD IN VERMONT.

from Florida and California alone. Needless to say you'll have company. But whether you are admiring the distant view of a mountain range or the close-up branches of a maple brushing against a town library, you will find the trip is worth the traffic.

Long regarded as one of Vermont's best-preserved towns, Newfane, a paragon of Greek Revival elegance, is your starting point. On Columbus Day weekend, the village green is the site of a craft fair, although it merits a close look at any time. The proud Windham County Court House standing grandly beneath the trees was built in 1825 while the oldest part of the Newfane Inn dates from 1787. The covey of buildings facing the green are all dressed in white paint and green trim and seem to be in uniform.

Following Route 30 north, you will pass on the right the Newfane flea market site, which is filled on Sundays from mid-spring into late October. For a while, the West River is your traveling companion, paralleling Route 30 on the right, then the left, as you travel through Townsend, sort of a toned-down Newfane with its own green bandstand and white clapboard buildings.

The Weston Country Store is as close to a turn-of-the-century emporium as you will find in the state.

The Scott Covered Bridge, 277 feet long and spanning the West River, can be seen on the left, although cement posts block cars from entering it. Just past the bridge is the Townsend Dam Recreation Area, while a flurry of bed and breakfasts and craft shops less than three miles farther welcome you to West Townsend.

A mile past West Townsend, Route 100 joins Route 30. Follow both for three miles into Jamaica, another village of homey craft and specialty shops. Jamaica State Park, on the right, affords an opportunity to examine the leaves close up and ingest some sustenance; it contains both hiking trails and picnic tables.

You will do some climbing and descending as you proceed along Routes 30 and 100. Where the routes split in Rawsonville, five miles from Jamaica, take a right onto Route 100 north toward Londonderry, site of the verdant ski slopes of Magic Mountain ski area. The West River is your travel mate once more, agreeably appearing in the foreground of your views of the color-packed trees.

The village of Weston also warrants a stop. The Weston Country Store (along with its branch in Rockingham) is as close to a turn-of-the-century emporium as you will find in the state, with rock candy and Common Crackers, and you might want to focus your Minolta on the Old Parish Church with its square bell tower and the little bandstand on the green.

Turn right (still on Route 100) for the village of Ludlow at the base of Okemo Mountain. While cruising along, your eyes will meet some stellar views of evergreens, deciduous trees, and deep blue mountains in the distance. A ski town, Ludlow is a fun place to shop or dine. At the intersection with Main Street, turn left to continue on Route 100; however, if you turn right and travel four-tenths of a mile, you will see the Baptist Church, all cream-colored with dark red trim and angled roofs, and the closest thing to a European building you will find in Vermont.

Continue on Route 100 north. At the intersection with Route 103, you can continue straight to visit the home of President Calvin Coolidge. Then take Route 103 to Route 140, across the spine of the Green Mountains. Wave to hikers as you cross the Long Trail and Appalachian Trail, or take their example and stretch at White Rocks Recreation Area where you will find foot trails and tables waiting for your picnic baskets. Or just relish the landscape of hills, leafy trees, and the clear, rolling brook, obviously crafted on one of nature's best days.

Slow down as you approach Wallingford, where those interested in local history can tour the historical museum (call (802) 446–2336 for an appointment) or press onward. At Route 7 take a left, cross Roaring Brook, and savor the spectacle of silos and farms and the jagged Green Mountains that you will find for the next 21 miles. Expect to see the prominent forms of Dorset Peak (3,804 ft.) and Netop Mountain (3,290 ft.) on your right, and Mount Tabor (3,043 ft.) on your left; the railroad tracks of the Vermont Railway parallel Route 7 on your left. Emerald Lake State Park, just south of North Dorset, has foot and nature trails and picnic tables.

The antique and specialty shops and historic sights of Manchester Center are inviting, but unless you are planning to stay overnight, are best saved for another visit. Instead, as you approach Manchester, exit onto Routes 11 and 30 toward Brattleboro and take advantage of the scenic view pullout on the right five miles later, where you will confront an exquisite view of mountains and valley and trees. At just less than a mile later, Routes 30 and 11 split; turn right onto Route 30 south and continue for nine miles, past Stratton Mountain Ski Area to the junction with Route 100 in Rawsonville.

Continue south, backtracking through Jamaica, West Townsend, Townsend, and Newfane. To see the longest covered bridge in Vermont, proceed five miles past Newfane along Route 30 to West

Dummerston. The entire loop trip is about 120 miles and should take up to four hours with no stops.

Trip #5: Pastoral Southern New England

YOU WILL CROSS no fewer than 12 brooks or rivers and several ponds or lakes on this fall excursion, focused on the quiet northeast corner of Connecticut and neighboring Rhode Island. Some of these waterways are moderate in size, others are mere trickles, and though none is a gushing monster, just about all invite you to indulge in a view of flowing water encompassed by the finest colors of a New England fall, in this sparsely settled section of the Constitution State.

It's worth some time to ponder the reflections of those who lived and died 200 years ago.

Your starting point is Union at the junction of Routes 171 and 190, just west of Bigelow Hollow State Park (take exit 74 off Interstate 84, just a maple leaf south of the Massachusetts border). You can begin your adventure with a relaxing picnic in the state park. Otherwise follow Route 171, then Route 197, both serpentine, narrow roads hemmed in by stone fences, bulky barns, and generous woods, for a bit less than ten miles from Union to North Woodstock. Then take a right onto Route 169 south, and cross the little bridge over English Neighborhood Brook, which in the thick of trees should present some palatable photo possibilities.

You'll meet more farm buildings, stone fences, and a grange hall, before reaching Woodstock 3.8 miles later. Not to be confused with the rock concert site in New York or the resort of the same name in Vermont, this Woodstock is the home of an immaculate town green, appealing apple orchards, a multibuilding academy, an ancient cemetery, and a peach-colored mansion; and every September it's the home of the unfeigned and bucolic **Woodstock Fair**, (203) 928–1228, complete with midway and horse-pulling contests. The prettiest view of the village is with your back to the Woodstock Academy (founded in 1801) looking across the green toward the First Congregational Church with its white steeple poking heavenward.

The cemetery beside the church contains markers dating to the mid-eighteenth century, and it's worth some time to ponder the reflections of those who lived and died 200 years ago. You will get to know these people as more than names on tombstones, as complex and diverse as anyone alive today. One gravestone, of a Mrs. Sarah Paine who died in 1857, reads:

Christian Reader Cast An Eye
As You Are Now For Once Was I
As I Am Now So Must You Be
Prepare Your Hearts To Follow Me.

On the other side of the green is candy-colored Roseland Cottage, all gables and angles, built in 1846 as the summer retreat of businessman Henry C. Bowen. Inside it's just as showy, with trompe l'oeil panelling, stained glass, and one of the oldest indoor bowling alleys in the country. (Long before bowling became identified with the Stanley Kowalskis of the world, it was a favorite of high society in Victorian times.) Bowen's guests included four Presidents: Grant, Benjamin Harrison, Hayes, and McKinley. The cottage is open weekends in fall. Call (203) 928–4074 for exact hours.

Motoring out of Woodstock you will see some clearings to the left, with wooded hills in the far distance. Continue on Route 169 through South Woodstock, crossing the Peake Brook, until you reach Pomfret, well regarded for the brick campus of the Pomfret School (founded in 1894), although the medieval-styled Clark Memorial Chapel looks like a transplant from the Rhine River Valley. Continue straight, crossing the Wappoquia and Mashamoquet Brooks, to the intersection with Route 101. You're only 29 miles from Providence.

Follow Route 101 for 9.3 miles, through an industrial section of Dayville and under Interstate 395, to the Rhode Island border. You will soon pass on your right Rhode Island's highest point, Jerimoth Hill. (Don't brag to your friends in Colorado—it's only 812 feet high.) At North Foster, take a left onto Route 94 heading north, and for about six miles you will keep company with thick, foliage-laden woods.

Route 94 ends at the junction with Route 44 at Bowdish Reservoir. You can take a right and scoot by the well-maintained George Washington Management Area, where there are picnic tables and camping is available. Otherwise, take a left and head west back into Connecticut. Route 44 brings you into Putnam and across several waterways—the Mary Brown and Keech Brooks and the Five Mile River—and the entrance to Quaddick State Park. Cross under I-395 and continue into a residential and not necessarily scenic part of Putnam.

Then take Route 171 west across the Little River

and the Peake, Sawmill, and Mascraft Brooks, and past Lake Bungee through South Woodstock and West Woodstock toward Kenyonville. Continue on Route 171 back to Union, where you will once more border Bigelow Hollow State Park, a fine locale to unpack a picnic lunch. The total trip runs about 70 miles and should take two hours of continuous driving or three hours or longer if you stop and see some sights.

TRAINS, BOATS, AND BALLOONS: OTHER WAYS TO SEE THE FALL FOLIAGE

If you have a craving to see the leaves without watching the road, you have two choices: hire a driver or select a different form of transportation.

The advantages of these car-free means of enjoying the colors? You are able to put all your energies into enjoying the view, you don't have to sit in traffic jams behind air-fouling tour buses, and you get perspectives unavailable on public roadways. The disadvantages? You can't stop whenever you'd like and step outside to take a walk or a close-up snapshot of that perfect blend of birches and sugar maples.

We recommend you try both methods of catching the yearly fall foliage show. For non-driving opportunities, Vermont has one train excursion that's hard to top.

The Green Mountain Flyer

The **Green Mountain Flyer** is the place to be when you are nostalgic for the immediate post-war years, when the American body politic wavered between "Give 'em Hell, Harry" and "I like Ike," and commuting by railroad was a necessity rather than a novelty. The Flyer trails the rails between Bellows Falls and either Chester or Ludlow, Vermont, taking tourists and train buffs on trips back to the time just before two-car families became commonplace and the interstate highway system was a reality.

A CONTEMPORARY YOUNG
CONDUCTOR PUNCHES TICKETS
OF FALL FOLIAGE FANS ON
THE GREEN MOUNTAIN FLYER.
THE TRAIN RIDE IS A THROW-
BACK TO THE IMMEDIATE
POST-WAR ERA.

In autumn, the Flyer embarks on special 54-mile-long **Fall Foliage Weekend** trips through three river valleys, from Bellows Falls to the cozy ski town of Ludlow. But even on the shorter 26-mile-long treks to Chester you will see a myriad of maples and oaks, farms and marshlands, a craggy, 100-foot-deep gorge, and a 100-year-old covered bridge.

The Flyer, owned by the Green Mountain Railroad, is named for a passenger train that ran in Vermont from the 1930s to the 1950s. This reborn Flyer, built in 1948 based on a 1939 design, is pulled by a diesel engine, and was started up as a replacement for Steamtown, the railroad museum that left the Vermont hills for the coal mining country in Scranton, Pennsylvania, in 1983. It is only appropriate that the first noteworthy point you pass on your ride out of Bellows Falls is the former site of Steamtown.

When we rode the Flyer we sat in a passenger car built in the 1930s for the Jersey Central Railroad in New Jersey. For an extra fare, you can choose to occupy either of two classic wooden coaches, built in 1891 and 1913.

The Flyer also has a pseudo-dining car, a former passenger car with 1940-ish-style brick-red vinyl seats, which also has about a dozen wooden tables, yellow walls, and posted prints of old trains.

Sandwiches, cookies, fruit, and other snacks are sold.

A commentary is given but is not constant. It is as if the conductor taps you on the shoulder now and then to direct your attention outside the window for a moment, then lets you continue your conversation.

One highlight is the Bartonsville Covered Bridge, built in 1870 and rebuilt in the 1980s, and the commanding Brockway Mills Gorge with its gushing water and jagged cliffs. On the return trip, the train comes to a halt at each sight for photo takers.

The scheduled stops in Chester and Ludlow give riders time for a quick stroll or a picnic lunch. If you have an aching to remove wrinkles from your wallet, consider browsing through The Mill, a refurbished industrial building in Ludlow, or at the many shops in the center of the colorful town. In Chester, there is an antique and craft center a short walk from the station.

Farther up is Chester Depot, where many will relish the small town atmosphere by heading into Munroe's Supermarket and Cummings's Hardware store, old clapboard buildings that seem to have been around since the initial rail was hammered into the hard Vermont soil.

But it would be a shame for anyone to neglect to step inside the Chester Depot train station, which has been in use almost continuously since it was built in 1872. The station was the stopping point for the Rutland Railroad through 1961, and has been used by Green Mountain Railroad since 1965. The snug quarters boast wooden benches and an old-time one-cent scale which generously gives your weight whether or not you drop in a penny.

The Flyer departs from Bellows Falls's Amtrak station. Reservations are taken for the fall foliage specials to Ludlow only; it is first come first served for the rest. For information on costs or schedules, contact the Green Mountain Railroad, One Depot Square, Bellows Falls, VT 05101; (802) 463–3069.

MORE RAILROADS

Vermont

COMPLIMENTING THE GREEN Mountain Flyer's exploration of southern Vermont is the **Lamoille Valley Railroad** that treks through the state's northern reaches. The diesel engine pulls passengers east on a round trip of about 40 miles to East Hardwick or west for about 14 miles, round trip, to Johnson. On the East Hardwick route you rumble through one of the last railroad covered bridges in use. On either trip you will parallel the Lamoille River and see farmland, woods, waterfalls, and possibly deer or other wildlife. Lamoille Valley Railroad, RFD 1, Box 790, Stafford Avenue, Morrisville, VT 05661; (802) 888–4255.

New Hampshire

NEW HAMPSHIRE CAN rightly brag about its own duo of excursion railroads. The **Conway Scenic Railroad** lumbers along track laid down through the early 1870s, through the Granite State's tourist-clogged White Mountains; the train trip is the perfect antidote to the traffic and crowds that jam this part of the state in fall.

Most of the time you'll be pulled along the 11-mile trip from North Conway to Conway by a huffing and puffing steam engine, although a newer diesel is called on as a pinch hitter once in a while. You can sit in an open air "cinder collector" car, an enclosed deep red coach, or a luxury Victorian Pullman Parlor observation car; whichever, the seats on the right side afford the best views, which include the Saco River, corn fields, cows and dairy farms, color-filled woods, and the commanding White Mountains. And the train depot is a yellow and maroon Victorian gem fringed with gingerbread and built in 1874; it is also home to a collection of railroading memorabilia. Conway Scenic Railroad, P.O. Box 1947, North Conway, NH 03860; (603) 356–5251.

The splendor of New Hampshire extends beyond its mountains to its lakes, and the **Winnipesaukee Railroad** will take you in a restored 1920s or 1930s coach past its eponym, the state's biggest lake. You can board at either Meredith, home of doll queen Annalee Thorndike and her shop and museum, or at Weirs Beach, honky-tonk capital of the Lakes Region. There is a choice of two trips lasting either just under one or two hours, and only rarely does the view not include Lake Winnipesaukee. The slopes of the Ossipee and Belknap Mountains are also magnets for the eyes. One of three diesel engines is used to pull the cars. Winnipesaukee Railroad, RFD 4, Box 317, Meredith, NH 03253; (603) 528–2330.

Massachusetts

At **Edaville Railroad** in South Carver, Massachusetts, the bright red of ripe cranberries ready for scooping is the dominant color as you chug along for five and a half miles on a steam train through the world's largest cranberry plantation. Also on the grounds are antique cars and fire engines, a petting zoo, and an antique operating carousel. Edaville Railroad, Route 58, South Carver, MA 02366; (508) 866–4526.

Cape Cod bound? The **Cape Cod Scenic Railroad**, which has the same owner as Edaville, is pulled by a diesel engine that runs round trips of about 35 miles between Hyannis, Sandwich, and Sagamore, past salt marshes, cranberry bogs, woods, open fields, and farmlands. An Edaville spokesman says the scenery gives riders a fair idea of what the Cape looked like 75 years ago, long before merciless development. Patrons ride on one of several restored coaches dating from the 1930s to 1950s, or a first class parlor car with swivel seats and small brass ceiling fans that was crafted in 1912. For information, call (508) 771–3788 in summer or fall, or write or call Edaville Railroad.

At the opposite end of the state is the **Berkshire Scenic Railway**, shuttling passengers through the

THE WHISTLE BLOWS AND EDAVILLE RAILROAD'S STEAM TRAIN TAKES VISITORS THROUGH THE WORLD'S LARGEST CRANBERRY PLANTATION, COLORED A RICH, DARK RED IN PEAK HARVEST SEASON.

foliage-filled hills along the Housatonic River. Expect to see waterfalls, historic mills, meadows, and wetlands. A museum with an operating model railroad, a caboose, and railroad videos is also on the property, on Willow Creek Road in Lenox. Berkshire Scenic Railway, P.O. Box 2195, Lenox, MA 01240; (413) 637–2210.

The mill yards of Holyoke have given birth to one of the Bay State's absorbing urban heritage parks. One park feature is the **Holyoke Heritage Park Railroad**, which operates special foliage trips, sometimes incorporating nature walks. Ride from Holyoke to Westfield in one of three World War I era cars pulled by a diesel locomotive. Other special events include train robbery and murder mysteries. Holyoke Heritage Park Railroad, 221 Appleton Street, Holyoke, MA 01040; (413) 534–1723.

The **Massachusetts Bay Railroad Enthusiasts** celebrate the fall with a day-long foliage railroad excursion from Boston to Albany aboard a modern diesel-powered train. The rambling rail jaunt is known for passing through rugged backwoods stretches inaccessible to automobiles. Expect to climb to the summits of the Berkshire Mountains. Massachusetts Bay Railroad Enthusiasts, P.O. Box 525, Bedford, MA 01730; (617) 489–5277.

Connecticut

IN CONNECTICUT YOU can combine a rail ride with a riverboat ramble thanks to the **Valley Railroad**. A steam locomotive, red and black with brass fixtures, and manufactured in China in 1989 (and that's not China, Maine), will pull you aboard antique and restored coaches down the Connecticut River Valley on a 55-minute-long round trip. Andrew Lloyd Webber, the composer of many classic Broadway musicals, stated that a ride on the Valley Railroad with his young son helped inspire him to complete *Starlight Express.*

As an additional option, you can pick up the reproduced Mississippi-style riverboat, *Becky Thatcher*, for an hour-long ride down the Connecticut, passing the Goodspeed Opera House, Gillette Castle, handsome private houses, and the multi-colored trees along the river's banks. The Valley Railroad Company, P.O. Box 452, Essex, CT 06426; (203) 767–0103.

BOATS

THERE ARE OTHER ways to see the best of fall while afloat on the Connecticut River, besides the *Becky Thatcher*, mentioned above. The **Lady Fenwick**, a reproduction of a mid-nineteenth-century steam yacht, and the **Aunt Polly**, a two-deck excursion boat named for actor and playwright William Gillette's private boat, both ply the river well into the fall. They are based in Hartford and Middletown, respectively. The last Saturday in October is reserved for a special day-long autumn cruise from Hartford to Old Saybrook. Deep River Navigation Company, P.O. Box 382, River Street, Deep River, CT 06417; (203) 526–4954.

Maine's massive Sebago Lake is the setting for fall cruises on the **Point Sebago Princess** as part of larger weekend getaway packages. The cruises might have murder mystery, Oktoberfest, or singles themes. The fall colors on the islands and lake shore are on the house. Point Sebago Outdoor Resort, RR 1, Box 712, Casco, ME 04015; (207) 655–7948.

Champ is Lake Champlain's version of the Loch Ness Monster, and some people in northern Vermont swear he exists. One such person is Mike Shea who gives tours on the paddle wheeler replica, **Spirit of Ethan Allen**, which takes folks on the lake for narrated cruises lasting an hour and a half. Mike recalls: "A group of about 70 had chartered the boat for a fiftieth wedding anniversary party. We were heading up toward Colchester Reef Lighthouse when something appeared about 400 feet off port side. It was about 25 or 30 feet long and followed us for about five minutes."

Even if you don't see the lively sea serpent you will be privy to a special view that should be savored, as you are sandwiched in between the Green Mountains to the east and the Adirondacks to the west. Green Mountain Boat Lines, Ltd., P.O. Box 4306, South Burlington, VT 05406; (802) 862–9685.

New Hampshire's aquatic behemoth, the glacier-formed, spring-fed Lake Winnipesaukee, is home to more than just a train. Also carrying passengers is a giant-sized cruising boat, the **Mount Washington**, which weaves in and around the lake's 274 islands offering foliage inspections that simply aren't available to those behind the wheel of a car. The boat can

be boarded at Weirs Beach, Center Harbor, Alton Bay, and Wolfeboro. Winnipesaukee Flagship, P.O. Box 5367, Weirs Beach, NH 03246; (603) 366–2628.

Smaller but no less foliage-fringed Lake Sunapee can be yours for an hour and a half aboard the **Mount Sunapee**. The mountain for which the boat is named can be seen during the entire cruise, while Mount Kearsarge can often be spotted in the distance. The other Lake Sunapee excursion boat, the *Kearsarge*, completes its tours before fall foliage season commences. MV *Mount Sunapee II*, P.O. Box 345, Sunapee, NH 03782; (603) 763–4030.

HOT-AIR BALLOONS

PHILEAS FOGG NEVER really took a hot-air balloon ride in Jules Verne's *Around the World in Eighty Days*, but you have the opportunity to do so in New England, and there is no better time than in autumn. Those who have viewed the fall harvest of color from above say the show is worth the hefty price tag. Hour-long balloon rides average $200 per person.

The cool air of early morning is most agreeable for hot-air ballooning, so most rides depart around 6:00

TIRED OF THE SAME OLD VIEWS OF FALL? THERE'S
NOTHING ROUTINE ABOUT A BALLOON RIDE.

in the morning, although in early fall a ride before sunset is probable, too. Depending on winds, you might travel anywhere from a couple to 15 miles in an hour. Some operations let you help attach the basket to the balloon or lend a hand inflating it. (Call the balloon an "envelope" when you are attaching it and you will pass as an expert.)

It is recommended that you arrive for a balloon adventure with your feet snugly entrenched in waterproof boots or shoes since launch sites and landing spots can be ripe with morning dew. Sunglasses are important, too. The temperature aloft will not be much different from that back on terra firma, so you won't need to take that winter overcoat out of storage, but you should dress as you would for any outdoor adventure in fall.

Most hot-air balloon rides end with a traditional glass of champagne, if not a full champagne breakfast. Supposedly the custom began in Europe when an early balloonist from France landed in a field in Germany. Since he couldn't speak the language, the balloonist showed his appreciation with a bottle of French wine, and the link between hot-air balloons and champagne had begun.

Some companies offering balloon rides in New England include:

Boland Balloon, Pine Drive, RD 2, Burlington, CT 06013; (203) 673–1307.

Balloon School of Massachusetts, Inc., RFD 1, Palmer (Brimfield), MA 01069; (413) 245–7013.

Aeronauts Unlimited, 27 Skyview Road, Lexington, MA 02173; (617) 861–0101.

Berkshire Balloons, P.O. Box 22, Old Ferry Road, Northampton, MA 01061; (413) 586–1755.

Balloon Adventures of New Bedford, 564 Rock O'Dundee Road, South Dartmouth, MA 02748; (508) 636–4846.

Balloon Inn Vermont, Silver Maple Lodge and Cottages, RR 1, Box 8, Fairlee, VT 05045; (800) 666–1946 or (802) 333–4326.

COLLEGES AND FOOTBALL

Yale's football team has played Harvard's since 1875. Yale has played Brown since 1880. Dartmouth has played Harvard since 1882. Yale and Dartmouth have played each other since 1884. Boston College's first gridiron outing took place in 1893. And Brown and Dartmouth have faced each other since 1894.

Our college football teams might not play before 90,000 fans in cavernous stadiums, and their efforts may not merit the glory of the Big Ten or the Pacific Ten. But our rivalries have been around longer than electric heat. Texas and Oklahoma is a drooling infant compared to Harvard and Yale. New England football might not have network coverage, but it has an enviable heritage.

In addition, our colleges proudly boast their own cultures, histories, and arts that you would be hard pressed to locate on the campus of a prairie or West Coast football factory. When visiting these campuses for a Saturday home game, keep in mind that there is much to do before the tailgate party and after the fourth quarter. Consider taking advantage of the extracurricular activities that abound at our colleges, and turn an afternoon of sports into a full-day outing. Keep in mind, though, that these campuses are enlightening places to visit any time of year and a football game is just a handy excuse.

New England football might not have network coverage, but it has an enviable heritage.

Harvard University

AROUND THE TURN of the century the sight of a squad of Harvard men in their football jerseys caused panic on football fields throughout the East. From 1890 through 1919 Harvard won seven national championships including a Rose Bowl victory. In 1887, Harvard slammed Tufts twice by scores of 68–0 and 86–0. Through the years Harvard has maintained winning records against most of its Ivy League opponents and has proved the spawning ground for National Football League players like Pat McInally, John Dockery, and Dan Jiggetts.

Many cities would kill for the wealth of culture that can be found at the oldest university in the country.

The campus itself is worth a tour, whether guided (daily except during winter vacations) or self-guided.

The **statue of John Harvard** in front of Bulfinch's University Hall is a photographer's jewel, although it has a dubious story. Known as the "statue of three lies," the Daniel Chester French work bears an inscription reading: "John Harvard, Founder, 1638." The facts are, however, that the college was named after but not founded by John Harvard and that the founding took place in 1636. In addition, the likeness is not that of John Harvard. Since no authentic portraits of John Harvard exist, French based his statue on the appearance of a well-liked and handsome student from the Class of 1882.

The oldest building standing on campus is **Massachusetts Hall**, built in 1720, which once housed soldiers of the Continental Army. Today it's home to the offices of the university president, vice presidents, and treasurer. The second oldest building is the clapboard **Wadsworth House**, dating from 1727, where General George Washington once quartered.

This is not to imply that Harvard University is only full of relics. The **Carpenter Center for the Visual Arts** is the handiwork of the distinguished French architect Le Corbusier. Completed in 1963, it is the only building he designed in North America. The ten-story **Science Center** was constructed between 1970 and 1972 by José Luis Cert, and the **Tanner Fountain** outside was dedicated in 1985.

Priceless items fill all of Harvard's museums but the **Widener Library**, third largest in the country, contains its own treasures including a Gutenberg Bible and Shakespeare folios. The library is easily recognized by its huge Corinthian portico.

Harvard's quartet of natural history museums is home to collections respected by scholars the world over, although young minds will also be intrigued by the artifacts. Watch a child's eyes widen as he or she takes in a glimpse of the largest turtle shell ever found or the whale skeletons in the **Museum of Comparative Zoology**, also known as the Agassiz Museum, or the masks in the **Peabody Museum of Archaeology and Ethnology**.

The Peabody is the oldest museum in this hemisphere devoted entirely to these two topics, and its largest collections are devoted to North, Central, and South American Indian cultures, although it also contains major ethnographic collections from Oceania and Africa. The **Botanical Museum** serves as the garden for 3,000 glass flowers made solely of glass

Many cities would kill for the wealth of culture that can be found at the oldest university in the country.

with a bit of wire reinforcement. The flowers were shaped mainly by hand, with the magnified parts blown after the glass had softened. **The Mineralogical and Geological Museums** hold exhibits on minerals, meteorites, gems, and ores.

Three art museums supplement the natural history showcases. The **Fogg Art Museum** is the place to see masterpieces by Rubens, Van Gogh, Renoir, Degas, and Americans Jackson Pollock and Winslow Homer. There are also major holdings of late medieval paintings and sculptures. For Oriental and Islamic art, head to the **Arthur M. Sackler Museum**, which opened in 1985, the newest of the university's art museums. Notable collections include ancient Chinese jades, Chinese bronzes, Roman sculpture, and Greek vases. The **Busch-Reisinger Museum**, devoted to art of central and northern Europe, is the only museum of its kind in the United States; it was renovated and reopened in 1991.

The two other Harvard repositories are the **Semitic Museum**, with its special exhibits on the Near East, and the **Collection of Historical Scientific Instruments**, complete with sundials, clocks, microscopes, telescopes, early computing devices, and vacuum pumps, among other such tools; they are closed Saturday.

To reach the Harvard Information Center, call (617) 495–1573. For Harvard's museums of natural history, call (617) 495–1910 for a recording or (617) 495–3045 to speak with a human. For Harvard's art museums, call (617) 495–2387 for a recording and (617) 495–9400 for a human voice. The Semitic Museum can be reached at (617) 495–3123, and you can contact the Collection of Scientific Instruments at (617) 495–2779.

Dartmouth College

ASK ANY FAN of college football to name the game's best coaches and you will ultimately hear the monikers of several men who have guided Dartmouth. Before he became famous as a World War I hero, the legendary Frank Cavanagh coached Dartmouth to a 42–9–3 combined record from 1911 to 1916. Jesse Hawley led Dartmouth to a national championship in 1925, with its first undefeated and untied season. Bob Blackman guided Dartmouth to an impressive combined record of 104–37–3, with seven Ivy League titles, from 1955 to 1970. A total of five Dartmouth coaches, plus six players, have been named to the National Football Foundation's Hall of Fame, regarded as college football's hall of fame.

On campus, most eyes searching for esthetics should be directed toward **Dartmouth Row**, a quartet of elegant Greek Revival buildings facing the College Green. The oldest of the white and black-trimmed structures are **Wentworth** and **Thornton Halls**, both built in 1829, although **Dartmouth Hall** is a 1904 copy of an original 1791 building destroyed by fire. Contrast these with the Romanesque-style **Rollins Chapel**, which has been an entity here since 1886.

Searching for art? First step inside the Georgian-style **Baker Memorial Library**, home of a massive fresco painted by noted Mexican artist José Clemente Orozco. The work is called *An Epic of American Civilization* and consists of panels depicting American scenes from pre-Columbian times to the industrial age.

Then take a walk through any of the ten galleries inside the **Hood Museum of Art**, where you will find a range of European Old Master paintings, American paintings and silver, Native American and African art, and twentieth-century creations. Some of

WORKS BY PICASSO, COPLEY, AND LORRAIN ARE ON DISPLAY IN DARTMOUTH'S HOOD MUSEUM OF ART.

the most noteworthy works include *Guitar on Table* by Pablo Picasso, *Portrait of Governor John Wentworth* by John Singleton Copley, *Shepherd and Shepherdess in a Landscape* by Claude Lorrain. (603) 646–2808.

The **Webster Cottage**, one-time home of New Hampshire's most famous statesman, Daniel Webster, and repository today of Webster memorabilia and Shaker furniture, is open Wednesday, Saturday, and Sunday until Columbus Day. (603) 643–2326.

Yale University

WITH A RESPLENDENT heritage consisting of countless football icons—from the superlative Albie Booth to the fundamental Walter Camp to the spurious Frank Merriwell to the canine Handsome Dan—the Elis still command respect on the gridiron. With over 750 all-time victories, Yale still leads all other schools in total wins in the history of college football.

The third oldest college in the country is home to a bumper crop of museums.

Yale's gridiron debut took place against Columbia on November 16, 1872, when Captain David B. Schaff led his team to a 3–0 victory. Since then Yale has produced two Heisman trophy winners, over 116 All-Americans, and more members (26) of the National Football Foundation's Hall of Fame than any other college. And Yale holds winning records against all of its Ivy League opponents.

Like Harvard, the third oldest college in the country is home to a bumper crop of museums. The **Yale University Art Gallery**, oldest college art gallery in the country, has five floors of sculpture, antiquities, and American, European, and Near and Far Eastern paintings. Van Gogh's *Night Cafe* and Picasso's *First Steps* are worth seeking out, although you will also find works by Gauguin, Cézanne, Pollock, Homer, Hopper, and Calder. (203) 432–0600. Across the street is the **Yale Center for British Art**, with works by Turner, Constable, and Gainsborough. (203) 432–2800.

Restless children who don't know Gainsborough from Gainesburgers will likely be awestruck by the riveting collection of dinosaur skeletons in the **Peabody Museum of Natural History**, also on campus. The imposing skeleton of a *Brontosaurus excelsus* overwhelms onlookers on the first floor, while the 110-foot-by-16-foot mural, *The Age of Reptiles*, is intriguing for visitors of any age. (203) 432–5050.

Spinets, harpsichords, virginals, and fortepianos, many animatedly decorated, join an Arabian oud and a Japanese koto as a few of the over 800 music makers in the **Yale Collection of Musical Instruments**, closed Saturday. (203) 432–0822. The **Sterling Memorial Library** contains Babylonian tablets, as well as more than four million volumes. (203) 432–1775. And in the **Beinecke Rare Book and Manuscript Library** is a Gutenberg Bible. (203) 432–2977.

The most famous landmark on campus is the **Harkness Tower**, 221 feet high and part of the Memorial Quadrangle, a Gothic-style block of dormitories. The oldest building and part of the **Old Campus** is **Connecticut Hall**, a Georgian-style brick edifice where colonial patriot Nathan Hale (Yale Class of 1773) boarded; the building dates to 1717. Call (203) 432–2300 for campus tours.

Brown University

NONE OTHER THAN John Heisman, whose name has become synonymous with college football excellence, is a Brown alumnus, Class of 1891. Brown has also made other contributions to the game, with longtime Penn State coach Joe Paterno, and Fritz Pollard, credited as the first black to be named All-American; in 1915, Pollard led Brown to the first official Rose Bowl, long before it became the domain of the Pacific-Ten and Big Ten conferences. Brown boosters still rave about their championship 1976 season, but it was a half century earlier, in 1926, when Brown played its only undefeated season, ending with a record of 9–0–1.

The spacious **College Green** on the Brown campus is an enticing, verdant carpet lying at the feet of the Greek Revival, Victorian Gothic, and colonial buildings that comprise the original section of the university. The most storied structure is **University Hall**, dating from 1770 and once used as a barracks and hospital during the Revolutionary War; today it's home to administrative offices. For a campus tour, call (401) 863–2378.

Other historic buildings are the several libraries. The **John Carter Brown Library** holds exhibits and maps dating to the age of exploration, including those written by Christopher Columbus. Some of the oldest books you might ever see, printed before the sixteenth century, are in the **Annmary Brown Memorial Library**, which also holds a permanent collection of American and European paintings. Named for Abraham Lincoln's private secretary and a

SOME ENTER BROWN'S JOHN CARTER RROWN LIBRARY JUST TO STUDY. OTHERS STEP
INSIDE TO SEE EXHIBITS AND MAPS DATING TO THE AGE OF EXPLORATION.

former Secretary of State, the **John Hay Library** houses Hay's papers, as well as celebrated American sheet music.

You will find art at the **David Winton Bell Gallery** in the List Art Center on campus. (401) 863–2932. However, the most distinguished repository of art in Providence is not a Brown property, but the **Museum of Art of the Rhode Island School of Design**. Inside are representatives of American furniture, Greek and Roman classical art, and American and European masterpieces. (401) 331–3511.

There is another Brown University museum worthy of mention, although it is located 17 miles from the main campus in Bristol, Rhode Island. The **Haffenreffer Museum of Anthropology** displays clothing and other artifacts of the native people of North, Middle, and South America, and the traditional arts of the people from Africa, Asia, the Middle East, and Oceania. (401) 253–8388.

Boston College

THE "MIRACLE IN MIAMI" might be foremost in the minds of New Englanders when they think of Boston College sports heroics, and the 47–45 thriller from 1984—won on a 48-yard pass from Doug Flutie to Gerald Phelan as time ran out—is a standout in the memory banks of the current generation of football fans. The crew from Chestnut Hill went on to a 45–28 win over Houston in the 1985 Cotton Bowl.

But the Eagles were bowl game participants long before the Flutie-Phelan duo was making headlines. The legendary Frank Leahy, who would later find fame coaching Notre Dame, led the Eagles to Cotton and Sugar Bowl appearances on New Year's Day in 1940 and 1941. B. C. has five alumni in the National Football Foundation Hall of Fame, and two—Art Donovan and Ernie Stautner—in the Pro Football Hall of Fame. And face it, the only place to see Class A Division I NCAA football in New England is at Alumni Stadium.

Stained-glass windows and rare books highlight the college's **Bapst Library**, which is closed on Saturday, but most of the cultural and historic attractions are off campus in the city of Boston. Within an easy drive from Chestnut Hill and close enough to get you back by kickoff are the sites of Brookline.

The **John F. Kennedy National Historic Site** is the birthplace and boyhood home of the charismatic president. Your guide through the house is Rose

Kennedy, thanks to the magic of a permanent audio tape. (617) 566–7937. The **Frederick Law Olmsted National Historic Site** is the home of the patriarch of American landscape architecture and the designer of New York City's Central Park. (617) 566–1689.

A late Victorian carriage house in Brookline's Larz Anderson Park contains the **Museum of Transportation**, in which you will find historic cars and other vehicles. (617) 522–6140. To learn about Christian Science founder Mary Baker Eddy, visit the **Longyear Museum**, with memorabilia and displays about her life. (617) 277–8943.

PICK YOUR OWN APPLES

Which state was first known as "The Peach State?" No, not Georgia.

Not even South Carolina.

Thanks to its proximity to large population centers, in the days before commercial refrigeration Connecticut was regarded as the home of the downy yellow fruit. It was essential for growers to be able to pick, pack, and ship to major markets within 48

CLIMB TO NEW HEIGHTS TO PICK YOUR OWN APPLES.

hours. In the winter of 1917–18, however, a killing frost ruined thousands of peach trees in the state, ending Connecticut's domination in the field.

We learned that fact while on a visit to Lyman Orchards in Middlefield, Connecticut, a popular center for picking your own apples that also includes a fully stocked store, a cider mill, a golf course, and a restaurant. Lymans' is just one of many enterprises in our six states bursting with apple appeal, where you can grab your own apples right off the tree.

Lyman Orchards

THE HERITAGE IS a long one. The Lymans have owned land here since John Lyman purchased 36 acres in 1741. It was Charles Elihu Lyman who helped spawn Connecticut's peachy image, when he grew 800 acres of peaches in the late 1800s.

Nowadays, thousands come during a normal autumn to pick McIntosh, Red and Golden Delicious, Mutsu, Cortland, Empire, and Ida Red apples, among others, that hang in profusion from the trees covering the central Connecticut hilltop where the Lymans have their orchard. The view from the summit is inspirational any time of year, but especially at harvest time, when the trees are lush with fruit. (Apple

JOHN LYMAN, EIGHTH GENERATION OF THE LYMAN FAMILY TO FARM IN MIDDLEFIELD, CONNECTICUT, IS A BONA FIDE APPLE EXPERT.

blossom time in spring, when the orchard is a cushion of white and pink, is another choice time to enjoy the panorama.)

A current John Lyman, member of the eighth generation to farm the land, appreciates the past but has an eye toward progress. In order to increase production, the Lymans have begun to replace many of the sprawling older apple trees with younger, dwarf trees. He says: "The smaller trees have the same blossoms as the big ones, but many people have a romantic attachment to those big trees with big limbs, the type that Andrew Wyeth painted. But it's important that they understand that these smaller trees help the grower get better utilization of the acreage."

In modern times of massive super stores and antiseptic convenience stores John realizes it's easy for consumers to have misconceptions about farming, which is one reason why he welcomes those who come to pick their own apples.

Says Lyman: "It's a connection of the people to the farm, a connection that we used to have but lost. Picking apples brings people in touch with agriculture. They learn that apples don't come right from the supermarket shelves. We help make people familiar with the way food is produced."

Why pick your own apples when you can more easily buy a bag at a supermarket? John says three

CIDER IN THE MAKING AT LYMAN ORCHARDS.

factors invite people into his orchards, and cost savings is certainly one. By picking their own fruit, consumers don't pay for added expenses associated with handling.

Yet cost isn't the main reason, says John, why his customers prefer shopping in the orchard. Freshness of fruit is a bigger draw ("There's nothing like an apple right off the tree," he smiles), while the activity itself is the biggest. The unspoiled open air—and there still is some unspoiled open air in Connecticut—initially greets apple pickers with open arms, but an hour in the orchard, enfolded by trees and rolling hills, offers an encounter with nature even a confirmed sofa spud can appreciate.

There is a lengthy list of fruits on the Lyman grounds. As well as apples, you can gather, in their proper seasons, your own strawberries, raspberries, blueberries, sweet corn, peaches, pears, and pumpkins. You can also make a point to stop at the Apple Barrel, the fully stocked round-like-an-apple country store, where you will find—in addition to the obvious—coffees (in such exotic flavors as cinnamon crème de noisette), cheeses from Connecticut and Holland, Indian pudding from Vermont, barbecue sauce from Texas, a deli and a bakery, and enough aromas to tempt an anorexic.

The Lymans also have a cider mill, though tours of it are limited to special groups. However, special events are planned throughout the year for all visitors. In February sugar on snow is served on one special day. There are an Easter apple hunt, drive-through tours in blossom time, a summer craft show, a fall art show, and an apple pie baking contest. And year round, the shouts of "fore" emanate from Lymans' 18 holes; call in advance for a tee time on weekends.

Lymans' is located at the junctions of Routes 147 and 157 in Middlefield, Connecticut. Their special pick-your-own hot line is (203) 349–1566. The main office can be reached at (203) 349–1793. The Apple Barrel farm store number is (203) 349–3673. And the golf club number is (203) 349–8055.

For Lymans' and any of the following pick-your-own centers, picking seasons are limited, and can vary from year to year. Just because you can buy Paula Reds in the store in October doesn't mean you can pick them at the same time. And a hardy crop in one year doesn't mean another the same time next year. Call before making a special trip.

OTHER PICK-YOUR-OWN PLACES

FOLLOWING IS A selection of places to pick your own produce in each state, as well as a few apple operations that specialize in cider pressing.

Connecticut

SILVERMAN'S FARM You can't pick your own here but there is cider pressing on old-fashioned cider mills. You can watch them in action any day in October and on weekends in late September and November. The process is explained through cartoons and labels. Also take the time to meet the resident emu, llamas, turkeys, pheasants, goats, sheep, and other animals of the petting zoo. Pumpkins, flowers, and plants are sold at the Silvermans' garden center store. 451 Sport Hill Road, Easton; (203) 261–3306.

BLUE JAY ORCHARDS The baker's dozen of apples you can pick here are McIntosh, Cortland, Red and Golden Delicious, Macoun, Rome, Stayman, Ida Red, Mutsu, Empire, Baldwin, Jonathan, and Paula Red. Bags are provided. You can hear a bit about cider pressing as you watch it take place. An abundance of apple products is sold here, including apple spice bread, apple crisp, apple sauce, apple pies, sugar free apple pies and sauce, and cider doughnuts. You can also purchase jams and jellies, honey, Vermont maple syrup, eggs, vegetables, ham, turkey, and range-fed chickens. On fall weekends, storytelling is offered and you can pick your own pumpkins; a hay ride brings you to the pumpkin patch. Other produce to pick includes strawberries and raspberries. 125 Plumtrees Road, Bethel; (203) 748–0119.

LEWIS FARMS Apple pickers can reach for McIntosh, Red Delicious, Cortland, Mutsu, and Empire. Containers are supplied. You can also pick your own strawberries and vegetables. Cider is pressed, and the Lewises' bakery sells 21 types of bread, several pies (apple, pecan, coconut custard, peach, to name a sampling), cookies, and strudels. Jams, jellies, and vinegars made at the site, as well as dried flowers and seasonal crafts can be purchased. 391 Bellevue Avenue, Southington; (203) 628–9736.

APPLEBERRY FARM Among the varieties one can pick here are Paula Red, Jerseymac, Northern Spy, McIntosh, Cortland, Macoun, Empire, and Red and Golden Delicious. Bring your own containers. Pickers can also pluck their own peaches, corn, raspberries, and strawberries. Cider, pies (apple and pumpkin), jams, jellies, fudge, and some vegetables are sold, too. 1576 North Stone Street, West Suffield; (203) 668–7252 or (203) 668–7013.

AVERILL FARM Many varieties are yours for the picking including McIntosh, Rhode Island Greening, Spartan, Rome Beauty, Ida Red, Northern Spy, and Mutsu. The Averills also permit you to pick your own pears, and at times, quinces. Some cider is sold, but it is not made on the premises. 250 Calhoun Street, Washington Depot; (203) 868–2777.

OAK CREST FARM McIntosh and Cortlands can be picked on weekends in September. Containers are supplied. Horse-drawn wagon rides through the orchards are offered during apple season. Pears and raspberries are sometimes available for picking. There is no cider pressing, but skeins of yarn from the resident sheep are sold. 234 Upper State Street, North Haven.; (203) 239–0474.

Maine

BROWN'S ORCHARD Cindy and Mike Brown let visitors pick McIntosh, Cortland, and Red Delicious. Containers are supplied. You can view cider pressing, done mainly on weekends. Pumpkins and other squash, jams and jellies, honey, maple syrup, and handmade wreaths are also sold. Taber Hill Road (three miles off Route 201), Vassalboro; (207) 923–3113.

HOPE ORCHARDS Come to this town six miles off Route 1 near Camden to pick McIntosh, Cortland, Red and Golden Delicious, Macoun, Northern Spy, and some antique varieties of apples. Containers are supplied. In addition to their own cider, owners Karl and Linda Drechsler sell many Maine-made foods such as jams, maple syrup, honey, pickles, chocolate sauce, mixes for candied and caramel apples, and mulled cider. Route 105, Hope Corner; (207) 763–4080.

THE APPLE FARM Owner Marilyn Meyerhans has McIntosh, Red and Golden Delicious, Cortland, Northern Spy, and Macoun for picking. Containers are supplied. She tries to have cider pressing take place on Saturday or Sunday when guests can watch. On one fall weekend, Marilyn offers an open house, where crafts are demonstrated and recipes and food samples are given away. (Another special event is **Honey Day**, where people can learn how to make and use the viscid fluid produced by bees.) Hay rides into the orchard are given on weekends and Marilyn also sells jams and jellies, bakery items, beeswax candles, and other handcrafts. Back Road (off Route 104), Skowhegan; (207) 453–7656.

DOUBLE T ORCHARD McIntosh and Cortland apples can be picked here. Containers are supplied and you can watch cider being pressed if you arrive at the right time. Also sold are maple syrup and jams and jellies. 17 Orchard Road (off Routes 100 and 26), Cumberland; (207) 829–3316.

LAKESIDE ORCHARDS "People pick largely for entertainment," confesses Penny Markley, orchard owner. "Sometimes the prices are just as good in the stores." So to add to the mood of the outing, she and husband Reed offer tractor rides to the orchards. For your picking pleasure, you can grab onto McIntosh, Cortland, and Red Delicious; a young orchard should be producing additional varieties in a few years. Bags are supplied. Penny also sells frozen ready-to-bake pies, jams and jellies, cheese, maple products, and crafts mostly made in Maine. Route 17, Manchester; (207) 622–2479.

KENTS HILL ORCHARD At this mid-Maine business 17 miles west of Augusta, you can pick McIntosh, Cortland, Red and Golden Delicious, Jersey Macs, Northern Spy, Gravenstein, Paula Red, and Vista Bella, a new variety. It is preferred that you bring your own container. Cider is pressed but no tours are given. You can also pick pears and strawberries. At the shop on the grounds you can buy baked goods, vegetables, jams and jellies, honey, maple syrup, cheese, and steamed hot dogs. Route 17, Kents Hill; (207) 685–3522.

HARDIE ORCHARD You can't pick your own here but you can watch cider in the making on a ratchet press dating from 1893. "I just went to have it repaired and the repairmen hadn't seen one for years," says owner Craig D. Sandler. A little explanation of cider pressing is given and samples are offered. Vegetables and pumpkins are sold, too. East Sennebec Road, Union; (207) 785–5289.

Massachusetts

HILLBROOK ORCHARDS Come here to pick a wide variety of apples including McIntosh, Cortland, Macoun, Red and Golden Delicious, Baldwin, Northern Spy, Red Rome, Paula Red, Empire, and Roxbury Russet. The tart-tasting Russet, says Hillbrook owner Andrew Rosenberger, is the oldest apple in America, and was brought from Roxbury, England, to Roxbury, Massachusetts, in 1635. Containers are supplied. Cider is pressed on weekends and an explanation of the procedure is offered by press operators. On weekends after you leave your car, you can hop onto a pony, a horse-drawn hay wagon, or a tractor to transport you from the parking area to the picking area. A farm stand is on the grounds, with home-baked apple pies, mulled cider, jams and jellies, and vegetables. You can also pick your own strawberries in season. 170 Old Ayer Road (off Route 119), Groton; (508) 448–3248.

CLARKDALE FRUIT FARMS McIntosh, Cortland, and Red Delicious are here for the picking. Half bushel bags are supplied and cider is pressed as you watch. Honey and maple syrup are also sold. Upper Road, Deerfield; (413) 772–6797.

HONEY POT HILL ORCHARDS After you have finished picking McIntosh, Cortland, or Red Delicious apples, you can spend some time petting the sheep, goats, pigs, rabbits, and other farm animals. Containers are supplied and cider is pressed periodically, often on Friday mornings. Honey is sold, too, and there are also blueberries to pick yourself. 144 Sudbury Road (off Route 62), Stow; (508) 562-5666.

PINE HILL ORCHARDS In the shadow of the Mohawk Trail you can pick McIntosh, Cortland, and Red Delicious apples, mainly on weekends. Visitors are taken to the orchards by tractor, and given a short tour of the grounds. Half bushel bags are supplied. Cider is pressed but on an irregular schedule and mainly on weekdays. There is a petting farm with sheep, goats, cows, ducks, and pigs, and a farm stand with homemade baked goods (pies, breads, cookies, doughnuts, and muffins). Greenfield Road (three miles off Route 2), Colrain; (413) 624–3325.

BAXTER'S ECHO HILL ORCHARDS
Fred Baxter, a native of the London suburb of Essex, England, and his wife, Margaret, let visitors pick several varieties, including McIntosh, Cortland, Empire, Macoun, and Red and Golden Delicious. Containers are supplied or you can bring your own. You ride out to the orchards on a trailer pulled by a tractor, and you can watch cider being pressed. The Baxters maintain a country store on the grounds, where they sell jams, jellies, and baked goods like cider doughnuts, breads, and cherry, apple, and other fruit pies. Other produce you can pick yourself includes peaches, nectarines, raspberries, both sweet and sour cherries, plums, apricots, and red and black currants. Wilbraham Road (off Route 32), Monson; (413) 267–3303.

CHENEY ORCHARDS
McIntosh and Cortland apples are picked here. Containers are supplied. Cider is not pressed here, but is sold along with apple pies, jams and jellies, tree-ripened peaches, honey, Vermont cheese, and maple syrup. Apple Road (off Route 148, four miles from Old Sturbridge Village), Brimfield; (413) 436–7688.

ZANE ARNOLD ORCHARDS
The varieties you can pick include McIntosh, Cortland, Red and Golden Delicious, Baldwin, and Ida Red. Containers are supplied. Cider pressing takes place but cannot be viewed. Apple pies, jams and jellies, maple syrup, and honey are for sale, too. 15 Spring Road, Westborough; (508) 366–2845.

RED APPLE FARM
A total of 25 varieties can be picked; the list includes McIntosh, Cortland, Red and Golden Delicious, Macoun, Northern Spy, Gravenstein, Spencer, Baldwin, Ida Red, Barton, and Empire. Bags are supplied. Cider is pressed but there are no tours. Fruit pies, apple dumplings, jams and jellies, honey, maple syrup, and cheese are for sale, too. Pumpkins and blueberries are also available for picking. Highland Avenue (off Route 2A), Phillipston; (508) 249–6763.

Keep in mind that Old Sturbridge Village also maintains its own cider mill, which can be visited with admission into the recreated nineteenth-century community. Sturbridge, MA 01566; (508) 347–3362.

New Hampshire

MEADOW LODGE FARM Those arriving to pick apples on fall weekends can expect a free tractor ride, as well as the chance to pick 20 varieties, including McIntosh, Cortland, Red and Golden Delicious, Empire, Mutsu, and Paula Red. Owner Dave Johnston supplies containers and throws his own harvest festival with food and pony rides on one fall weekend. There are a few picnic tables and you might catch cider pressing in progress if you are lucky. Jams, jellies, herb vinegars, honey, and maple syrup are sold, too. Route 129, Loudon; (603) 798–5860.

BROOKDALE FRUIT FARM, INC. The Hardy family, in town since 1752, allows pickers a choice of McIntosh, Cortland, Red and Golden Delicious, and Granny Smith. You can also pick pumpkins, strawberries, and blueberries. Containers are provided. There is no cider pressing but there is a large retail stand offering homemade baked goods like breads (Irish soda, fruit nut, and French garlic, among others) and pies (Swedish apple, cherry peach, pear, pecan, and pumpkin, to name a few). The Hardys also make their own ice cream. 38 Broad Street, Hollis; (603) 465–2240.

YE OLDE ALLEN FARM Pick your own McIntosh, Cortland, Northern Spy, Red and Golden Delicious, Macoun, and others. There are also hay rides on weekends for visiting pickers, and cider pressing. Containers are supplied. Picnic tables are on the grounds and pies, jams, jellies, honey, and maple syrup are sold. Route 101, Greenland; (603) 436–2861.

GOULD HILL ORCHARD The Leadbeater family grows 41 varieties of apples and hopes to have over twice that in the future. Available for picking now, among others, include McIntosh, Cortland, Red and Golden Delicious, and Northern Spy. Cider pressing is ongoing but you have a better chance to see it in progress on weekdays than weekends. The view of Mount Washington is always there (except in the worst weather) and Rick Leadbeater says his farm is a great spot for sighting hawks migrating in fall. Vegetables including squash, handcrafts like stoneware and baskets, jams, jellies, pastries, and breads are sold at the orchard store. (A mile off Route 103), Contoocook; (603) 746–3811.

APPLE RIDGE You can pick Cortland and McIntosh at this family farm northwest of Concord. Cider is pressed, usually on weekdays, with blends of mainly Cortland and McIntosh, but sometimes including Delicious, Empire, and Tydman, an English variety. There are also jams and jellies, apple pies, Vermont cheddar cheese, salad dressings, wreaths, and flowers for sale at the farm garden center. Water Street, Boscawen; (603) 796–2654.

NORWAY HILL ORCHARDS This is a small farm in the state's Monadnock Region where you can pick McIntosh, Cortland, Baldwin, and Red Delicious. Containers are supplied. There is no cider pressing. Norway Hill, Hancock; (603) 525–4912.

Rhode Island

ROSS APPLE STORE Offered for picking are McIntosh, Red Delicious, Baldwin, Cortland, Macoun, and Opalescent. Containers are supplied. Cider pressing is done on some weekends on an old hand press. Pears can also be picked and pony cart rides take place on some weekends. Also for sale are honey, maple syrup, jams and jellies, frozen apple pies, apple cider, pumpkins, and Indian corn. Paine Road (off Route 6), Foster; (401) 647–7230.

JASWELL'S FARM At these family farm orchards you are able to pick McIntosh, Red Delicious, Empire, and limited amounts of Rhode Island Greening, Cortland, and Ida Red. Bags are supplied or you can bring your own. You can view cider pressing and ask questions of the operators. "There is always someone here glad to answer your questions," says Pat Jaswell. Strawberries and rabe (mustard greens) can also be picked and homemade jams and jellies are also sold. Swan Road (off Route 116), Smithfield; (401) 231–9043.

MATTEO'S FARM There are McIntosh, Red and Golden Delicious, Macoun, Baldwin, Cortland, and Rhode Island Greenings for picking. Containers are supplied or you can bring your own. Cider made from the Matteos' apples is sold but not pressed on the premises. Peaches, pears, and pumpkins grown on the grounds are also for sale. Swan Road (off Route 116), Smithfield; (401) 231–4393.

HILL ORCHARDS You are welcome to pick McIntosh, Cortland, Red and Golden Delicious, Empire, and a small amount of Baldwin. Bring your own containers. Cider is pressed here and is for sale, but the pressing is not open to the public. There are also pumpkins to pick, and honey is sold, too. When coming to pick apples, check in first at the sales office at the corner of Route 5 and Commerce Street in Smithfield. Windsor Avenue, Johnston; (401) 949–2940.

PIPPIN ORCHARD Available for picking are McIntosh, Cortland, Red and Golden Delicious, and Rome. Containers are available but it is preferred that visitors bring their own. Jams and jellies, assorted fruits and vegetables, and flowers are sold, too. 751 Pippin Orchard Road (between Routes 12 and 14 off Interstate 295), Cranston; (401) 943–7096.

Vermont

COLD HOLLOW CIDER MILL Come to this large retail store to watch cider being pressed and to taste a sample made from a blend of McIntosh, Delicious, Cortland, and Northern Spy apples. Pressing takes place daily in fall, less often the rest of the year. You can also screen short films about cider making (shown continuously) and maple syrup making (shown on request). Also sold are apple butter, apple sauce, maple apple granola, cider doughnuts, and several other baked goods in a natural foods bakery, as well as jams, jellies, and gift items. No pick-your-own apples. Route 100, Waterbury Center; (802) 244–8771.

WOOD BROTHERS ORCHARD The varieties of pick-your-own apples here include McIntosh, Empire, Red Delicious, and Northern Spy. Bring your own container. If you are here at the right time you might see cider pressed, but most pressing is done at night. Quarry Road (one mile east of Middlebury Inn), Middlebury; (802) 388–2110.

ALLENHOLM FARM Pick-your-own apples include McIntosh, Cortland, and Macoun. Containers are supplied. A little cider pressing is done. Jellies and jams are also sold. Other pickable fruit includes cherries. South Street, South Hero; (802) 372–5566.

CHITTENDEN CIDER MILL There are no pick-your-owns for the time being, but there is a cider mill and an observation room where you can watch cider making in progress. Tours are given by appointment, though you can watch at any time. Cider is made with McIntosh as the base apple, but might also include Delicious or Cortland as part of a blend. Pies and other pastries, jams, and jellies are also sold. 1580 Dorset Street, South Burlington; (802) 862–4602.

SHELBURNE ORCHARDS Pick-your-owns are mainly McIntosh and Delicious. Containers are supplied. You can watch pressing in progress but there are no tours. One Orchards Road (just south of the Shelburne Museum off Route 7—follow the signs), Shelburne; (802) 985–2753.

ATWOOD'S ORCHARD The picnic area with its inspiring view of the Adirondack Mountains is as much of a draw as the extensive pick-your-own apples list, which includes Paula Red, McIntosh, Cortland, Red and Golden Delicious, Macoun, Northern Spy, and Empire. Bags for picking are supplied, and orchard tours are available by appointment. Other pick-your-owns include both sweet and sour cherries and, to a lesser extent, plums. Doug and Tammy Atwood also operate a fruit stand on Route 22A in Shoreham featuring apples, cider, pies, syrup, honey, T-shirts, and sometimes crafts. Barnum Hill (three miles south of the village), Shoreham; (802) 897–5592.

EDGEWOOD ORCHARDS Ride to the orchard in a tractor-drawn hay wagon to pick your choice of McIntosh, Cortland, Empire, Red and Golden Delicious, and Northern Spy. Containers are furnished. You can have a look at the cider mill and chat with the attendant, or make your own cider on a small, hand-operated cider mill. There are also pumpkins to pick, nature trails, and a petting zoo with llamas, goats, pigs, sheep, pheasants, and peacocks. Baked goods, Indian corn, jams, and jellies are sold and in early October you can attend Edgewood's harvest festival, featuring a chicken barbecue, crafts, clowns, and games for children. Cider Mill Road (west of Middlebury between Routes 30 and 125), Cornwall; (802) 462–2729.

HALLOWEEN IN NEW ENGLAND

On Halloween it is permissible to expose both our darker and lighter sides, our sinister or mischievous personas that we repress the other 364 days of the year. With our lengthy heritage of witch hunts and pirates and long-dead patriots, there are ample opportunities in New England to exploit Halloween to the fullest.

A Visit to Salem

"DO YOU BELIEVE in witches?"

So asks a ghoulish voice as you gather in a dark room at the **Salem Witch Museum** and stand around a strange symbol—a spiral with names of victims of the infamous Salem witch trials—that reeks of the occult.

"Millions of your ancestors did," the voice challenges you.

Some in Salem might still believe in witchcraft. How else could it be explained that the witch trials of 1692, a minor footnote in American history, continue to rank as the single attraction luring so many people to travel by train, bus, boat, car, and just about everything but broomstick to this harbor city 20 miles up the coast from Boston? A visit to the Salem Witch Museum will put one in the proper mood for Halloween regardless of the time of year, although Salem's festive Haunted Happenings in late October is the prime time for some serious scaring.

After we heard that our ancestors believed in witches, our attention was directed above and to the right of us. There light beams focused on wax figures depicting a West Indian slave named Tituba and several young girls listening intently, as Tituba tells them legends of witchcraft in her homeland. Recorded dialogue simulates Tituba teasing their minds with her tales, followed by a narrator describing the staid and stoic seventeenth century, a time when people were unable to express themselves naturally and as a result, let their imaginations run wild.

Rebecca Nurse was one Salem woman convicted in court of practicing witchcraft and ultimately hanged. Her trial is recreated visually and orally in the museum. Then there was Giles Cory, pressed to death with boulders in an attempt to force a confession. And museum-goers see in the background of these court scenes a laughing, diabolical devil. (508) 744–1692.

Several of those accused of witchcraft were brought to the big, bulky dwelling standing today at 310½ Essex Street. Known nowadays as the **Witch House**, it was the home of Jonathan Corwin, a judge of the witchcraft trials. When you walk the steps of the narrow staircase to Corwin's study, you will be retracing the path of many of the accused brought here to face preliminary examinations. The house dates from 1642 and is filled with seventeenth-century furnishings. (508) 744–0180.

Nathaniel Hawthorne cemented the city's reputation for witches in 1851 when he wrote *The House of the Seven Gables*, a novel of sin and witchcraft set in Salem. Hawthorne described the house in this manner:

"Halfway down a by-street of one of our New England towns stands a rusty wooden house, with seven acutely peaked gables, facing towards various points of the compass, and a huge, clustered chimney

When you walk the steps of the narrow staircase to Corwin's study, you will be retracing the path of many of the accused brought here to face preliminary examinations.

in the midst. The street is Pyncheon Street; the house is the old Pyncheon House. . . ."

There never was a Pyncheon Street in Salem and no Pyncheon family ever lived in this historic house. But thanks to Hawthorne, this "rusty wooden house" would forever be known as the **House of the Seven Gables**.

Having read the classic novel is not a prerequisite for visiting. Clearly, most of those who tour the home have not read it. Many for that matter don't even know what a gable is. (The Second College Edition of the *American Heritage Dictionary* describes it as "the triangular wall section at the ends of a pitched roof, bounded by the two roof slopes and the ridge pole.") But you can get a clearer visual image on a scale model of the house shown on the tour.

And you will also hear the story of the house and why Hawthorne chose it as his setting. Original builder John Turner came to Salem from Boston and quickly became a prosperous merchant and ship owner. He constructed this home in 1668.

The house passed through two generations until his grandson, John Turner III, who lacked in business sense what he had in expensive tastes, lost much of the family fortune and had to sell the home in 1782.

Captain John Ingersoll, whose wife, Susannah, was Hawthorne's cousin, was the next owner of the house. It would be inherited by their daughter, who Hawthorne visited often. As a result, he was inspired to write his novel about this quirky old dwelling.

If you recall reading the novel back in 11th grade English class, you will naturally be drawn to the notorious judge's chair, Phoebe's and Hepzibah's rooms, and the recreation of Hepzibah's cent shop where she sold trinkets, candies, and toys that cost only a penny.

Not all the rooms nor all the artifacts, though, reflect the seventeenth century. While the 300-year-old English wine chest with the double-H hinges (standing for "heavenly" or "holy" with the idea that such initials would keep evil spirits from entering the wine) fits in perfectly with the novel's time frame, an original Hawthorne family bed in Phoebe's room, the Chippendale chairs around the dining room table, and the Black Beauty sled (a forerunner of the Flexible Flyer) in the garret are representative of the illustrious author's day, the mid-nineteenth-century. In 1990, a sewing room filled with Chinese export furniture like Susannah Ingersoll used was added to the tour.

Obviously, any house with over 300 years of history to its credit is bound to have some idiosyncrasies. Cupboards and closets hidden into the walls fascinate most visitors although the darkened and narrow hidden staircase alongside the main chimney is a favorite of all but the most portly or claustrophobic visitors.

Upon leaving the House of the Seven Gables, you enter a courtyard where you will see four other historic buildings. These are Hawthorne's birthplace, circa 1750, moved here from another part of Salem; the Retire Beckett House, built in 1655 and now the museum gift shop; a circa 1830 counting house; and the Hooper-Hathaway House, built in 1682 but not on the tour. 54 Turner Street; (508) 744–0991.

We came face to face with Hawthorne and Presidents George Washington, John Quincy Adams, and William Henry Harrison in the portrait gallery of one of America's premier museums, the **Essex Institute**. But don't get the idea that this is a deadly place to take restless children. Introduce them to someone like Emmaline, an eighteenth-century wooden doll, or to Lulu, one of her Victorian-era playmates. Then you can feel less guilty heading off to the pewter porringers or Hepplewhite chairs. 132–134 Essex Street; (508) 744–3390.

But Salem is filled with history and legends that transcend both the witch trials and Hawthorne.

But Salem is filled with history and legends that transcend both the witch trials and Hawthorne and envelop the city with layers like the skin of an onion. Peel off one and there is another right behind it.

To gaze at some of the riches brought here from the far corners of the world when the city was a thriving port, head to Salem's other highly regarded repository, the **Peabody Museum of Salem**. The China Trade collection is a must-see, but plan to spend some time eyeing the curiosities from other countries, too. For example, the small statuette of the war god Kukailimoku, mouth open in an agonizing grimace, was brought back from the Sandwich Islands—today, Hawaii—and is one of just three extant in the world. 161 Essex Street; (508) 745–9500.

In the early nineteenth century one would have found harborside warehouses overflowing with casks of rum from the West Indies, barrels of coffee from Arabia, and delicacies from the Orient and other points on the globe. The closest to one that you will find today is the Bonded Warehouse, a relic from 1819, filled with tea chests, rum barrels and other containers, part of the multi-building **Salem Maritime National Historic Site**. Derby Street; (508) 744–4323.

In front of the Bonded Warehouse stands the Custom House, widely recognized by its granite steps and carved eagle. It was from this 1819 structure that port business was administered. One of the many who worked here was a middle-aged man who would lose his job after three years, due to political squabbles. His name? Nathaniel Hawthorne, proof that the layers of Salem history can't help but overlap.

In his novel *The Scarlet Letter*, Hawthorne described the customhouse as "cobwebbed and dingy with old paint." You will find it significantly cleaner today.

Also part of Salem Maritime National Historic Site are the Derby House, home of a prominent eighteenth-century merchant; the 1826 Scale House, still containing original equipment; and the West India Goods Store, still selling imported goods and foods as it did 170 years ago.

Yet on those mellow fall days when walking through the halls of a museum or old house is as enticing as cleaning your bathtub, head to **Pickering Wharf**. As late as the early 1970s, it was a decaying center of oil storage tanks. A few years and $8 million later, it became a glowing example of a rejuvenated city center. There are more than 80 shops and restaurants here, and you can spend hours feasting on falafel, mulling over muslin curtains, or checking out Chinese cork carvings. Many of the stores offer crafts and imported items with nautical themes. The wharf is located between the harbor and Derby Street; (508) 745–9540.

Salem's Haunted Happenings

THE MID-AUTUMN moon lights up the wharves and you can see shadows of the buildings of Salem dancing with each other in the streets. It's an apt setting to hear tales of pirates and witches, some of the activities scheduled during Salem's ten-day-long spell of Halloween fun called **Haunted Happenings**.

Fall in behind a guide like Hazel Trembley, who dons bright silks, striped pants, ruffled socks, ankle boots, and everything but a parrot on her shoulder, as she hoists a Jolly Roger flag with skull and crossbones. Though it might be natural to think of this Salem tour guide at this time of year as Witch Hazel, at this event Trembley becomes Pirate Hazel. An interpreter at Salem Maritime National Historic Site, Hazel wears full pirate regalia, explains to doubters that there truly were women pirates, then leads inquisitive people by candlelight lantern from the Custom House along the trail of crushed stone to the lighthouse on Derby Wharf on special tours called **Pirate Walks**.

In proper spirit for Halloween, Hazel embellishes the historically accurate with the gruesome truth in relating stories about pirates with a Salem connection. So after Hazel explains the technical differences between privateering and piracy, you might hear how a dog's tongue was once nailed to the floor as a scare tactic or how unfortunate victims had limbs lopped off by ruthless pirates who were trying to force them to divulge information.

You never know who might be leading you on a tour during Haunted Happenings. At the House of the Seven Gables, it is an actor in character as Nathaniel Hawthorne himself, resurrected specifically to take you through his old haunting ground as part of a holiday program called **The Spirits of Seven Gables**. His wife, Sophia, and *Seven Gables* fictional characters Hepzibah and servant Mary Connolly also come to life to tell you about each of the candle-lit rooms in the 1668 house from their points of view.

At **Eerie Events at the Essex Institute**, the otherwise formal multi-building museum complex gets to put on its Halloween best as storytellers—grotesque and creepy and in seventeenth-century garb—inhabit the ancient abodes to entertain you with tales of the bizarre from Essex County history. They don't have to go far to find source material; the Essex's own Gardner-Pingree House was the site of a brutal murder. There is also a video presentation about the 1692 witch trials, *luminaria* lighting up the walkways, and often a bonfire to warm up by.

Children who might be frightened by tales of terror might opt for a treasure hunt at either the Salem Maritime National Historic Site or the famed Peabody Museum. Winners might get to keep some of their finds, like chocolate doubloons in a hidden treasure chest. And all youngsters get to show off their newest Halloween outfits at Sunday's **Children's Costume Parade**.

What else is there to put you in a Halloween state of mind? Discover the art of reading tarot cards or the secrets of palmistry and numerology at the annual **Psychic Festival**. Learn the skill of casting a spell, or take in the true facts behind the notorious witch trials by joining a guided tour along the **Witch Trial Trail**. Costumed balls with music and masquerades occur throughout the city and you might even get to meet Laurie Cabot, modern Salem's resident witch. (508) 744–0004.

Halloween "Graveyards and Goodies" Tour

THE MYSTERIOUS TOUR guide known only as the "Wizard of Bos" leads brave souls on a 90-minute-long Halloween night tour of Boston's famous graveyards and other spooky sights, followed by an hour and a half at a classy Boston watering hole for feasting on champagne, cheese, and dessert. This **"Graveyards and Goodies" Tour** is Uncommon Boston's offering for Halloween.

The wiz, clad in cape and mask, will lead you to (though not inside) King's Chapel Burying Ground, site of Colonial Governor John Winthrop's grave; Granary Burying Ground, with Paul Revere's, John Hancock's, and Mother Goose's graves; and Central Burying Ground, which includes the unmarked graves of many British soldiers who died at the Battle of Bunker Hill.

The Wiz of Bos, who won't reveal his daytime identity, stays in character through the whole tour, and alternates facts with some tongue-in-cheek communications with the dead.

"Oh, if only we had closed our eyes, we might have lived," says a British Bunker Hill veteran through the wizard, while the ghost of master of the macabre Edgar Allan Poe utters, "I curse the day I was born in this city," as the tour passes the site of his birthplace.

Costumes are welcome but not necessary—on one tour, Madonna and Ben Franklin were on hand—but you are asked to bring a flashlight. Uncommon Boston, 437 Boylston Street, 4th floor, Boston, MA 02116; (617) 731–5854.

The Witch's Dungeon

AN EVIL LAUGH welcomes you into the Bristol, Connecticut, Halloween attraction called **The Witch's Dungeon**, followed by the cautioning words of legendary screen actor Vincent Price.

"Welcome poor mortal to this witch's dungeon of nightmares. As you journey through these dark corridors you will encounter all those ghoulies, ghosties, and long-legged beasties that go bump in the night. Beware, and gather up all your courage, for we are about to begin."

And you hear Price chortle.

Step inside this singular place, which its creator Cortlandt Hull refers to as a "horror museum," wander through the narrow corridors, and you encounter a baker's dozen of life-sized realistic replicas of age-

"THE MASQUE OF THE RED DEATH" AND "ERIK" MENACE CORTLANDT FROM BEHIND, AS HE HOLDS A WAX BUST OF CHANEY SR.

less movie monsters brought to the screen by famous fright masters like Price, Boris Karloff, Bela Lugosi, and Lon Chaney.

Hull pays strict attention to detail and in some cases, uses original costumes or monster heads from the actual films. Included are cinematic chillers like the Phantom of the Opera, Frankenstein's monster, Count Dracula, and the Wolfman, who thanks to edited movie soundtracks all speak to you. Admonishes Lon Chaney's Wolfman: "Even a man who's pure of heart may become a wolf."

The Witch's Dungeon, on Battle Street in Bristol, is only open in late October and only after dark. It takes about ten minutes to explore the museum, but since only a handful are admitted inside at a time, the wait to enter has been known to last for an hour or two. Still, Hull reports visitors come from as far away as Maine and New Jersey, and some make annual pilgrimages. A nominal fee is charged and the Witch's Dungeon is not recommended for children under six. For specific dates and directions, call (203) 583–8306.

Terror on the Trolleys

BOTH CONNECTICUT'S TROLLEY museums serve up Halloween scares. At the **Connecticut Trolley Museum** in East Windsor, visit **Rails to the Dark Side**, a half-hour-long haunted trolley jaunt on which you will hear a spooky ghost story, like the one about the trolley tracks built over a graveyard. Then you will meet a gaggle of ghouls who hop on board carrying menacing chain saws or severed heads (no, not real ones). One time a man set his arm on fire (a real-life stunt man and master of illusion, we were told). Parental discretion is advised for children under 13. For hours and other details, call the museum toll free at (800) 252–2372 outside Connecticut and (800) 223–6540 within Connecticut, or locally at (203) 627–6540.

The Constitution State's **Shoreline Trolley Museum** in East Haven presents **Trolley Tricks 'n' Treats**, where you might encounter the ghost of a motorman killed in a turn-of-the-century trolley crash, or possibly witness trolley lights flashing for no apparent reason, followed by the appearance of other ghostly beings. A spokesman says the adventure might be too strong for little children. After the 30- to 40-minute-long ride, Halloween treats are served indoors. For hours and further information, call (203) 467–6927.

Rutland's Halloween Parade

AS WITH MOST parades, this one consists of marching bands, floats, and majorettes. Unlike most parades, all the participants in this one march down the streets in costume. School bands might be decked out in ghostly sheets, while an entire cheerleading squad can tramp through downtown Rutland, Vermont, wearing elephant heads. Other groups have been known to dress en masse in flannel nightgowns, black witches' outfits, and cuddly Smurf costumes. The audience has been known to decorate the sidelines in costume, too.

The Halloween night parade starts at 6:30 from the old Firestone end of the Rutland Shopping Plaza and proceeds from Merchants Row right onto Center Street, left onto Wales, left onto West, right onto Cottage, left across State, and right onto Merchants Row. For a good seat, it's best to arrive by 6:00, and one parade observer says the best spots are along Merchants Row and Center Street. Find a seat near the opera house and you should have an agreeable vantage point.

The Rutland Recreation & Parks Department, parade sponsors, also presents a children's Halloween party, a haunted mansion at the Lawrence Recreation Center, and a haunted hobgoblin hike, where you might encounter a werewolf or other ghastly monster in Giorgetti Park, before the holiday. (802) 773–1822.

The Haunted Monastery

The **Cumberland Company for the Performing Arts**, a Rhode Island–based theatrical troupe performing throughout the year, combines horror and humor in its annual **Haunted Monastery** production. (The group's main base of operations is an old Gothic-style monastery in Cumberland.) The company members, who integrate circus-like acrobatics and stunts into their presentations, entertain with a different original thriller every Halloween season, usually incorporating contemporary or newsworthy themes. Once the show delved into environmental issues, featuring a "toxic avenger" and an industrial villain who dumped toxic chemicals in the monastery catacombs. The actual setting, an outdoor courtyard with trees growing into and through the theater sets, contributes to the production's eeriness. (401) 333–9000.

THANKSGIVING DAY AWAY FROM HOME

You will probably find dinner served by people wearing outfits like those crafted on the looms and spinning wheels of early New England.

Dare to break the routine of Thanksgiving dinner at home and you can partake in one consisting of delicacies like mussels steamed in beer, Marlborough pie, moose burgers, and lumbardy tart.

That doesn't mean you have to part with long-standing conventions like pumpkin pie and drumsticks. After all, only a miscreant with the ideology of Joseph Stalin would forego turkey on the fourth Thursday in November.

But it does mean you can supplement your usual tradition by visiting some of New England's historic towns and recreated villages, where you will sup on victuals not found on the dining room table of Aunt Phyllis and Uncle Joe. You will probably find dinner served by people wearing outfits like those crafted on the looms and spinning wheels of early New England.

Thanksgiving is, after all, a New England creation, a fact accepted everywhere, with the possible exception of the area within a 30-mile radius of Berkeley Plantation in Charles County, Virginia. It was on the site of Berkeley, Virginians say, that the crew of 39 men aboard the English ship *Margaret* uttered the first official words of Thanksgiving per order of King James I, on December 4, 1619.

According to the staff of Plimoth Plantation, the recreated Pilgrim village in Plymouth, Massachusetts, Pilgrim leader William Bradford's diary and a letter sent by settler Edward Winslow both mention a harvest feast in 1621. It took place between September 21 and November 9, and included cod, sea bass, fowl (duck, goose, and swan, for example), turkey, cornmeal, and five deer brought by Indians. It is likely that shellfish were not included, since they were regarded as food for the poor and not fitting for a feast.

Louise Miller, co-administrator of Fort at No. 4, a living history replica of a colonial stockade in Charlestown, New Hampshire, reports eighteenth-century journals record a full Thanksgiving dinner in the 1740s. It is also known that President George Washington declared national Thanksgivings in 1789 and 1795, and some presidents followed suit for the next two decades.

According to researchers at Old Sturbridge Village, an advertisement in the *Greenfield* (Massachusetts) *Gazette* on November 19, 1804, asked for "articles necessary for Thanksgiving," such as "Rum, Brandy, Molasses, Loaf and Brown Sugars . . ."

By the 1830s, say Sturbridge staff members, Thanksgiving was already an excuse for New England families to gather together at home and feast with one another. Many were the Thanksgiving dinners celebrated in conjunction with a reunion or wedding. By this time the holiday was starting to spread its way west into New York State and the Northwest Territory.

In a typical 1830s New England household, hungry folks would gather around tables stacked back to back, with a few of the family's usual ten or so children standing, since spare room was a rare commodity. There were no appetizers, soups, or salads. Turkey resting in a torrent of gravy was the main dish and was served first.

Then came a parade of seasonable vegetables—boiled squash, turnips, and onions—followed by homemade breads and cheeses and a tray full of condiments. A traditional dessert was Marlborough pie, a filling apple tart with a custard pudding baked over the layer of apple. Other popular dessert pies included apple, mince, pumpkin, and cranberry, which would have been kept frozen in a guest bedroom, the frigid night air all that was needed to keep them from spoiling.

Those New Englanders still making their living off the land might have excused themselves from the house now and then to check the fields and barns. Upon returning they would likely see in progress fireside games such as "Blind Man's Bluff," "Charades," "Run Around the Chimney," and "Button, Button, Who's Got the Button."

Wealthier families might have employed live music in the form of a fiddler and offered dancing in the main hall. The poor were at the mercy of the rich, who, depending on their generosity, would leave baskets and bags of ingredients like flour, sugar, and raisins for those who couldn't afford to buy them. Some would even leave entire pumpkins, potatoes, chickens, or desserts.

By the 1850s, most states held their own Thanksgiving holidays, although some Southern states, slow to embrace a Yankee tradition, did so reluctantly. In 1859, only Delaware, Missouri, and Oregon didn't celebrate Thanksgiving.

The first modern national Thanksgiving holiday

was declared by President Lincoln in 1863, thanks in large part to a New Hampshire woman, Sarah Josepha Hale. Author of the nursery rhyme, "Mary Had a Little Lamb," Hale was the editor of a prominent magazine called *Godey's Lady's Book* and campaigned long and hard for a national Thanksgiving holiday, refusing to concede until her dream reached fruition. In spite of the Civil War that was raging, Americans still felt there was much to be thankful for.

It wasn't until the late 1800s that the Pilgrim story began to play an important role in the celebration of Thanksgiving. For about a century, beginning in the years just before the American Revolution, New Englanders and others commemorated the Pilgrims' landing with a December holiday called Forefathers' Day. As celebration of Thanksgiving spread in the nineteenth century, the popularity of Forefathers' Day abated. By 1890, the Pilgrims and their original harvest celebration had become integral themes in the observance of Thanksgiving.

Over the years, the traditional Thanksgiving dinner has survived in both the best and worst of times.

Over the years, the traditional Thanksgiving dinner has survived in both the best and worst of times. Take the year 1932, for example, perhaps the bleakest in our century. The typical middle-class family cooked their holiday turkey in an electric stove and kept their food fresh in an electric refrigerator, its bulky motor as prominent as Jimmy Durante's nose. Those who couldn't splurge for electric time and step savers utilized their coal stoves and ice boxes that had served them faithfully for so many years.

They still fixed potatoes with hand mashers, but made pumpkin pie with canned pumpkin and served canned cranberry sauce for the first time. It would have saved bundles of time in preparing a dinner for 12, consisting of both immediate family members and unemployed relatives and spouses.

In grocery stores in Keene, New Hampshire, in 1932, the cost of turkeys ranged from 35 to 39 cents a pound, although one radio store in town gave away a free ten-pound turkey with the purchase of any Philco radio. Those who already had radios in their living rooms might have spent the holiday listening to traditional Thanksgiving Day football games like Brown at Colgate, Holy Cross at Boston College, or Carnegie Tech at NYU, and might have wondered why people would fight the crowds and traffic to see a football game in person when they could hear the same one over the radio for free.

After dinner, they might have loosened their belts and ignited a cigar or cigarette while listening to Thursday night radio shows like the "Rudy Vallee

Hour," "The Jack Benny Show," "Amos and Andy," or "Death Valley Days."

Those who ventured to a restaurant for the holiday dinner might have encountered a menu like the following offering from the Doukas Cafe in Keene, New Hampshire, as printed in *The Keene Sentinel*, November 25, 1932:

Oysters on half shell or fruit cocktail.
Cream of mushrooms soufflé.
Hearts of celery and olives or sweet mixed pickles.
Roast young Vermont turkey, chestnut dressing with
    giblets sauce, fresh cranberry sauce, mashed sweet or
    white potato.
Baked squash or boiled young onions in cream. English
    plum pudding, sherry wine sauce, pumpkin, or hot
    minced pie.
Mixed nuts, raisins, or grapes.
Tea, coffee, or milk.
Total price per person: $1.00

We can't guarantee a Thanksgiving dinner at 1932 prices or a trip through a time tunnel to the nineteenth century, but in the following places you will be offered a taste of an earlier Thanksgiving Day in New England.

Thanksgiving at Old Sturbridge Village

ACCORDING TO THE long-defunct *Massachusetts Spy*, the harvest of 1813 was one for the books. On November 24 that year, the *Spy* boasted, "The season has been remarkably favourable, the earth unusually prolifick and the husbandman has reapt an hundred fold as the fruits of his labour . . ."

The newspaper sums up the mood of the time when Thanksgiving, though not a federal holiday, was a literal occasion during which those who survived on what the ground could muster gave fervid appreciation for their bounty. Now, eighteen decades later, you can spend a few hours at **Old Sturbridge Village**, feasting in the manner in which early nineteenth-century New Englanders did.

At no time of the year is it too early to think of Thanksgiving at Sturbridge. Bookings for Thanksgiving dinner start in spring and can fill by early September. The thought of a nineteenth-century feast and early New England ambience lure potential

Turkey Day diners from throughout New England and the Northeast.

Your dinner tickets admit you to the entire recreated village which, of course, includes all those special demonstrations or performances you'll witness as you walk out by Freeman Farm or along the village green.

We happened to be strolling by the fully stocked Knight Store when a husky young man in a stove pipe hat and carrying a musket made his way past us toward an open grassy area near the green. He was immediately joined by an older bearded man, similarly armed. Moments later, a turkey shoot began as the two men aimed their muzzle-loaded weapons, then fired at paper targets, substitutions for the live game that would have drawn their fire long ago.

You might also step inside the 1832 Greek Revival-style meetinghouse that faces the green. If you are there at the right time, you will hear a costumed villager in the role of the village minister preach directly from an authentic nineteenth-century text, while a choir in period garb renders hymns while accompanied by an antique organ.

As you leave the meetinghouse and continue walking around the grounds, the rich, appetizing smells of home cooking—turkeys roasting in tin reflector ovens, Marlborough pies baking in brick hearths—will grab you like an outstretched hand, taking you out of the cold late November air and into the village homes. Feel free to pump Sturbridge's costumed interpreters for information, with questions like how long it takes to prepare a turkey using 1830s methods, what's the best way to produce a tangy mince pie, or how they would have preserved food so it would last all winter.

The staff members will gladly accommodate you with one exception; you can't sample the fresh-from-the-oven victuals. Cooking methods and sanitary conditions have changed drastically since those early days, and health regulations prohibit serving any of these delectables to guests. All you can do is look and drool and wait for dinner to be served.

There are four seatings in the village tavern: one in late morning, two in the afternoon, and one in the evening. The afternoon slots are most popular and usually fill first. Since the rest of the village is closed when the evening seating takes place, those attending it receive a complimentary admission pass for another day.

Our party of six sat at a table placed against a stone-lined wall and was greeted with a plate of relishes, cups of locally mulled cider, and an oyster bisque.

After whetting your appetite, you are ready for the traditional Thanksgiving meal which, some might be surprised, was not much different from our holiday dinner today. Then again, what would Thanksgiving dinner be without roast turkey, giblet gravy, cranberry sauce, and butternut squash? A tasty cornbread and herb stuffing was a welcome substitute for today's bland packaged stuffing mixes.

While you may not have the familiar warmth of your own dining room, with the obligatory television set blasting a balloon parade or football game in the background, the food is no less—and possibly more delectable—than that you had while growing up. Dinner is, after all, catered by the highly regarded Publick House, a Sturbridge institution.

Pumpkin pie headed a list of dessert offerings, although plum pudding with hard sauce, mince pie with Vermont cheddar cheese, and an apple square with cream cheese frosting were just as tempting.

The obvious connections to the nineteenth century are the early tavern atmosphere—from the furnishings to the floor-length gingham dresses and white bonnets of the women servers—and the fact that all food is prepared according to the guidelines of actual period cookbooks.

In one such book, *The American Frugal Housewife*,

written in 1832, author Lydia Maria Child discussed the proper way to cook mince pies. "Put in a gill of brandy," she recommended. "Make it [the pie] quite moist with cider. I should not think a quart would be too rich; the more moist the better, if it does not spill out into the oven."

Except for the absence of the quart of cider or the brandy, it's likely that Lydia Maria Child would approve of the offerings at this early American Thanksgiving banquet. Old Sturbridge Village, Sturbridge, MA 01566; (508) 347–3362.

Plymouth, Massachusetts

THIS BOSTON SUBURB on the Bay State's South Shore might seem the most obvious place to make a Thanksgiving pilgrimage. You might smell the aroma of roasting turkey as you walk along Sandwich Street. Your nose will lead you into the Harlow Old Fort House, built in 1677, where a typical Pilgrim dinner is prepared in the home's ancient kitchen. Kids can help churn the butter and adults may be allowed to turn the spit, but as at Sturbridge, this meal is for demonstration purposes only.

To satisfy your taste buds, you can attend an ample Thanksgiving dinner at **Memorial Hall** on Court Street. Celebrants looking for the traditional meal will be pleased. Fresh-roasted turkey with herb stuffing and giblet gravy, potatoes, butternut squash, and several kinds of bread dominate the offerings.

On the other hand, those looking for a taste of early America will also be happy. Included in the meal are cornmeal pudding, walnut cornbread, rum-orange butter, and cranberry-orange relish, all prepared according to old Plymouth recipes. For dessert there is a choice of apple dumpling or Indian pudding, a regional concoction made from cornmeal, milk, and molasses.

Should you obtain tickets for the first seating you will be in for a double treat when a re-enactment of the first **Pilgrim's Progress** marches through Memorial Hall. Others can gather in the center of Plymouth at 10:15 A.M., when men, women, and children representing the first colonists in dress and number will assemble "by the drum" and walk to the First Church, in a carbon copy of the Pilgrims' first procession to church. A non-denominational service is held inside; you will give thanks when you discover it is greatly shorter than the marathon the Pilgrims would have attended.

If you can't get a seat for the city's annual Thanksgiving Day dinner, consider attending **Plimoth Plantation**'s version of the sumptuous holiday feast. The time period for this particular meal is Victorian New England. While you dine on New England clam soup, oysters on the half shell, roast native turkey with giblet gravy, creamed onions, Indian pudding, pumpkin pie, and more, you are entertained by strolling singers in Victorian dress. There are two seatings with room for 150 at each. Reservations are taken as early as August 1 and are usually filled by September 15.

As with many of the sights in New England, the majority of the smaller ones in Plymouth shut down after Columbus Day and do not reopen until the spring. On Thanksgiving however, much of Plymouth puts out the welcome mat for visitors.

One of the oldest houses in the country is the Richard Sparrow House, built in 1640. The only house remaining in Plymouth where Pilgrims actually lived is the Jabez Howland House (1667) with its corded beds and early American quilts. Pilgrim Hall Museum, the only Plymouth museum open year round, could easily be called the Pilgrims' attic, with its many original Pilgrim possessions.

At **Cranberry World Visitors Center**, open through November, you can inspect the workings of

THANKSGIVING VISITORS TO PLIMOTH PLANTATION ARE ENTERTAINED BY VICTORIAN-ERA SINGERS WHILE THEY DINE.

a scale model cranberry farm and pick up a few new recipes. And yes, by the waterfront, under its handsome portico, is **Plymouth Rock**, although this time of year there is no guide on duty to tell its tale.

To break from the masses and undertake something a little non-traditional, make reservations for Plimoth Plantation's seventeenth-century English harvest dinner. This is an autumn banquet with surprises for those who think only of turkey and winter squash this time of year. Seaside dwellers that they are, Plimoth folk serve steamed mussels in beer and a lightly seasoned oyster soup to compliment the expected entrées of turkey baked with pudding in the belly and sweet potatoes. They also add a bit of period cuisine in the form of "frittors of spinage" (spinach fritters), pear tart, and lumbardy tart.

What's a lumbardy tart? The hostess or another representative of seventeenth-century Plimoth Plantation, in full costume and character, will inform you it's a savory beet root tart; she'll also explain the whats and whys of this repast of long past.

As at Old Sturbridge Village, dinner tickets entitle you to admission to the recreated village, as well as the *Mayflower II*, an accurate reproduction of the merchant vessel that carried the Pilgrims to their new home. Keep in mind that at both attractions, the guides play the roles of actual settlers in the 1620s and can only answer questions concerning their time

THE *MAYFLOWER II* IS AN APT SIGHT TO EXPLORE IN LATE NOVEMBER. ACCURATELY DRESSED STAFF MEMBERS PLAY THE ROLES OF PILGRIM SETTLERS ON BOARD.

and place. Plymouth Area Chamber of Commerce, 91 Samoset Street, Plymouth, MA 02360; (508) 746–3377, for information on the Thanksgiving dinner in Memorial Hall. Plimoth Plantation, P.O. Box 1620, Plymouth, MA 02360; (508) 746–1622.

Thanksgiving Dinner at Fort at No. 4

LONG BEFORE PLACES like Plymouth became thriving communities, many were little more than forts and outposts dotting the New England wilderness. At the edge of the frontier in 1746 was **Fort at No. 4**, hugging the banks of the Connecticut River in present-day Charlestown, New Hampshire. Come to the recreated fort on Thanksgiving and you can dine by fireplace and candlelight in the Great Chamber, a long open hall reserved for important gatherings, or some of the fort's private residences. Two afternoon seatings are offered.

Dinner music straight from the eighteenth century is provided on an Italian box virginal and a dulcimer by music masters dressed in long coat, vest, and knee breeches, while servers donning 1746 fashions bring your dinner. Expect to sample roast turkey with corn bread and sausage stuffing, chicken pie (chicken and gravy in pie crust—hold the vegetables, thank you), giblet gravy, potatoes, turnips, herb butternut squash, creamed onions, cranberry sauce, and sweet breads. Dessert consists of steam pudding and three types of pie: mincemeat, pumpkin, and Marlborough pie. Fort at No. 4, P.O. Box 336, Charlestown, NH 03603; (603) 826–5700.

The Bradford Wild Game Supper

THIS ANNUAL EVENT wasn't planned to be a Thanksgiving event. It was chosen to take place the Saturday before Thanksgiving, since it coincides with the Vermont hunting season. But since it is so close to the holiday, says supper co-chairperson Eris Eastman, it is linked with Thanksgiving in the minds of the many patrons who dine on the exotic in a little church in this village on the banks of the Connecticut River.

With the streamlined efficiency of any of Boston's best restaurants, the staff of volunteers from Bradford's United Church of Christ serves up a filling buffet, usually with portions of venison steak, wild boar sausage, rabbit pâté, moose burgers, pheasant, bear, beaver, and raccoon, as well as seasonal side dishes of squash, potato, and bread. So diners can keep track of what they eat, each portion is color coded with a toothpick.

It's not unusual to find a faithful following making annual three- and four-hour-long treks from Massachusetts, New Hampshire, and other nearby states, and even visitors from the West Coast and Europe have been known to reserve a seat in order to munch moose burgers and wild boar sausage.

Then there was the first-time guest who, when asked what exotic item she liked best, responded, "The squash, the potatoes, and the roll."

Some people just have no sense of adventure. United Church of Christ, Bradford, VT 05033.

Thornton W. Burgess Society's Old-fashioned Thanksgiving

Oh, the good old-fashioned dinner
Of the good old-fashioned days,
Served as only grandma served it
With her quaint old-fashioned ways!
Thornton W. Burgess

IF THE WILD game supper seems a bit too exotic, consider a stop at the Cape Cod home of author and naturalist Burgess, where you are welcome to get a taste of Thanksgiving a few weeks before the holiday. In early November the staff cooks up a time-honored traditional feast in the center's turn-of-the-century kitchen.

While you won't be given a full meal, you can plan to indulge in samples of mincemeat, cranberries, turkey with stuffing, pumpkin breads, and hot mulled cider. The kitchen, which doubles as the reception area, contains an old wood stove, a hand pump sink, and a Hoosier cabinet, and is worthy of a few long glances. A special exhibit, usually involving antique tableware or kitchen utensils, is also often scheduled for this early holiday celebration. Thornton W. Burgess Society, 6 Discovery Hill Road, East Sandwich, MA 02537; (508) 888–6870.

Thanksgiving at Shelburne Museum

HOLIDAY PREPARATIONS, nineteenth century–style, are yours to tackle at this major Vermont attraction. In past years the holiday workshops held in early November have given visitors a taste of either the coming Thanksgiving or Christmas. If the staff prepares for Turkey Day, you might be asked to help roast the bird in an open fire pit or lend assistance stirring a pot of Brunswick stew—an early American holiday dish made with turkey, beef, squirrel, and other game. If it's Christmas you make arrangements for, you might help create homemade cookies. You also get to sample what you prepare.

You will also likely help out in craft making, whether it be arranging a nineteenth-century holiday centerpiece with hand-dipped candles and dried flowers, or producing an orange pomander or Victorian toys. All the while you will be serenaded by a Vermont fiddler or other musicians rendering appropriate period holiday tunes like "There Was a Pig Went Out to Dig" and "Apple Tree Wassail." Shelburne Museum, Shelburne, VT 05482; (802) 985–3346.

The Turkey Olimpics

TURKEYS, TURKEY ENTHUSIASTS, and spectators with a penchant for the odd gather at the Inn on Lake Waramaug in New Preston, Connecticut, the Sunday before Thanksgiving. It is here that real turkeys (no, not goofy people but actual gobbling, wrinkly-necked turkeys) compete in contests measuring their jumping, racing, and eating abilities.

Turkeys are dressed (with clothing, not stuffing) for the event, and they are also graded on their outfits. Past turkey competitors have come garbed as Pilgrims or weekend athletes wearing jogging shirts and sweat bands. Human owners are awarded with prizes such as dinners at the inn, while gold-medal gobblers might receive wreaths of Indian corn. Inn staff member David Reardon says the outing is not cruel and animals rights activists have had no beef about this turkey competition. A brunch and refreshments are served to humans, of which several hundred usually gather together for the outing. The Inn at Lake Waramaug, 107 North Shore Road, New Preston, CT 06777; (203) 868–0563.

WHO NEEDS TO TRAVEL TO MIDTOWN MANHATTAN? SPRINGFIELD, MASSACHUSETTS,
HOSTS ITS OWN GIANT BALLOON PARADE ON THANKSGIVING WEEKEND.

Springfield's Balloon Parade

THE GRAND MACY'S Thanksgiving Day Parade in New York City isn't the only one to feature humongous balloons depicting cartoon characters and mythical beings dazzling kids and adults alike. A similar parade takes place in downtown Springfield, Massachusetts, the morning after Thanksgiving Day.

The **Downtown Springfield Giant Balloon Parade** often includes as many balloons as Macy's, though there are some differences. Several of Springfield's balloons are not helium filled and must rest on floats, and Springfield cannot accommodate the 100-foot-long record breakers, such as Macy's Popeye.

Still, they are big and formidable and impressive, and have included in the past both generic pink elephants or snowmen as well as big-name balloons like cartoon tough-cat Heathcliff, Felix the Cat, and Pop 'n' Fresh.

The balloons tour the country like musical and theatrical groups do, and arrive big and flat in trucks in Springfield on Thanksgiving Day. It takes several trucks to transport balloons, ropes, and other accessories from one city to another.

While most of us are recovering from Thanksgiving dinner, the parade crew inflates the ground balloons with generators and air late Thursday. The crew will stay in area hotels and will start inflating the helium balloons about 4 A.M. Friday. It takes about 75 healthy humans to bring life to Heathcliff and Felix and the rest, and about 250 to 300 to hold them down to earth during the parade. All are volunteers, lending a hand in exchange for a parade T-shirt (given only to volunteers) and the satisfaction of helping make the parade a reality.

The parade steps off Main Street in front of the Springfield Newspapers building and continues down Main Street to its end at Court Square, taking about an hour and a quarter to an hour and a half. (413) 787-1548.

MYSTIC IN WINTER.

WINTER

Don't expect sympathy from winter. The harsh season shuns loafers but welcomes with open arms those willing to meet it halfway. The time of year that seems forbidding and foreboding is both gracious and frivolous if you take some time to look past the stern exterior. Melting in the warmth of a welcoming host and savoring hospitality are natural during the cold months, which of course, are only cold in a skin-deep sense.

And contrary to popular assumption, winter is not for skiers only. None of the activities and events discussed in this chapter entails skis, poles, or boots.

Winter is a time for romance. A raging fire in a cozy inn and a ride through the woods in a horse-drawn antique sleigh do more to rev up the heart's palpitations than a hot, muggy day at the town pool; you might be surprised to hear how many marriage

WINTER WELCOMES WITH OPEN ARMS THOSE WILLING TO MEET IT HALFWAY. THIS SPECTACULAR TABLEAU IS COURTESY OF THE BALSAMS IN DIXVILLE NOTCH, NEW HAMPSHIRE.

proposals take place on sleigh rides under frosty New England skies.

This is a season of whimsy, of 30-foot-high dragons made of snow, or of outhouses sliding on runners across a frozen lake. At New England's winter carnivals what's ludicrous becomes expected and what's arctic becomes lauded. Instead of coping with cold and ice, we celebrate it.

We hitch up our sled dogs and watch them race. And we attach snowshoes to our feet and walk on white frozen water; snowshoeing is the perfect antidote to the frenzied, fashionable world of skiing.

Our tourist attractions are unruffled. Though many shut their doors by Columbus Day, others, like Mystic Seaport in Connecticut, keep their fires burning throughout winter. This is the time to supplement your usual summer sightseeing and gain insight into nineteenth-century life during a different season. You will find, too, that guides have more time to share their reserves of knowledge when they are not surrounded by tourists from Anaheim, Peoria, and Boca Raton.

Finally, we have our winter holidays. Toy trains and popcorn chains garnish Victorian mansions and cottages in Newport and elsewhere, where sips of wassail or snacks of sugar cookies are usually on the house. And the feasts of the arts known as First Nights, which began right here in New England in 1976, entice New Year's Eve partiers out of their homes into the safe, sober center of the city.

Only a southern Californian could believe there is nothing to do in New England all winter long.

DASHING THROUGH THE SNOW

Old-fashioned sleighs are still seen throughout New England and not just on greeting cards. You can admire sleighs on parade in a classic rally or can hop on board and take a ride through the woods and fields in the afternoon sun or under a starry sky. Plenty are the opportunities to make this romantic dream reach fruition.

The Hampden Sleigh Rally

HAMPDEN, MASSACHUSETTS, IS the place to be when you are overtaken by a warm feeling of nostalgia, an emotion reserved for still winter mornings when the smoke from a wood stove wisps into clear skies and you can almost feel the pace of life as it was when General Grant was president.

It is here in late January or early February that horse and sleigh owners from New England and New York show off their sleighs and style as they compete for honors based on authenticity, condition, gracefulness, and other qualities.

The scene looks like a Currier and Ives lithograph that has come to life: a circle of horse-drawn sleighs, some bright red and sleek, others black and bulky or with racing stripes, parading proudly on a field of snow. The sleigh drivers, called reinsmen, wear clothing from an earlier time: top hats, buffalo robes, bear skin gloves, or beaver skin hats. They look as if they stepped off of a Christmas card.

Peter Webster from Belchertown, Massachusetts, is a veteran of these rallies. He sits grandly in a piano-box sleigh, named for its shape, with his formal top hat adding an extra half a foot to his proper demeanor; a young woman fully decked in Victoriana sits by his side as he holds the reins of his 16-year-old Morgan stallion, Townshend Don Bird.

THE HAMPDEN SLEIGH RALLY.

Webster, who wins one ribbon after another, explains the purpose behind the rally. "It is depicting old times—the late 1800s and early 1900s—when horses were a means of transportation, with or without snow. Horse shows were held in all seasons but when they were held in wintertime, they had to be hitched up to a sleigh. That's what we are recreating here.

"But rallies like this are few and far between," Webster continues. "It's hard to predict snow and then get the judges and concessionaires needed for this kind of event."

Another participant, Norman Krohn from Connecticut, rides in a grand, green sleigh about 100 years old. Krohn confides his sleigh is a horse-drawn wagon converted by removing all four wheels.

"That's what we did in the old country, in Canada. We were too poor to buy a sleigh," he smiles as his Arabian, Jamie, pulls him around the ring.

Horses here don't need to pull their weight as they do in summer fairs; there are no tractor-pulling or weight-pulling contests, which is just as well.

Says Peter Webster: "It can be tough on the horse. In winter, they're not used much and are not building their muscles and so are not in peak condition."

The emphasis at the sleigh rally is on appearance and style, and the types of horses establish categories: pony to drive, western-type horse to drive, English-type horse to drive, and draft horse to drive, for example.

Where horses don't set the classes, their human reinsmen do: gentlemen to drive, ladies to drive, and juniors to drive.

What is considered in selecting a blue ribbon winner? According to Rally Judge Bobbie Paradis, when horses establish the categories, the horses' movement counts for 75 percent of the scoring. For example, horses are asked to trot at three different strides, which should be lengthened or shortened. The cadence should remain the same, and a horse is docked points if he quickens or slows his pace rather than changing his stride.

When drivers establish the categories, their movements count for 75 percent of the total score. The less their hands and wrists move when controlling their horse, the higher the score. For Webster, Krohn and others who like dressing the part, there's the Currier and Ives class with ribbons given to the reinsmen looking most like they steered their sleighs through a time tunnel; in this class, the sleighs must be certified antiques, and one hears sleigh bells clinging and clanging with every step the horses take.

Ah yes, sleigh bells. Their ringing euphony is as much a part of winter as is snow itself. Ever since a Connecticut minister named J. S. Pierpont wrote "Jingle Bells" for a Sunday school performance, the sounds of sleigh bells on a clear winter night have turned even the most hardened cynic into a maudlin sentimentalist with a heart of mush.

Peter Webster breaks through the mawkishness, discussing and demonstrating the original uses of sleigh bells and telling the practical tale of how they came to be.

Sleigh bells, simply, were early traffic horns. Because snow naturally muffles sound, and since earmuffs were commonly part of winter wardrobes in days long past, bells were placed on horses to alert pedestrians that a sleigh was on the way.

But like cars today, sleighs and sleigh bells became status symbols—the more and the fancier the bells, the greater the status. Webster holds a bell strap today worth three to five hundred dollars which sold in the 1902 Sears and Roebuck catalogue for $2.07. (A good sleigh at the time ranged between $16.95 and $22.50).

In the same vein, the announcer enlightens the crowd with a Currier and Ives version of Trivial Pursuit while sleighs are setting up for events. For example, why was the lighter colored horse of a two-horse team always placed on the left side? Answer: so an oncoming sleigh was as visible as possible on a dark street at night.

At times, participants offer sleigh rides for a nominal fee, usually about one dollar, though this often depends on the conditions of the snow and the horses. But even if you can't hop on board, watching others do the same affords one a chance to step back in time for a taste of life as it was lived when horsepower had a literal meaning. Hampden Sleigh Rally, 608 Center Street, Ludlow, MA 01056; (413) 566–2221 or (413) 566–3043.

Shelburne Museum's Sleigh Ride Festival

ON ONE WINTER Sunday usually in February, the Shelburne Museum teams up with the Morgan Horse Association to offer victims of cabin fever (and any-

one else) an opportunity to see the popular northern Vermont site in its winter clothing. A handful of sleighs, probably a two- and a four-seater and a larger one that seats about a dozen, are used to transport visitors across the museum grounds. The sleighs are antiques and the rides last 15 to 20 minutes.

A blacksmith performs magic with metal (or another craftperson will ply his or her trade) and selected museum homes, trade shops, and galleries are open for exploring. Shelburne Museum, Shelburne, VT 05482; (802) 985–3346.

TAKING A SLEIGH RIDE

IF YOU CAN'T attend either of the two special events but the falling snow out your window makes you want to jump head first into an overly sentimental Christmas card, plan to patronize any of several New England establishments offering sleigh rides.

Since our ancestors first connected three poles on a platform of sticks, sleighs have been a way of life in colder climes. Though used today for recreation rather than practicality, sleigh rides are as enjoyable as they ever were. Maybe even more so, since today others can do all the work while you go along for the ride.

"There's the challenge of the cold and briskness and the beauty of snow," says Alfred Sawyer, owner of **Silver Ranch Stables** in Jaffrey, New Hampshire, one of many New England enterprises offering sleigh rides for winter worshippers. "We associate sleigh rides with pleasure that progress has taken from us, that simple, emotional appreciation of life when people got by by doing things like cutting their own wood and growing their own food.

"There's the respect and survival in conjunction with animal friends," continues Sawyer, "and this is something that's gone today. But everyone today accepts sleigh rides as some of the loveliest experiences, don't they?"

The Sawyer family has been offering sleigh rides for recreation ever since what Alfred Sawyer terms "the fall of the horse empire." The car replaced the horse, and in terms of sleighs and sleigh rides, romance replaced necessity.

We associate sleigh rides with pleasure that progress has taken from us, that simple, emotional appreciation of life when people got by by doing things like cutting their own wood and growing their own food.

But even in the eighteenth and nineteenth centuries, when sleighs were used to shuttle lumber or hides or people from one place to another, few passed up a leisurely ramble in a sleigh on a lovely winter night.

Alfred Sawyer relates the story of his great-grandmother, who was pregnant one winter and adhered to the medical beliefs of the day by avoiding all strenuous activity, including sitting in a bustling, jostling sleigh. After giving birth in May, she complained to her husband that she hadn't taken a sleigh ride all winter. So a team of horses was hitched up and she rode in the spring sunshine on a field of clover.

If you take a ride on the runners at Silver Ranch, chances are you will be in a sleigh that dates from the mid-nineteenth to early twentieth centuries, and is one of around 150 carriages and sleighs the Sawyer family has to sell, trade, offer for rides, or just admire.

How authentic are they? Alfred Sawyer laughs, "After a while they become like George Washington's hatchet, with two new heads and four new handles."

They do need painting every two or three years, and when not in use are placed on wooden blocks, a practice that's been around for years. This prevents the sleigh from becoming excessively wet, which would cause the wood to rot.

Relatively modern developments have made life easier for both human and horse alike. An implement called the *snowball pad* is only a few decades old, but is something New Englanders could have used a century ago. It's a half-spherical pad placed between a horse's shoe and foot to keep out snow and slush, preventing discomfort and easing the horse's movements. All Sawyer's horses wear snowball pads while dashing through the snow.

Regardless of whether you are transported aboard an antique pung or a work sleigh built last winter, you will, at any of the following places, be most likely pulled by bell-bedecked horses on back roads or through isolated woods or fields under clean, country skies. And for an hour or so it might really seem that life was better back in the days before the combustion engine, air pollution, and oil companies.

Some outfits supplement their rides with hot chocolate or other snacks, or bonfires. At most, nobody will care if you bring along a wine flask, just as long as behavior doesn't get out of hand. While one sleigh owner says that people always find ways to keep warm in the back of a sleigh, it's still a good idea to wear a hat, gloves, and boots, regardless of whom you sit next to. An extra blanket can be handy. It is also suggested that jewelry be kept home. Looking for a lost ring amid piles of snow is no fun.

If there is no snow on the ground, many of the following places will take you out on a hay wagon. The majority also require reservations and charge a minimum price regardless of the number of people in your group. Calling ahead to check snow conditions is always a smart idea.

NORTHERN NEW ENGLAND

Maine

NORLANDS LIVING HISTORY CENTER For one or two days on weekends in January and February this living history complex, known mainly for its unique multi-day live-in programs, embarks on "Jingle Bell Rides." A team of Percherons pulls 10 to 18 persons in a big, old-fashioned logging sled around Norlands's woods and fields. Afterward, participants warm up by a black wood stove where they can pop corn and sip hot chocolate. Diversions, such as wool-spinning demonstrations and nineteenth-century games, are scheduled, and you can also take a walk to the barn to visit Norlands's resident animals. Norlands Director Billie Gammon estimates that most visitors who take "Jingle Bell Rides" spend two hours at Norlands, of which the actual ride lasts about a half hour. RD 2, Box 3395, Livermore Falls, 04254; (207) 897–2236.

NORTON'S STABLE Rides are given on an old, rebuilt double sled pulled by two Percheron draft horses. From 20 to 25 riders can be accommodated. The rides go through woods and open fields and last about an hour. Snacks and hot chocolate are available by request. 613 Blackstrap Road, Falmouth; (207) 797–4418.

HORSEFEATHERS STABLE, INC. The Mitchell family takes groups of up to 18 people on a newly made sleigh through adjacent woods. Pulling your sleigh will either be Belgian draft horses or Amish bay chunks. Rides take a half hour and patrons can warm up in a log cabin afterwards. 178 County Road, Gorham; (207) 839–2243.

HOOF 'N' PAW FARM Up to 15 people enjoy 30-minute-long rides in a new sleigh pulled by a team of Percheron mares. You are taken across fields and through woods, and there is a warm-up hut where free cocoa is offered. Route 134 North, New Sharon; (207) 778–3903.

NORTH WOODS SADDLE EXPEDITIONS In this snowy part of Aroostook County, sleigh rides can be given as early as the first week of November. Owner Mike Luchetti restores old sleighs and uses about six antique ones for his sleigh rides. There is room for as many as a dozen passengers in the largest. The rides last about 40 minutes and traverse a dirt road in a wooded setting. Luchetti uses Belgian horses to do the work. Patrons warm up afterwards drinking hot chocolate by a wood stove. Parties are available. Route 11, Portage; (207) 435–4371.

LEDGEBROOK FARM Percherons pull a box sled with room for 10 to 12 adults across fields and along the shoreline of Keoka Lake. Rides take a half hour to 45 minutes. The property has been featured on the cover of an L. L. Bean catalog. Weddings and other special parties can be arranged. Routes 35 and 37, Waterford; (207) 583–6603.

SMILING HILL FARM Rides here are given on a new sleigh built to resemble an antique that holds up to 30 adults. The rides last about 45 minutes and include a stop for hot chocolate in a cabin on the grounds. 781 County Road, Westbrook; (207) 774–8356.

New Hampshire

NESTLENOOK FARM The two sleighs most used at this White Mountains setting were custom-built in Austria and contain cushioned benches, big brass lamps, wrought iron, and red-and-black-painted Alpine ornaments. They seat 13 passengers each and are pulled by Clydesdales. Two rustic New England–made sleighs that seat up to 25 persons can also be used. The rides last a half hour and go over arched bridges and past a river, the paddocks, and a gazebo. Riders also get to feed reindeer in the nearby woods. Afterwards, hot cider, hot chocolate, old-fashioned popcorn, and peanuts are served. Dinsmore Road, Jackson; (603) 383–0845.

EASTERN SLOPE FARM Dr. Eugene Hussey, a veterinarian, and his Percherons take riders in any of three old bobsleds dating from the 1920s and 1930s. Vistas of Mt. Washington and Moat Mountain are yours as you are pulled through woods and fields in New Hampshire's north country. You can bring your own refreshments to serve after the ride. West Side Road, North Conway; (603) 356–5538.

SILVER RANCH STABLES Three large sleighs for groups and any number of sleighs for two to four persons are employed in taking passengers across fields and into the woods. Most are antiques and are pulled by either half-Morgans or cross-breeds. Hot chocolate and square dancing are provided if requested. "If you don't know how to square dance we'll teach you," offers Silver Ranch's Lee Sawyer. Route 124, Jaffrey; (603) 532–7363.

INN AT EAST HILL FARM One sleigh fitting 15 to 18 persons is used for 45-minute-long rides along country dirt roads, in woods, and across fields. Hot chocolate, coffee, and snacks are free. Patrons can see resident farm animals and can use the inn's public rooms for relaxing after rides. Jaffrey Road, Troy; (603) 242–6495.

STONEWALL FARM Belgian draft horses haul two sleighs, capacity about 20 adults each, on rides of about 45 minutes. Rides along wooded trails include a hilltop stop affording a stellar view of Keene below. Roast marshmallows over an outdoor campfire, or indulge in hot cider and doughnuts afterwards. 350 Chesterfield Road, Keene; (603) 357–7278.

BARDEN TREE FARM Bay draft horses will take you on an hour-long sleigh ride through the Barden family's managed wood lots. Stopping points along the way offer expansive views of the seacoast 25 miles away. You can use either or both of two two-horse box sleighs that can accommodate 16 people each. 357 Meaderboro Road, Rochester.; (603) 332–0082.

POINT OF VIEW FARM A ride in a Currier and Ives–style Sweetheart sleigh is perfect for two; dinner and dessert in a private dining room is optional. There are also two large sleighs for groups of about 16 each. Belgian horses pull patrons on hour-long rides through the woods on farm property. Hot chocolate and cookies or other snacks can be provided for an extra charge. 160 South Street, Deerfield; (603) 463–7974.

NORTH STAR LIVERY Rides here go through open fields and along a bluff past the Connecticut River as well as through a wood lot. Owner John Hammond uses Percherons, Belgians, or Suffolk punch horses to pull a 12-foot bench sleigh, with a capacity of about 12 persons. The rides last about 45 minutes and hot drinks are offered. Route 12A, Cornish; (603) 542–5802.

Vermont

ADAMS FARM At this farmstead in southern Vermont's Mount Snow Valley you can embark on a 90-minute-long sleigh adventure that includes a warming stop in a woodsy cabin and a narrated tour. During the 45-minute-long break in the cabin, you can sip hot chocolate and listen to music courtesy of a player piano. A narration provides information about maple sugaring and sleigh construction. The three sleighs utilized were made by farm owner Bill Adams, can hold 15 to 20 persons each, and are drawn by a team of Belgian draft horses. The rides, Bill says, "go through meadows and over hill and dale." Higley Hill, Wilmington; (802) 464–3762.

SANTA'S LAND This small children's attraction closes its doors to its Christmas village after the holidays but remains open for sleigh rides. Small draft horses called Austrian Haflingers will pull you on one of two antique sleighs. There is a hefty Woodstock sleigh, low to the ground with seats on the sides that can hold 12 to 15 people, and a three-seater that can hold six or seven patrons. Rides last 15 to 25 minutes and go along roads and paths through woods and on open fields. There are farm animals, a pancake house, and a small collection of antique sleighs on the grounds, too. Route 5, Putney; (802) 387–5550.

STANLEY BILL'S SLEIGH RIDES Rides here take place on refurbished antique sleighs and last from a half hour to two hours. There are two sleighs that can hold about 20 each and a snug single sleigh with room for just two. Bill uses Percherons and Belgians to pull his sleighs along an old town road and across open fields. Route 30, Townsend; (802) 365–7375.

BAILEY FARM One sleigh (old runners, new body) is used to take passengers through woods and across fields for half-hour-long rides. Suffolk punch horses are used and a bonfire after the ride is yours by request. Upper Dummerston, Road Brattleboro; (802) 254–9067.

WINDHILL HORSES AND TACK SHOP Rides lasting an hour on old sleighs traverse woods and fields. A dozen to 15 people can be held on each. Two teams of Belgians and Percherons are used. Manchester Center; (802) 362–2604.

KEDRON VALLEY STABLES Paul and Barbara Kendall use half-Arabian light workhorses to draw up to 32 persons around on mostly antique sleighs. Patrons are taken across open meadows and through a bit of woods. Route 106, South Woodstock; (802) 457–1480.

SLEIGH RIDES AT TIMBER VILLAGE Two farm-type sleighs—one old, one new—transport up to 14 passengers. You can take a 10-minute-long ride around a field or a 30- to 40-minute-long ride on a field and in woods. Restaurants are within walking distance. Route 4, Quechee; (802) 295–2910.

VERMONT ICELANDIC HORSE FARM A newly made sleigh drawn by a team of Belgians can haul 10 to 14 people. Rides go mainly through meadows and into a bit of woods. Hot chocolate, hot cider, and snacks like cookies or popcorn are included. Waitsfield; (802) 496–7141.

ROUND BARN FARM INN Warren Kingsley takes up to fourteen patrons out in a *cross-chain travis-style* *sled* (with rear runners that steer along with front runners) that he built. Kingsley's rides last 45 to 50 minutes and go mostly through fields and along the edge of woods. Snacks of hot cider with cinnamon are offered. Waitsfield; (802) 496–6261.

POND HILL RANCH Harry O'Rourke uses a team of Belgians to pull a couple of new sleighs that can hold up to 20 passengers. The rides last an hour to 90 minutes and go along dirt roads through a wooded area. For an extra charge a bonfire will be built to warm chilled riders. Pond Hill Road, Castleton; (802) 468–2449.

VERMONT BRAND LLAMAS & CAMELS Edgar and Marie Brand supplement their summer llama trekking trips with wintertime sleigh rides. Imported European Belgian horses ("a sturdier and heavier breed," says Marie) do the work, pulling any of four sleighs Edgar built. There are a European vis-a-vis sleigh in which up to six passengers face each other, box sleighs that seat eight and 18, and a two-seater for couples. Rides last from a half hour to an hour and are followed by hot chocolate—possibly with other snacks—served in a heated tack room. Marie says people also enjoy seeing the Brands' llamas and Kublai Khan, the resident camel. Route 73 East, Brandon; (802) 247–6015.

STOWEHOF INN Perfect for romantics, Juliet O'Neil's sleighs are authentic antiques with room for two adults (and perhaps one or two children if you wish to skip the romance). You have your choice of a stately Kingsbury sleigh, a fast and sleek Albany cutter, and a pragmatic Surry sleigh. The horses, mixed Morgans and Percherons, wear plumes and bells; and guests are given fur muffs. Juliet says there have been many marriage proposals given on her rides, which last 25 to 30 minutes and head over open meadows and past Stowe's fully lit Christmas trees (still lit well past Christmas). Afterward, riders have complimentary hot spirits and hors d'oeuvres in the inn bar. Five-course dinner and sleigh ride packages are also available. Edson Hill Road, Stowe; (800) 422–9722 or (802) 253–9722.

SMUGGLERS' NOTCH STABLES Proposals while on board these sleigh rides aren't unheard of either. There is a black sleigh for one or two couples and two refurbished travis sleighs for up to 16 adults. Rides last 50 to 55 minutes depending on the guests. Driver Wayne Terpstra says, "A lot of city folk don't want to sit in the hay out in the cold while others feel just the opposite." The rides go along roads past a reservoir and through a covered bridge. Jeffersonville; (802) 644–5347.

ROSE APPLE ACRES FARM BED & BREAKFAST The
Mead family has both a *pung* (a low box sleigh with room for three persons) and a six-passenger two-horse wagon sled, which are pulled by Belgian and standardbred mares. Both sleighs are antiques. Riders are taken mostly across fields, and hot cider and cakes or doughnuts are served afterward. East Hill Road, North Troy; (802) 988–4300.

WHITCOMB'S SLEIGH RIDES A narrated tour of a
working dairy farm is a bonus on Whitcomb's rides. You might hear about milking cows, crop rotation, or the farm's computer feeding system, as Belgian horses Buster and Baldy pull you about the grounds. The rides are on a restored travis sleigh with bench seats, and last about an hour. A campfire is yours by special request and there is a petting area. Essex Junction; (802) 879–6291.

SOUTHERN NEW ENGLAND

Connecticut

FLAMIG FARM Rides emanating from this farm cross
open fields and logging roads and wind through neighboring woods. Four sleighs, of which three are antiques, are used. Two large ones hold 16 adults each, and there are smaller sleighs just right for two or four riders. A team of Belgians pulls you about. A party room might be available depending on scheduling. West Mountain Road, West Simsbury; (203) 658–5070.

WIMLER FARM A duo of work sleds, capacity about
20, are employed in rides lasting about an hour and a half. Belgians haul patrons through the woods. Route 77 (Guilford Road), Durham; (203) 349–3190.

WINDY HILL FARM, Two antique bobsleds take rid-
ers around the open fields of this dairy farm located (appropriately) atop a windy hill. One bobsled holds 15, the other 20 to 25, and both are pulled by American Belgians or heavier-boned European

Belgians. Jaunts here last about an hour and a barn is yours afterwards if you wish to bring your own snacks or refreshments. The Scanlon family loves giving sleigh rides; Louise Scanlon says: "If no one has reserved a ride, we'll round up our neighbors and friends, put the bells on the horses, and brave the cold." Kick Hill Road, Lebanon; (203) 642–6188.

HORSE AND CARRIAGE LIVERY SERVICE Antique sleighs with curved dashes drawn by Belgians and Percherons can be seen clip-clopping across the fields and through the woods around northwestern Connecticut. You can ride in either of two large sleighs with capacities of 18 and 10 or a romantic sleigh built for two. The rides last from 40 minutes to an hour and are followed by warming sips of hot mulled cider or cocoa. A raging bonfire can also be yours depending on conditions. Loon Meadow Drive, Norfolk; (203) 542–6085.

WOOD ACRES Ken and Joyce Wood take winter enthusiasts out on either of two bobsleds through woods or across fields. Capacities are six and 16 persons. Percherons do the pulling for rides lasting a little under an hour. The Woods also maintain a horse-drawn trolley. You also have the use of a heated barn for an hour after the ride, but must bring your own snacks. A bonfire can be made if the conditions are right. Griffin Road, Terryville; (203) 583–8670.

Massachusetts

WINDY KNOLL FARM Ralph Rotondo has an old bobsled and a team of Belgians he uses to haul up to ten adults over the back roads and through woods in the southern Berkshires. The rides last an hour to an hour and a half. Stringer Avenue, Lee; (413) 243–0989.

RICHARD ODMAN Odman has a vintage 1890s six-seat express sleigh, once used to carry people from the Northfield train station to the Northfield Inn (both long gone) as well as three old bob sleighs with new beds that handle up to 14 adults each. Odman uses Belgian draft horses that pull passengers for approximately an hour and 15 minutes, across a pasture but mostly through woods. A sugarhouse is available for your use after the ride, but you must bring your own snacks or entertainment. Main Road, Gill; (413) 863–9618.

DOUGLAS KIMBALL The retired Kimball keeps horses and offers sleigh rides as a personal favorite pastime. Over 300 acres of farmland including open fields and logging roads are traversed. Up to 20 adults can be accommodated on rides lasting about an hour. Route 119, Ashby; (508) 386–2219.

WILDER HILL FARM Peter Bravmann's motto might be "have sleigh, will travel." Peter will transport his newly built sleigh—capacity about 15 adults and five children—and bay Percheron cross-breed horses to any locale you wish for your own sleigh ride. Or you can take a sleigh ride near his farm, across fields, through woods, and over abandoned roads. Bravmann's rides last about an hour. Wilder Hill Road, Conway; (413) 625–6567.

Rhode Island

JOHN W. COLE, INC. Cole uses two pungs he built for half-hour to 45-minute-long rides. The capacity is 14 persons for the bigger of the two. Two Belgian horses draw riders through woods. "The horses are bilingual," Cole says. "They take commands in both French and English." Route 100, Chepachet; (401) 568–9303 or (401) 568–7659.

CARNIVALS ON SNOW

His eyes were narrow slits, peering forward, dead straight ahead. His mouth was a flat even line. His nose was strong. He looked determined, forthright, in command.

A robed sleeve draped his right arm as he raised a magic wand in the air, far up above us. In his other hand was an open book. Even as we stood as far back as Main Street we could clearly see its pages and front and back covers. We could even determine the close-clipped fingernails of this giant Merlin the Magician, a creation crafted of ice and snow for the Dartmouth Winter Carnival.

Hanover, New Hampshire's storied Ivy League college throws its giant-sized winter carnival every February, but it is just one of numerous such celebrations, mostly scheduled for mid-winter, when the memories of the holidays have faded into a blur and the word "winter" conjures up thoughts of brown slush, rather than Frosty the Snowman and walks in a snowy white wonderland.

Winter carnivals are one of the activities for the non-athlete in the cold months. Attending one is the winter equivalent of the summer sightseeing trip in a national park. You need neither strong legs nor stamina. You don't need to be able to maneuver on skis. You don't even have to sweat. You just have to bundle up, stand, and watch. The winter carnival is the perfect antidote to those mid-season blahs, the consummate reminder that there is enjoyment out there if you know where to find it.

New Hampshire

THE DARTMOUTH WINTER CARNIVAL Not far away from Merlin stood a dragon, his teeth welded together as if constructed of wax that had long since melted. His bones, protruding from his back, were dulled; some were broken, victims of wear and tear caused by 12-year-olds who used him like a slide in a public playground.

There was also a knight on horseback, although where the horse ended and the knight began had become a bit hard to discern. A behemoth of a helmet guarded the entrance to a brick, pillared building, and nearby a man stood straining, perpetually trying in vain to pull a sword imbedded in a white powdery stone. He would pull until completely melted.

A few years earlier a great white whale attempting to escape a harpoon swam in the spot where Merlin stood. Instead of knights and dragons there were King Neptune, a bulging treasure chest, a smiling and friendly frog, a slithering sea serpent, and a well-endowed mermaid. And they too remained on view until the mercury rose.

Like the multi-hued canyons of the vast West and the floral concoctions at the Tournament of Roses Parade, the grandeur of massive snow sculptures cannot be appreciated until they are seen close up and in person. The details of Merlin's fingers or Moby Dick's eyes are most impressive while you are standing next to them. Television, films, or photographs reduce the mammoth undertakings so much that it becomes similar to admiring the Lincoln Memorial pictured on a postage stamp.

There is a bit of luck involved, since the weather plays a major supporting role. An unexpected thaw or steady cold rain would have turned Merlin into mashed potatoes. One staff member of the Dart-

The grandeur of massive snow sculptures cannot be appreciated until they are seen close up and in person.

COLOSSAL SNOW SCULPTURES ARE THE RULE AT THE LEGENDARY DARTMOUTH WINTER CARNIVAL.

mouth College News Services recalled one legendary warm spell.

"One year, it is said, there was so much rain that all the snow melted and there was almost a lake on the central campus. Instead of offering sleigh rides, people brought canoes and offered canoe rides. Of course, I'm not sure how much truth there is in that story."

Canoes, however, do play a major role in the Dartmouth Winter Carnival. There is a downhill canoe race—on snow—at the Hanover Country Club. And visitors from outside the campus community are invited to watch this tongue-in-cheek "sporting" event.

How did the Dartmouth Winter Carnival get started? William Howard Taft was in the White House when Brattleboro, Vermont, native Fred Harris, Dartmouth Class of 1911, took his skis into the woods around Hanover one bright, winter day while his fellow classmates stayed indoors, huddled around stoves.

To Fred this seemed like a big waste of winter. So he put his feelings into writing in the form of a letter to the campus newspaper. And thanks to Fred Harris, the Dartmouth Outing Club was formed. Harris later founded the Brattleboro Outing Club and became instrumental in the popularization of winter sports across the country. Subsequently he was enshrined in the National Ski Hall of Fame in Ishpeming, Michigan.

Soon after the birth of the Dartmouth Outing Club, the Dartmouth Winter Carnival debuted, with a snowshoe race and some ski sprints. As the carnival grew with added events, a Winter Carnival Committee was formed. A cultural event, like a play or concert, became a permanent part of the carnival; that begat the snow sculptures, which begat a dance and carnival queen, which begat a figure skating exhibition, which begat the showing of a real honest to goodness full-scale Hollywood production about a college romance at the winter carnival. It starred Ann Sheridan, Richard Carlson, and the campus of Dartmouth College.

In the 1920s and 1930s and even into the 1940s this was the year's biggest weekend. Only the most hapless bumbler didn't have a date arriving in White River Junction across the Connecticut River on a special New Haven Railroad run that picked up women passengers from Connecticut College for Women, Vassar, Smith, and Mount Holyoke.

Things changed in the 1960s and 1970s, mainly a result of the feminist movement and the college becoming coeducational. The carnival queen went the way of the raccoon coat, and the tradition of dates arriving by train from women's colleges became unnecessary.

Dartmouth Winter Carnival is no longer the ultimate in weekends, though it remains a major event. Dartmouth officials stress that the carnival is primarily a campus-wide event open to Dartmouth students and their guests. But the general public is invited to witness the cross-country ski race, the downhill canoe race, the basketball games and other intercollegiate meets, and most definitely the snow sculptures.

Actually, the snow sculptures are slush structures. Because it must be below zero for the freezing process to work, water is added to the snow and brave students are usually out under the lights after dark forming their creations.

About one thousand man-hours are involved in making the biggest snow sculpture on the green in the center of campus. Included in the creative process are the formation of a massive snow base and the addition of chicken-wire frames for appendages like arms, legs, and head. The finished product usually weighs in at 200 to 300 tons of snow.

Snowless carnivals? There have been a few, such as the dry winters of 1980 and 1989. But in 1980 students borrowed snow-making machinery from Killington Ski Area, a demonstration Mack Truck fire pumper from New Jersey to provide water pressure to make snowy ice crystals, diesel fuel from three local oil companies, water from the Hanover Water Company, and advice from the Hanover Fire Department. An Olympian sculpture was built, and there was enough snow left over to make a ski jump to be used in competition. Excitement like that you don't see in Florida.

The Dartmouth Winter Carnival always takes place on the second weekend in February. Many who come to see the snow sculptures or athletic competitions extend their excursion by exploring the shops in downtown Hanover or Dartmouth's Hood Museum of Art (See page 192) (603) 646–2255.

WINTER CARNIVAL AT KING PINE This winter bash in tiny East Madison, just south of Conway, New Hampshire, was born in 1990 and emphasizes family participation in numerous events. You might be asked to climb over a bale of hay in a ski obstacle race, bop a volleyball over a net in a spirited, snow-filled contest, or sled downhill on a plastic garbage bag. An outdoor barbecue brings a taste of summer to this mid-winter carnival. (603) 367–8896.

Vermont

BRATTLEBORO WINTER CARNIVAL The same Fred

Harris credited with founding the Dartmouth Winter Carnival also started the cold weather party in this southeastern Vermont town. Brattleboro has been a ski jumping center since the early 1920s, but when it was named an All-American city in 1956, Harris decided to celebrate the honor with a three-day winter festival. The initial celebration included a ski ball, a fashion show, a parade, and, of course, a ski jumping contest.

Today up to 50 events take place around the town during this week-long frosty fiesta, the high point being the two-day, 70-meter Harris Hill Ski Jump competition, drawing entrants from across the United States and other countries. Also scheduled at times have been a parade, a sleigh rally, a sled dog exhibition, sugar on snow, and competitions in ice fishing, skating, and cross-country and downhill skiing. (802) 254–4565.

STOWE WINTER CARNIVAL

There was a winter carnival in Stowe back in the 1920s, but it focused mostly on athletic competitions. The event was discontinued in 1924 and reinstated a half century later in January 1974, as a draw for tourists in an otherwise slow period.

The cold-season tribute lasts eight or nine days and involves about 25 events. There is sled dog racing and ski racing, and on Village Night folks dressed as cartoon characters parade about town. There is more clowning around during the snow golf competition, in which costumed adults practice their putting with a rubber ball on a golf course of snow.

How do mountain bikes perform in the snow? You'll see during the Mountain Bike Derby. Indoors one will find a game night and a casino night, while snow sculptures decorate restaurant and lodge properties along Routes 100 and 108. (802) 253–7321.

BRANDON WINTER CARNIVAL

This small town between Rutland and Middlebury, Vermont, hosts a mid-winter carnival lasting nine days and consisting of ice and snow sculpturing, figure skating demonstrations, sledding, tobogganing, and plenty of skiing. A couple of dances and an ethnic food fair are some of the events to warm up by indoors. (802) 247–6401.

NEWPORT'S WINTERFEST

In Newport, Vermont, on the shore of Lake Memphremagog near the Canadian border, winter comes on like a runaway moose and stays and stays and stays. Rather than fight it, locals fete it, taking full advantage of their northern exposure and lakefront geography.

The wintertime trio of snow golf, snow bowling, and snow volleyball, all played on ice or snow, offers some seasonal impediments to these traditional sports. You might also be privy to visions of outhouses on runners speeding across Lake Memphremagog, all part of the friendly neighborhood outhouse race. For the more conventional there is an ice fishing contest, for the creative there is a snow sculpture competition, and for the canine there are sled dog races. (802) 334–7782.

Rhode Island

THE OTHER NEWPORT'S WINTER CARNIVAL
Don't think that Rhode Island's biggest leisure city is only worth visiting in a T-shirt or tank top. Fireworks on the beach; ice, sand, and snow sculpturing contests; recreational skating; dog sled competitions; and a polar-bear plunge from Easton's Beach into the shivery waters of Newport Bay are reason enough to spend some time at the ten-day-long Newport Winter Carnival. The annual block hunt gives youngsters the chance to dig for prizes in the snow and sand, while the scavenger hunt allows their parents to scout the streets of Newport for clues leading to prizes like free dining and lodging. (401) 847–7666.

Maine

BELFAST WINTER CARNIVAL In 1990, people in mid-coastal Maine, knowing that their winter was as lasting as anyone else's, decided they could commemorate the season as spiritedly as people in New Hampshire and Vermont. And so in February, 1991, they threw the first Belfast Winter Carnival. Hallmarks of winter blowouts, like snow sculpture competitions and town-wide dances, were on the three-day agenda, but Belfast residents also got to swing away in a snow softball game, mush up a storm during the dog sledding exhibitions, and take their Flexible Flyers out of dry dock for the sledding party. And what better way to get such an undertaking off to a roaring start than with a blazing bonfire? (207) 338–2151.

OXFORD WINTER CARNIVAL Another weekend-long snow celebration occurs in Oxford, Maine, a community of 600 near Auburn. You can take a ride on a dog sled, give ice fishing a whirl, play a game of snow volleyball, or watch a caravan of variegated

snowmobiles—their headlights covered with cellophane of different colors—parade by in an eye-riveting event. In the Anything Goes Race, kids and others get to test their homemade cardboard sleds and other sliding concoctions for speed, while one can always warm up at the bonfire at Lake Thompson or while chowing down pancakes at the Sunday morning breakfast. (207) 539–4848.

CARIBOU WINTER CARNIVAL In the northern reaches of Aroostook County, Maine, where winter comes early and lasts long, hardy folks have been paying homage to the surliest season since the 1930s. Their fest lasts ten days and includes a snowmobile poker run although the royal flush of activities could easily be the annual outhouse race. Cross-country competitors vie for top ranking in the ski race from New Sweden to Caribou, and the artistic can craft sculptures in the snow. You can show your gliding skills at the skating party outdoors, then trade in your blades for wheels for the roller skating party inside. Arm wrestling, basketball, and dancing complement the outdoor events. (207) 498–6156.

WINTER WEEKENDS FOR NON-SKIERS

Whether you love the high life or the low life, some say there is no life for non-skiers in winter in New England. Believe that and we'll sell you some mountaintop property in Florida. The weather is at best an asset and at worst no detriment. And you never even have to look at a pair of skis.

What is defined as pleasure to some may not be so to all. But in the following selections there is something to strike a note of enjoyment with anyone willing to turn off the television set and leave the house.

What to do during the day? Horse-drawn sleigh rides seem to bring out the sentimentalist in many of us and are perfect for special occasions. For hedonists, massage is the message attainable during health spa weekends; for masochists, rugged exercise workouts precede massages.

Should you just want to go out and taste the wine, you can do just that on special theme weekends. Indoor entertainment doesn't necessarily mean watered-down lounge music. It can also take the form of an early American magic show or the sampling of a culinary feast cooked eighteenth-century style. For those whose greatest passion leans towards shopping, downtowns and college towns await.

Some of the following hotels, inns, and lodges do offer skiing—very good skiing—often on trails or slopes right outside their front door. But that's for another audience.

On the other hand, the following packages and activities are not for non-skiers only. They are for anyone who wants a wintertime diversion.

Massachusetts

SALEM CROSS INN For their **Hearthside Tradition Dinners** on Friday evenings, the Salem family prepares an entire meal as it was done in the 1700s. So instead of food processors and pasta makers, the Salems employ a circa 1700 *roasting jack,* incorporating two spits that turn by means of pulleys and weights, based on a principle devised by Leonardo da Vinci. Innkeeper Henry Salem boasts that it's the only working roasting jack he knows of in the country. Show up by 6:30 P.M., when the inn is engulfed with the scents of home cooking, and you'll see the roasting jack in action, slowly turning six prime ribs of beef at once.

HEARTHSIDE DINNER PREPARATIONS AT THE SALEM CROSS INN.

We grabbed a hot mulled wine—made with the help of a fiery hot mulling iron—and watched Henry's daughter Margaret Salem peel and core apples on a hand-operated apple peeler dating from the early 1800s. Another staff member was grinding nutmeg by hand for the night's apple pie dessert. At their urging, we put down the hot glasses of mulled wine and gave the apple peeler a try, doing fairly well with our peeling but having less success with our coring efforts. Margaret also offered us a sniff of fresh nutmeg, and we inhaled its potent and floral fragrance before sampling crackers and a cream cheese dip.

Meanwhile, Dick Salem, Henry's brother, was dropping fresh fish, diced onions, diced potatoes and other ingredients into a 50-quart black iron cauldron suspended over the fireplace, preparing seafood chowder as the wife of John White, the original property owner, would have done when the house was built in 1705.

Hearthside Dinners are preceded by a sleigh ride and a guided tour of the inn. A pair of Belgian horses will pull you in an antique sleigh for about 15 to 20 minutes across the expansive inn grounds. Wool blankets and hay are provided as warming agents but you will still want to wear your coat to shield yourself from what can be a biting winter chill.

On the house tour, you will hear the tale of the Salem Cross Inn and the actual Salem Cross. The cross, which you can see on the inn's front door latch and which resembles the letter X with a line across its top, middle, and bottom, was a common sight in the Massachusetts Bay Colony and was meant to protect a dwelling from witchcraft. You might wonder whether it was a kind of sorcery or just pure coincidence that led the Salem family to purchase the Salem Cross Inn from descendents of John White in 1950.

Son David Salem leads the tours, on which you will hear about the inn's punctilious restoration and see the Salems' collection of antiques and collectibles. In one small dining room, named the Peregrine White Room for John White's ancestor, born on the Mayflower, are portraits of a Colonial era boy and girl. David explained that the works were painted by an itinerant artist, one of many in that day, who traveled the countryside in winter with paintings he made of children's torsos; when he found a family that wanted a likeness of their children, he simply filled in the faces.

In the kitchen, which dates from the 1830s,

Patrons dine family style, sitting at rectangular tables, and there is no extra charge for friendly conversation with your neighbors.

lanterns and herbs hang from rods below the ceiling. Years of scraping away wallpaper and paint turned up original plastering concocted by using oyster shells as a prime base and horsehair as paste. The barn—today the dining room where you are served—is the location of the beehive oven, built in 1699 at a nearby tavern. It is in this oven that the apple pies we had helped prepare earlier were baked.

The banquet that followed included seafood chowder, prime rib, squash muffins, pecan rolls, squash, and spinach pie. Portions are generous, and those of us used to other restaurants were shocked to be offered seconds on our appetizer, the fish chowder. Patrons dine family style, sitting at rectangular tables, and there is no extra charge for friendly conversation with your neighbors.

You will know dessert is nigh when Henry enters the dining room holding a deep wooden bowl overloaded with heavy whipped cream, looking like a portable iceberg. Forget about cholesterol watching for the night; your apple pie will be liberally topped with dollops of whipped cream.

Expect to spend three and a half to four hours at the inn for a Hearthside Tradition Dinner. Dress is casual. There is no overnight lodging on the grounds. Reservations are required. Salem Cross Inn, Route 9, Ware Road, West Brookfield, MA 01585; (508) 867–2345 or (508) 867–8337.

PUBLICK HOUSE

"Leave the twentieth century far behind," urges the staff at the Publick House. Spend two nights here during one of their Yankee Winter Weekends and you will appreciate the time when the Whigs occupied the White House.

Arrive on Friday evening and you are greeted with a sing-along led by costumed minstrels. If you would rather eat than sing, help yourself to early nineteenth-century treats like mulled cider, syllabub (an alcoholic beverage mixed with sweetened cream), clam chowder, and Joe Froggers (cookies).

Saturday starts with breakfast and continues with a day at Old Sturbridge Village highlighted by a buffet lunch and a hay or sleigh ride. For dinner, order from the Publick House's regular à la carte menu or indulge in a game dinner—entrées can include wild boar or venison.

After-dinner entertainment consists of a period magic show back at Old Sturbridge Village, where staff member Bob Olson plays both Harry Ames, a fictional nineteenth-century English street magician, and Richard Potter, the first successful American-born magician, who really did perform in New England in the early 1800s.

A buffet breakfast is offered Sunday. One-day weekend extensions are available. Yankee Winter Weekends are offered early January through late March. Publick House, P.O. Box 187, Sturbridge, MA 01566; (508) 347–3313.

CHARLES HOTEL AT HARVARD SQUARE Why do people spend hundreds of dollars to rack their bodies to exhaustion? Because at the Charles Hotel pleasure joins pain in a special health and fitness package offered by the hotel and the plush Le Pli Health Spa and Salon next door.

"There is always a carrot dangled in front of you," says hotel spokesperson Martha W. Sullivan. "After vigorous exercise, you get a massage. After water aerobics there's a facial."

Key to the workouts are personal consultations with Le Pli's nutritionist and trainers, and a fitness program tailored to each individual's needs. The program is expensive, but includes five meals (Friday dinner through Sunday breakfast).

The Charles has two other winter packages. The Bed & Breakfast Weekend comes with one night's lodging and continental breakfast. The Wine & Dine Weekend includes one night's lodging, dinner, full breakfast or brunch, and tickets to a live jazz concert at the hotel's Regattabar. Access to Le Pli can be added to either package. Charles Hotel at Harvard Square, One Bennett Street, Cambridge, MA 02138; (800) 882–1818, or (617) 864–1200. For information on the Le Pli Weekend only, call Le Pli at (617) 868–8087.

New Hampshire

INN AT EAST HILL FARM Known best locally as a cross-country ski center, this inn also offers both Square Dance Weekends and a wealth of indoor recreational facilities. To keep pace at Ron Libby's Winter Wonderland for C-2 level square dancers you have to be a pretty adept mover.

Regular winter weekend packages include, in addition to trail fees, use of the game room, hot tub, sauna (have quarters handy), and indoor pool. And the bells jingle as horse-drawn sleighs take guests across the snow-filled fields of southern New Hampshire.

All weekend package costs include two nights'

THE BALSAMS GRAND RESORT HOTEL, DIXVILLE NOTCH, NEW HAMPSHIRE.

lodging and six meals from Friday dinner through Sunday lunch. Sleigh rides are extra. Inn at East Hill Farm, Troy, NH 03465; (603) 242–6495.

THE BALSAMS What is there for a non-skier to do in this grand resort at the rooftop of New England? There are hay wagon rides, skating parties, bonfires, movies (the resort has its own theater), guided natural history tours (conducted on snowshoes for non-skiers, or on cross-country skis by the hotel naturalist), cooking demonstrations, kitchen tours, an artist in residence (a silversmith at the time we went to press), and a profusion of nightly entertainment.

There are also two other pluses: gourmet dining the likes of which you will be hard pressed to find elsewhere in northern New England, and the pleasure of really getting away from it all—and we mean *really* getting away. This is a land of logging trucks and tiny towns in true wilderness, rugged terrain a snowball's toss from the Canadian border. Expect a three and a half hour drive from the New Hampshire–Massachusetts border. Weekend packages include two nights' lodging, two dinners, two breakfasts, and all activities. The Balsams, Dixville Notch, NH 03576; (800) 255–0600 outside New Hampshire, (800) 255–0800 or (603) 255–3400 inside New Hampshire.

Maine

LAKE HOUSE This four-room inn built circa 1786 in western Maine is the place to taste the wine. Wine-tasting dinners are scheduled monthly in winter, with each dinner focusing on one theme and consisting of five courses and at least four wines. Bob Bartlett of Bartlett Wines, based in the state of Maine, usually speaks at one dinner for which "Maine Food and Wines" is the topic. He usually brings along his most popular wines, including pear, blueberry, and raspberry.

Other dinners are likely to focus on Italian, French, and American foods and wines, although natural or German wines might also be the specialty on a given evening. In addition, during each month, Lake House owners Michael and Suzanne Uhl-Myers offer a selection of wines coinciding with each theme. Exact menus are available two to three weeks before each scheduled dinner. You don't need to be an overnight guest to participate. Lake House, Routes 35 and 37, Waterford, ME 04088; (207) 583–4182.

NORTHERN PINES: A HEALTHY RESORT Nancy
Reagan and Joan Baez might not have much in common, but both would be intrigued by weekend programs at this spa and alternative health resort tucked amid the pine trees in Maine's Sebago Lake region. Astrology and folk singing are two topics that have been explored here.

Body conditioning, yoga, vegetarian cooking classes, reflexology, massage, and general recreation are commonly the chosen activities of guests. But in winter special programs are offered, too. In addition to the favored pastimes of Baez and Reagan, tarot cards, ayurvedic medicine, transcendental meditation, and holistic medicine have all been featured. There have also been special sessions devoted to helping dysfunctional families and coping with co-dependency and addiction.

The people here don't ignore their exquisite surroundings. There is often a special outdoor trek on snowshoes or skis into the woods, in which the goal is to track non-human forms of winter wildlife. Northern Pines: A Healthy Resort, RR 1, Route 85, Box 279, Raymond, ME 04071; (207) 655–7624.

Vermont

MIDDLEBURY INN One of New England's handsomest hostelries, this 77-room inn is located within the center of one of New England's classiest college towns. One staff member calls it a "village inn" as opposed to a country inn, stating that guest rooms in country inns are not often stocked with telephones and television sets.

In winter, the Middlebury serves up murder mystery and Romantic "Inn-Terlude" weekends. The murder mystery packages, called Detectives Alert! weekends, consist of two nights' lodging, two breakfasts, two dinners, afternoon tea, one night's entertainment, and the opportunity to test your sleuthing skills to discover what culprit committed what crime.

The Romantic "Inn-Terlude" weekends offer, in addition to nearby cross-country and downhill skiing, access to a fitness center, gourmet dining in the inn, and the village of Middlebury, an enticing place to walk in any season, and nirvana for the discriminating shopper.

Within strolling distance are book, clothing, and specialty shops, as well as the Frog Hollow Craft Center, one of Vermont's most complete craft emporia. The 1827 inn also boasts its own craft and gift shop. The Middlebury Antique Center is about three miles away and the staff will plan an itinerary for an avid antique hunter.

Included in the romantic weekend package are two nights' lodging, two breakfasts, one dinner, and afternoon tea. Middlebury Inn, P.O. Box 798, Middlebury, VT 05753; (800) 842–4666 or (802) 388–4961.

Body conditioning, yoga, vegetarian cooking classes, reflexology, massage, and general recreation are commonly the chosen activities of guests.

Connecticut

EARLY AMERICAN HEARTH TOURS Have lunch
prepared over an open hearth with Noah Webster,
nibble on nineteenth-century Adelaide cookies after
eavesdropping on a gaggle of women gossiping
about who's doing what to whom in 1830s
Connecticut, celebrate George Washington's birthday
at an elegant Federal period tea, or spend an afternoon at a colonial tavern being entertained as you
would have been in the 1770s.

These are just some of the featured parts of winter
programs called **Early American Hearth Tours** that
have been offered on Saturdays by the Farmington
Valley/West Hartford Visitors Bureau. Horse-drawn
sleigh rides, colonial cooking demonstrations, historical stage shows, and museum tours are also likely to
be included. If you are planning on staying overnight, consider taking advantage of the Warm Up to
Winter packages offered by several area lodgings.
The packages might include sleigh rides, discounted
ski passes, and discounted admissions to area museums and historic sites.

You can take an Early American Hearth Tour with-
out staying overnight or you can also take part in a
Warm Up to Winter package without joining the spe-
cial Hearth Tour. The choice is yours. The
Farmington Valley/West Hartford Visitors Bureau,
P.O. Box 1550, 41 East Main Street, Old Avon Village,
Avon, CT 06001; (800) 468–6783 or (203) 674–1035.

STONEHENGE Leave your Mercedes at home. A
chauffeur-driven limousine is yours for the duration
of the two-day, one-night weekend. It will pick you
up at your home or office within 100 miles of
Ridgefield (or at an airport within 100 miles) and will
be your means of transport to the Aldrich Museum of
Contemporary Art, Danbury's historical Scott-Fanton
Museum, or any other attraction on your agenda. It is
also yours if you wish to embark on a shopping or
antiquing tour. While on your luxurious wheels,
champagne and hors d'oeuvres, or afternoon tea with
sandwiches, are offered for your dining pleasure.

While at the inn, you will have a personal captain,
a private bar, and an individually tailored dinner
served either in your suite or in the dining room.
Breakfast is yours on the terrace or in your suite, and
an extensive brunch is provided before the limousine
takes you home or to the airport. The price as we
went to press was $1,500 per couple. Stonehenge

Inn, Stonehenge Road, Ridgefield, CT 06877; (203) 438–6511.

Other significantly less extravagant outings at Ridgefield, Danbury, or Bethel lodgings are offered as part of Winter Revels packages. Most are two days, one night, and can include dinner, breakfast, or welcome baskets. Housatonic Valley Tourism Commission, 72 West Street, Danbury, CT 06813; (800) 841–4488 or (203) 743–0546.

Rhode Island

BELCOURT CASTLE You are taking what seems to be a standard tour of this Newport mansion with your guide pointing out Belcourt's treasures, like the rosewood Chinese table from the Imperial Palace in Beijing in the grand hall, and the Indian bed with the elephant feet, made for the Maharajah of Jaipur.

Then your guide calmly brushes over a corpse covered with a sheet, acting as if there is nothing to be alarmed about. As the tour winds down, an individual playing the role of a chief detective tells you and the rest of the visitors that you are all suspects in the murder of the unfortunate victim seen earlier.

Welcome to the Mystery Tour With Dinner at Belcourt Castle. Who is the villain? That is for you to discern while munching on chicken Kiev or rice pilaf in the castle's banquet hall. But don't handle the corpse or any evidence, or you will be sentenced to three hours of imprisonment; and dinner in prison is served from the leftovers on the buffet line.

One or more public Mystery Tours are scheduled in winter, although Mystery Tours for private groups can be arranged. Belcourt Castle, Bellevue Avenue, Newport, RI 02840; (401) 846–0669.

NEWPORT STAR CLIPPER DINNER TRAIN A four-course dinner is served while you rumble along the western shore of Aquidneck Island in a train that recalls the elegance of rail travel of years past. On Monday nights, the Star Clipper serves up a murder mystery. Newport Star Clipper, 102 Connell Highway, Newport, RI 02840; (800) 462–7452 outside Rhode Island, (800) 834–1556 or (401) 849–7550 in Rhode Island.

DAYS OF TINSEL AND HOLLY

Puritanical as they were, New Englanders were among the last Americans to celebrate Christmas as a festive holiday. Considering it a solemn occasion, they saw no good in marking December 25 with pagan customs like wreaths and Christmas trees. It wasn't until 1845 that the first state in New England, Connecticut, legalized the holiday.

Even so, it is said that the first recorded Christmas tree in New England was in a Boston home in 1832, although one didn't appear in the White House until 1856, ironically during the administration of New Englander Franklin Pierce.

It was also that year when Henry Wadsworth Longfellow, living in Cambridge, Massachusetts, wrote to a friend: "We are in a transition state about Christmas here in New England. The old Puritan feeling prevents it from being a cheerful, hearty holiday, though every year makes it more so."

Times change. Today you can revel in holiday cheer in New England without the slightest bit of Puritan guilt. And there are plenty of places to be festive. Just remember that the following events are described as we experienced them, but are discussed mainly to convey atmosphere. You might see different decorations or activities when you visit.

Today you can revel in holiday cheer in New England without the slightest bit of Puritan guilt.

Christmas in Newport

While sitting in a wicker chair on the glassed-in veranda at John F. Kennedy's Newport, Rhode Island, presidential retreat, **Hammersmith Farm**, we found the perfect antidote to the holiday season rat race. Slowly nursing a hot mulled cider, snacking on cookies, and listening to happy songs about merry gentlemen and snowmen and roasting chestnuts, we looked out the windows and watched the gentle blue waters of Narragansett Bay lap against the shore. And suddenly the obtrusive holiday crowds and traffic seemed as far away as Neptune.

Christmas in Newport is a month-long array of events, music, food, and millionaires' mansions decorated as they might have looked had their owners been around in December. As the melodious sounds of "Hark the Herald Angels Sing" bathed our ears and the late fall sun our faces, we glanced around the Hammersmith Farm veranda, admiring a green wreath dotted with holly berries that adorned a window, and other wreaths made from blue mussel shells that fit perfectly in this seaside setting.

This isn't to say, however, that such a Yuletide respite is wholly typical. You will encounter crowds at Christmas in Newport, especially on weekends, and at times the bus tours might seem suffocating, as they descend like swarms of locusts upon the gold ballroom of Marble House or encircle the 35-foot-high Christmas tree in the great hall in The Breakers. A lot depends on the luck of good timing, but if you should find yourself surrounded by 39 Instamatic-toting tourists from Scarsdale, just tune in on the holiday music and the decorations and think about the theme of the season. It won't clear the hall but it might clear your mind, and you will concentrate more on the attractions than the distractions.

At Hammersmith Farm all the rooms—including the bathrooms—are decorated with symbols of the season as Hugh and Janet Bouvier Auchincloss, their daughter Jacqueline Bouvier Kennedy, their son-in-law John Fitzgerald Kennedy, their grandchildren Caroline and John, Jr. (and their other children and grandchildren from previous marriages) might have had them.

President Kennedy's study, dominated by his oil portrait, is garnished with a Christmas tree ornamented with miniature patriotic landmarks such as the White House, the Capitol, and the Liberty Bell. Similarly, the kitchen Christmas tree is trimmed with tiny rolling pins and fresh popcorn, while the table-top tree in the room of Jamie Auchincloss, Hugh's half-brother who loved the ocean, is decked with ornaments resembling sailboats and captain's wheels.

Unlike the garish and ostentatious mansions on Bellevue Avenue, Hammersmith Farm is quite underwhelming, with wicker and light taking the place of the baroque and heavy. And the Christmas decorations follow suit. The foyer, where young bride Jacqueline threw her bouquet at her 1953 wedding reception, is embellished unpretentiously with wreaths adorned with green apples.

The dining room table in the most formal room is decorated simply, set for a luncheon of eight with a single wrapped gift on each plate and green and silver drapings on the mirror and mantel. John, Jr.'s homey yellow and white bedroom is noticeable for its teddy bears and garlands of green.

Hammersmith Farm is quite underwhelming, with wicker and light taking the place of the baroque and heavy.

THIS MEMORABLE CHRISTMAS TREE AT NEWPORT'S MARBLE HOUSE
IS COMPOSED OF OVER 400 INDIVIDUAL POINSETTIA PLANTS.

In the rustic, sprawling deck room is the biggest Christmas tree, sheltering a Buster Brown doll, a set of blocks, and other Victorian toys on the floor. Gifts waiting to be unwrapped sit atop the piano and there's a bowl with candy canes and walnuts for holiday revelers.

But people coming to Newport want to see lavishness and luxury and you will find that in the resort town, too. Every year the Preservation Society of Newport County, which maintains eight area mansions and other attractions year round, decorates three of them for Christmas. The list varies from year to year, but when we visited Marble House, The Breakers, and Green Animals were dressed for the holidays.

What might seem like a poinsettia on steroids is the center of attention in the ballroom of **Marble House**. The 22-foot-high poinsettia tree is actually composed of over 400 individual poinsettias, and its vibrant red contrasts vividly with the gold leaf on the room's walls and ceiling.

Poinsettias are in profusion in Marble House: pink ones on the floor of the Gothic Room, white ones in Consuelo Vanderbilt's bedroom, red ones in the guest bedroom where the Ninth Duke of Marlborough once slept, and in the library, trunks of two different colored kinds of poinsettia twisted together to appear like one with both red and white blossoms.

Over at that other stately Vanderbilt villa, **The Breakers**, a towering 35-foot-high tree trimmed with white doves and red and silver balls stands like a fir colossus in the Great Hall. Between the tree and the Grand Staircase is a black, curved sleigh out of the Gay Nineties, packed with giftwrapped presents. Overhead hangs a flowerpot of red poinsettias, while lining the red carpet along the staircase is a line of white poinsettias standing like tin soldiers. It's a tableau that would have suited Cornelius Vanderbilt II grandly.

There's another Christmas tree in The Breakers. It is in the library and wears a proper gown of Victorian white; hanging on its branches are white beads, white lights, white snowflakes, and white electric candles. Underneath is a crèche with a model train set, a big, stuffed bear, and several boxes still to be unwrapped.

From the library you step inside the music room, where strains of "O Come All Ye Faithful," among other carols, are heard on a newly manufactured but old-fashioned-appearing music box. Perhaps you will hear "O Christmas Tree" while you admire the cone-shaped, dark green topiaries and the pomegranates laced with ribbons at their bases.

Even the doll house dons Christmas greens at the Brayton House, the main residence at the seven-acre estate called **Green Animals**, ten miles north of Newport in Portsmouth. Best known in summer for its sculpted topiaries that make a zoo of green, in December it's the house's toy collection that is spotlighted.

A proud and patriotic Victorian Christmas tree in the Brayton House brims with paper fans, miniature flags, tiny French horns, lace hearts, rosy red apples, toy soldiers blowing bugles, and paper doll chains. Underneath are occupants of a nineteenth-century toy chest: Indian clubs, dolls, cradles, and a Chinese checkers set. In another room is a stuffed giraffe wearing a red ribbon for the occasion, and in the children's play room you can see floral arrangements of snapdragons and carnations, proving that there is Christmas flora beyond the poinsettia.

The holiday decorations are not limited to toys at Green Animals's Brayton House. An 1870s sideboard is swathed with balsam, holly, pine, pinecones, and fresh fruit such as apples, pomegranates, and some hardy, dwarf oranges grown right on the mansion grounds, over a thousand miles north of sunny Florida.

Because of heavy visitation at Christmas, the Newport Preservation Society dispenses with guided tours and lets you explore the mansions on your own. At each place your visit is concluded with some holiday munchies like Christmas cookies, cold cider, and eggnog.

Each Sunday a different mansion hosts live music and sometimes a visit from the jolly, red-suited one, too. When we visited we ran into Santa at Green Animals and watched him hand out candy canes to little ones while a trio of musicians on clarinet, bass, and guitar serenaded us with "Santa Claus is Coming to Town" and other timely tunes.

Should these peeks into the life of the upper crust rouse your interest, you can join the cream of high society at a Victorian Christmas Dinner with the Astors, presented at **Mrs. Astor's Beechwood**, the Bellevue Avenue mansion where it's always 1891 and your guides are actors and actresses playing Mrs. Astor's guests and employees.

For two and a half hours you will dine on gourmet entrées like roast turkey with sausage meat stuffing or braised leg of lamb in wine, while the Astors and their guests entertain you with "It Came Upon a Midnight Clear" or "Angels We Have Heard on High," and the distinguished Mr. Stuyvesant Fish explains

Each Sunday a different mansion hosts live music and sometimes a visit from the jolly, red-suited one, too.

the derivation of the wassail bowl before all drink up. A holiday tour of the mansion is also on tap, and you can learn about Victorian traditions and party games like "Ring, Ring, Who's Got the Ring?"

If you can't join the Astors for dinner, you can still take a 45-minute-long guided tour, as someone like John Jacob Astor IV leads you about his festively decorated home. In the Music Room, the butler, head housekeeper ("who happens to be a marvelous soprano," says young Mr. Astor), and distinguished guests like Mr. James Roosevelt and Mrs. Stuyvesant Fish practice songs around the piano. The housekeeper, Mrs. Florence Lightfoot, then solos with, "I Wonder as I Wander," before the whole group renders "Deck the Halls."

The Music Room Christmas tree, meanwhile, is resplendent in pure Victorian white. As we enter the room, Mrs. Fish says to a tourist wearing a dress hanging above her knee, "My dear, you have a terrible shrinkage problem."

At **Belcourt Castle**, just down the road from Beechwood, you might not get to pamper yourself with a full Gilded Age meal but you do have the luxury of sampling the choicest of desserts at the two-hour-long Sunday afternoon Christmas tea. For the first hour, you assemble in the castle's French Gothic Ballroom, known for its original suits of armor and thirteenth-century stained glass, for a concert of carols performed on organ and recorder and by the silk-toned voices of the Rhode Island Touring Ensemble.

For the second hour, you head downstairs to the Italian Banquet Hall, where spread before you is a table topped with a glutton's fantasy feast of desserts. We counted hazelnut torte, chocolate brownies, sugar cookies, chocolate fudge torte, nut breads, Danish, and coconut chocolate chip cookies, and we stopped counting when we were too stuffed to breathe. Oh yes, to wash it down there are tea, eggnog, and holiday punch.

All the while you are encouraged to sing along as the ensemble renders time-honored carols like "Away in a Manger," "I'll Be Home for Christmas," and "Joy to the World" (no, not the one by Three Dog Night). We joined in for the few seconds when we weren't chowing down on some cookie, cake, or brownie.

Along with the pastry and music, admission entitles you to a tour of the castle, a Gilded Age medieval-style chateau built by banker Oliver Belmont, and currently home to caretakers and collectors Donald Tinney and family. (You can regularly tour the castle at other times, too.)

We found wreaths of green on the secret doors in the library, and the Tinneys' tree of peace, trimmed with likenesses of doves and white lights, in the family dining room. The largest tree, arrayed with garlands and balls of silver, stood in the upstairs ball room, while the hand-carved wood staircase, all 365 balusters of it, was covered with pine and red ribbon. A wreath of statice and pink poinsettia proved that the color red doesn't enjoy a monopoly on their Christmas embellishments.

Of course, the Christmas decorations only supplement the castle's year-round abundance of treasures like the German throne chairs, the desk from China's Ching Dynasty, and the tenth-century bed made for the Maharajah of India. Of these gems, guide and resident Harle Tinney says, "We are caretakers. It is important that we take care of them and share them with other people."

And regarding the luscious tea, she adds, "It is the type of thing that would have been conceived in the Victorian era. Having a party like this is the best reward of living at Belcourt."

Numerous other special events have become part of the Christmas in Newport celebration. The official opening, always on December 1 in Washington Square, starts off with a bang as cannons fire their blasts welcoming the eagerly anticipated festival. A warming bonfire, a carol sing, and cookies and cider are further opening trademarks.

The **Festival of Trees** is a forest of firs, about 70 in all and each decorated differently, that takes place at the Naval Underwater System Center gym. James Van Alen, former President of the International Tennis Hall of Fame, another Newport landmark, routinely recites Clement C. Moore's " 'Twas the Night Before Christmas" and there are ample offerings of children's stories, carol sings, and teas served up by area museums or churches. On the three days after Christmas, you can embark on a look into Newport's private world as candlelight house tours of historic private homes are given.

For a calendar of events or other information about Newport's big December blowout, contact Christmas in Newport, P.O. Box 716, Newport, RI 02840; (401) 849–6454 evenings. For questions specifically about the mansions, call (401) 847–1000.

THE MANSION AT BLITHEWOLD GARDENS AND ARBORETUM IS
DECKED WITH A 20-FOOT-HIGH CHRISTMAS TREE.

OTHER CHRISTMAS ACTIVITIES

WHAT OTHER WAYS are there to celebrate the season in New England? Try the following state by state sampler.

Rhode Island

NEWPORT HOLDS NO exclusivity on Christmas splendor in the Ocean State. **Blithewold Gardens and Arboretum** in Bristol, which closes its doors for the season in October, reopens in December with the 45-room mansion dressed in its best holiday apparel. The theme changes every year, but you can always count on seeing a two-story-high Christmas tree in the front hall decorated in glowing turn-of-the-century style.

One year, when the theme was "A Child's Christmas," Chinese lanterns and sugar plums dangled on the tree's branches and a replica of an old-time toy train wound its way around its base on the floor. Another year, when the *Nutcracker Suite* was the theme, tiny musical instruments bedecked a wall wreath and tiny toy ballerinas hung from the king-sized tree.

When "Winter Wedding: A Romantic Christmas" was the theme, the home was heavy on flowers, with a bridal Christmas tree trimmed in silver and gold sheltering wedding gifts underneath it. Hot mulled cider is always served. Blithewold Gardens and Arboretum, Ferry Road, Bristol, RI 02809; (401) 253-2707.

In Providence, the elegant Georgian **John Brown House** at Power and Benefit Streets sports different Christmas decorations yearly. One December the house was abounding in Edwardian-style holiday decor. Another time, the parlor with an eighteenth-century piano was arrayed with silver miniature French horns and other musical instruments, while apples, lemons, and limes combined with laurel and other greens to beautify the dining room. The pre-Victorian room, however, is almost always a repository for children's toys.

A nineteenth-century German music box is the source of the classic Christmas melodies heard as you tour the mansion. An open house with free admission and live music is scheduled on one Sunday in December. Rhode Island Historical Society, 110

THE MERRY BOAR'S HEAD PROCESSION CLOSES THE SHOW AT A CELEBRATION OF TWELFTH NIGHT IN WESTERLY.

Benevolent Street, Providence, RI 02906; (401) 331–8593.

Say goodbye to Christmas on the weekend closest to January 6, in Westerly, with a 90-minute-long rollicking Renaissance-style program called **A Celebration of Twelfth Night**, where you drink wassail from royal goblets and watch entertainment provided by court jesters, jugglers, magicians, and mimes. The 200-voice Chorus of Westerly joins bagpipers, brass players, and other musicians, as they render holiday sounds as disparate as the fifteenth-century "Good Ale" and the standard "O Come All Ye Faithful," in celebration of Epiphany.

Then there are customary acts like the peasants' feast and the boar's head procession, and the sometimes-customary acts like "Twelve Days of Christmas" acted out on stage by actors and actresses dressed the parts of drummers drumming, pipers piping, lords a-leaping, maids a-milking, a partridge, and a trio of French hens. And wait until you see the French hens! The Chorus of Westerly, P.O. Box 132, Westerly, RI 02891; (401) 596–8663.

DURING MYSTIC SEAPORT'S YULETIDE TOURS, YOU'LL MEET MANY RESIDENTS OF THE NINETEENTH CENTURY DRESSED IN THEIR SEASONAL BEST.

Connecticut

At **Mystic Seaport** in Mystic you may find Christmas trees in some unexpected places, like atop the 100-foot-high masts of the ships *Charles W. Morgan* and *Joseph Conrad*, for example. This custom dates to the turn of the century, when sailors on ships in port would observe the holiday by placing an evergreen tree at the top of the rigging. Local garden clubs help decorate many of the village doorways with traditional greens and arrangements.

Annual traditions at Mystic are daytime Yuletide Tours and evening Lantern Light Tours. **Yuletide Tours** vary but might consist of a look inside the Burrows House with a tree decorated with handmade ornaments followed by a concert of sea chanteys.

On the **Lantern Light Tours** you will be led around the village, where you will find a cast of players in nineteenth-century costume portraying the townspeople of 1800s Mystic. You might ride in a Victorian-style omnibus behind a team of horses, or possibly spend time melodizing a round of carols in the village tavern. Lantern Light Tours tickets are quite the item in Connecticut. They go on sale October 1 and have a habit of selling out immediately.

You can always get a glimpse of a nineteenth-century seaside December without taking a special tour, since the village decorates for the holidays and keeps regular hours throughout the month. Mystic's planetarium presents seasonal shows in December, which in the past have focused on theories of the origin of the Christmas star and a look at winter's celestial events. Mystic Seaport, 50 Greenmanville Avenue, P.O. Box 6000, Mystic, CT 06355; (203) 572–0711.

A Victorian Christmas is portrayed at Wethersfield's **Captain James Francis House** where, true to Victorian tradition, you might see a Christmas tree, three to five feet high, set on a table and replete with hand-blown German glass ornaments and bead decorations. Open hearth cooking demonstrations and Christmas stockings filled with homemade candies might too be on tap. Wethersfield Historical Society, 150 Main Street, Wethersfield, CT 06109; (203) 529–7656.

Christmas on Main Street is an urban Victorian Christmas in downtown Hartford. The **Butler-McCook Homestead**, a rare clapboard home in the center city, was arranged, one year, according to family diaries. The paper-covered wooden boxes supporting a modest tree were used by the McCooks from 1875 to 1933, and the toys on view were part of the house collection. The dining room was set for Christmas dinner, thanks to the McCooks' Rose Medallion export porcelain. In some years, Hartford's **Isham-Terry House** may be garbed for the holiday instead of the Butler-McCook House. Another seasonal display is **Holidayfest**, an arts and crafts display at Hatheway House and the King House Museum in Suffield. The Antiquarian and Landmarks Society, Inc., 394 Main Street, Hartford, CT 06103; (203) 247–8996.

An old letter is the basis for the Christmas arrangements in another Hartford landmark, the **Harriet Beecher Stowe House**. The author's teenage daughter described the family tree as being topped with a fairy doll "in white gauze with gilt spangles and a gilt wand with a star on the end and gauze wings spangled with gold." And so one year there was a doll at the tree's summit when twentieth-century visitors filed by. The **Mark Twain House** next door is also duly decorated. Stowe-Day Foundation, 77 Forest Street, Hartford, CT 06105; (203) 525–9317. Mark Twain House, 351 Farmington Avenue, Hartford, CT 06105; (203) 247–0998.

It is not known how distinguished actor and playwright William Gillette costumed his eccentric mansion for the holidays, but in a tribute to Sherlock Holmes, Gillette's most famous character, **Gillette Castle** in East Haddam is dressed according to an English Victorian theme. You can likely see a 15-foot-high cedar Christmas tree, upwards of 50 wreaths hanging from the woodwork, poinsettias, green garlands, a representation of Santa's workshop, and an English village. Gillette Castle State Park, East Haddam, CT 06423; (203) 526–2336.

Santa trades his sleigh for trolley tracks at both of Connecticut's trolley museums, where trolley cars are decorated with lights, wreaths, or tinsel, and Santa meets kids on the grounds. Connecticut Trolley Museum, Route 140, P.O. Box 360, East Windsor, CT 06088; (203) 627–6540; Shore Line Trolley Museum, 17 River Street, East Haven, CT 06512; (203) 467–6927.

Maine

BILLIE GAMMON, DIRECTOR of Norlands Living History Center in tiny Livermore Falls, emphasizes, "There's no plastic at **Country Christmas at Norlands**," a weekend when the Washburn homestead dons a mirthful circa 1853 Christmas outfit, with a tree sporting popcorn and cranberry strings, and lace paper fans. Leave your diet at the door as you start the day with a hearty farmer's breakfast, perhaps consisting of scrambled eggs, ham, home-fried potatoes, biscuits, muffins, and coffee. The outing continues with a horse-drawn sleigh ride through the Maine countryside, followed by carol singing in the old church. A country noon meal is also served, and there's wassail served by the fire in the Israel Washburn parlor. Norlands Living History Center, RD 2, Box 3395, Livermore Falls, ME 04254; (207) 897–2236.

Santa arrives by lobster boat—naturally—at Kennebunkport's **Christmas Prelude**. This seaside season's greeting also has included a lighthouse lighting, outdoor candlelight caroling, hay rides, a fish chowder supper, a lobster dinner, and a community *Messiah* sing. The lighting of the outdoor Christmas tree in Dock Square is the official kickoff for the Prelude, which lasts over two weekends. Kennebunkport Business Association, P.O. Box 1178, Kennebunkport, ME 04046; (207) 967–0858.

Massachusetts

THE GOTHIC-STYLE great hall in Gloucester's majestic **Hammond Castle** is the setting for a series of Christmas concerts, while the castle's pipe organ—claimed to be the largest in any private residence in the world—is the source of the music. The programs are highlighted by both traditional favorites and classical selections, but there might be a sing-along to some of the melodies we have known since Mrs. Crosby's third grade music class. Hammond Castle, 80 Hesperus Avenue, Gloucester, MA 01930; (800) 649–1930, or (508) 283–2081.

Pick up some decorating ideas for your home at Cape Cod's **Thornton W. Burgess Museum**, which hosts its Victorian Christmas Open House one weekend in early December. The museum's tree will be trimmed with natural decorations based on those illustrating Victorian magazines or books. You might also hear seasonal sounds performed by a harp player, bell ringers, or a choral group, as you sample Christmas punch or pastries. Youngsters can keep busy making ornaments or other handcrafts in the museum's discovery room. Thornton W. Burgess Society, 6 Discovery Hill Road, East Sandwich, MA 02537; (508) 888–6870.

Over 200,000 multi-colored lights transform a five-and-a-half-mile-long train ride into a Christmas enchantment in November and December at **Edaville Railroad** in South Carver. Amid the lights and trees are 30-odd holiday displays depicting elves at play, winter settings, or Santa Claus, all seen as you chug by aboard the steam railroad. Edaville Railroad, Route 58, South Carver, MA 02366; (508) 866–4526.

The Shaker tradition of donating toys and foods to the less fortunate is continued as part of **Hancock Shaker Village**'s Christmas weekend. Visitors are requested to bring a new toy or can of food, which will be distributed to needy people by the Salvation Army. In return you get free admission, a look at the village's 1830 Brick Dwelling arranged in Shaker 1930s style, a chance to make small ornaments out of natural materials, a sampling of cookies baked in the brick oven, and a swallow of hot mulled cider warmed on the wood stove.

The decorations are accurate reproductions based upon photographs and descriptions by Shaker sisters. The Shaker building, as one might expect, wore a festive but not gaudy face, with red and green paper chains in the dining room, a modestly decorated tree, and paper birds hanging from the dining room ceiling. Hancock Shaker Village, P.O. Box 898, Pittsfield, MA 01201; (413) 443–0188.

The famous Shoppers' Stroll, part of **Nantucket Noel**, takes place down Main Street in the nineteenth-century village of Nantucket on a Saturday in early December. Costumed carolers, a brass ensemble, magicians, and mimes might entertain you as you browse or buy at any of the shops or at shows sponsored by groups like Nantucket Artists' Association and Nantucket Craft Alliance. To give your purse a break, join one of the house tours of private homes decorated for the holidays. Nantucket Island Chamber of Commerce, Pacific Club Building, Nantucket, MA 02554; (508) 228–1700.

Out in the Berkshires, the Lenox Chamber of Commerce presents its own **Christmas House Tour** of private homes. The Lenox event occurs the last Saturday of the year and features costumed hosts in decorated homes with period music and refreshments. Lenox Chamber of Commerce, 75 Main Street, Lenox, MA 01240; (413) 637–3646.

Halloween isn't the only time for Salem to shine like a magic wand. The Witch City's month-long **Holiday Happenings** have included house tours, gift-making demonstrations, caroling, candlelight tours of the House of Seven Gables, storytellers, mimes, musicians, and a Christmas art show. The Peabody Museum often offers their Winter Moon Celebration with crafts, games, and food centered around our only natural satellite. The man in the moon won't be in attendance but children will probably find Santa Claus in his place. Salem Chamber of Commerce, 32 Derby Square, Salem, MA 01970; (508) 744–0004.

THREE CROWN-TOPPED CAST MEMBERS HOLD MAYHEM, THE RESIDENT FOOL, IN BOSTON'S FESTIVAL OF LIGHT AND SONG.

Long before the existence of Jesus, humankind was celebrating the winter solstice and the renewal of light that continues the cycle of seasons for eternity. The rejoicing continues with Boston's **Annual**

Festival of Light and Song, a musical and multi-cultural tribute to this grand phenomenon of nature. The chorus interprets songs of pagan, Jewish, and Christian origin, and always banishes a mid-winter demon as part of its performance. And don't be surprised during the two-hour-long program if a performer hops into the audience and hands you a *survachka* (an adorned tree branch and Bulgarian good luck symbol) or a *dreidel* (a small top children play with during Chanukah). Audience participation is a major part of the show. SONG, P.O. Box 27, Cambridge, MA 02140; (617) 861–0649.

Uncommon Boston takes strollers on a Victorian Christmas tour, which customarily includes a walk around Beacon Hill, looks at some area homes dolled up for the holidays, and a stop in a Victorian parlor for a sip of holiday grog. The outing lasts about three hours, usually on a Saturday afternoon. Uncommon Boston, 437 Boylston Street, 4th floor, Boston, MA 02116; (617) 731–5854.

New Hampshire

YOU WILL FIND a Victorian atmosphere on the streets of Hanover during the city's annual **Dickens of a Christmas** when merchants dress in top hats, ruffled shirts, and other Victorian garb, and choral groups interpret songs of the season while shoppers rush in and out of downtown stores; these live renderings sure beat the canned Muzak you will hear ad nauseam in department stores. You might also inhale the scents of roasted chestnuts in the chilly New Hampshire air, or taste English treats like *bangers and mashed* (translated into American as mild sausage and mashed potatoes) or fish and chips at Hanover's restaurants. Hanover Chamber of Commerce, P.O. Box A105, Hanover, NH 03755; (603) 643–3115.

Also in Hanover is the annual performance of the **Christmas Revels** at Dartmouth College. The Revels honor the coming of the winter solstice and revival of light with a combination of dance, song, theater, and yes, revelry. Each year the minstrels, puppeteers, singers, and actors take you to a different time and place. In the past they have journeyed to medieval Russia, Renaissance Italy, Victorian England, and the American Old West. (603) 646–2422.

THE HISTORICALLY ACCURATE TABLE-TOP VICTORIAN CHRISTMAS TREE,
TRIMMED WITH BEADS, GLASS ORNAMENTS, AND PAPER FANS,
CAN BE FOUND AT STRAWBERY BANKE'S GOODWIN HOUSE.

The **Candlelight Stroll** at Strawbery Banke, the living museum neighborhood in Portsmouth, is designed to illustrate the evolution of the Christmas celebration in America and New England. So while the Chase House, where George Washington kissed Stephen Chase's three young daughters following a 1789 reception, is all dried flowers and greenery, the Victorian mode of the Goodwin House means a pinecone wreath on the front door, gilt letters spelling out "MXMAS," and a table-top Christmas tree trimmed with beads, glass ornaments, and paper fans.

Lights and luminaria illumine the narrow streets of dirt and gravel. Saint Nicholas, wearing a purple bishop's gown, might make an appearance and the dining rooms of the historic houses can sport everything from a gingerbread village in the circa 1795 Winn House to a splendorous setting of roasted goose with quince jelly, peas, beets, and mashed potatoes in the Georgian- and Federal-style Walsh House. Craftspersons such as a cooper, a potter, and a weaver might be on hand to demonstrate their skills, and music can be heard as you fill up with hot mulled cider and doughnuts. And the Dunaway Store, with its crafts and other quality gift items, is always open for shopping. Strawbery Banke, P.O. Box 300, Portsmouth, NH 03801; (603) 433–1100.

Vermont

THE HIGHLIGHT OF Woodstock's four-day-long **Wassail Christmas Celebration** might be the old-fashioned sleigh procession, where 50 sleighs (or carriages if nature doesn't cooperate with snow), led by reinsmen in nineteenth-century clothing like tall silk hats and riding habits, parade through town. The burning of a yule log on Woodstock's spacious village green follows. The Revere Handbell Choir usually rings out a round or two of holiday songs, there's a Wassail Royal Feast at the Woodstock Inn, a Wassail Cotillion with big band music, a *Messiah* sing-in, and a visit from Santa in a horse-drawn wagon. Woodstock Chamber of Commerce, P.O. Box 486, Woodstock, VT 05091; (802) 457–3555.

A **Victorian Christmas at Billings Farm & Museum**, the combination working dairy farm and 1890s agriculture museum in Woodstock, means tasting hot wassail in the kitchen and drinking in the nineteenth-century atmosphere, like hemlock and spruce draped over the mantels, windows, and doorways of the farm manager's house, on weekends in December. Reflecting the agrarian setting, many of the Christmas tree ornaments are items you'd find growing on this type of farm, and include dried apples, pinecones, and acorns, as well as other more exotic produce like oranges. Billings Farm & Museum, P.O. Box 489, Woodstock, VT 05091; (802) 457–2355.

During **Christmas at the Shelburne Museum**, visitors get a peek into the diverse holiday settings found in the period homes of different nineteenth-century Vermonters in this multi-building museum complex. The elegant Oriental silks and porcelains in the home of a wealthy retired sea captain contrast sharply with the homemade wooden toys in the simple Sawyer's Cabin. And while you are here, hop aboard a horse-drawn sleigh or carriage, watch a wood carver fashion a toy duck, or participate in a yule log search. Shelburne Museum, Shelburne, VT 05482; (802) 985–3346.

FIRST NIGHTS

It seems that ever since Guy Lombardo first led the Royal Canadians in "Auld Lang Syne," people wanting to celebrate New Year's Eve have had two simple choices: stepping out to a wild party and dodging drunk drivers on the way, or being a stick in the mud and staying home.

That is until 1976, when a group of aficionados of the arts in Boston started the tradition of **First Night**, a day-long festival supplying culture and entertainment without alcohol and the obligatory buffoon with a lamp shade on his head.

First Nights have since spread across the country like the common cold in a crowded office, and as we went to press there were over a dozen First Nights taking place on New Year's Eve throughout New England.

From Boston to Stamford to Burlington, Vermont, revelers spend December 31 staring at stilt walkers, appraising ice and snow sculptures of monumental proportions (a life-sized Concord coach graced the State House Plaza in Concord, New Hampshire, one year), gaping at 12-foot-tall puppets meandering through downtown streets, and enjoying entertainment provided by comedians, jugglers, marionettes, ventriloquists, storytellers, mimes, and musicians of

every style, before witnessing a grand finale of fireworks exploding with bursts of color and noise in the
winter sky.

KINGS, A QUEEN, AND A
JOKER ON PARADE AT FIRST
NIGHT BOSTON.

At most First Nights, the crowds, usually top-heavy
with kids, begin assembling in the afternoon, some as
early as noon, and can be seen weaving through the
thoroughfares or populating the sanctuaries of Gothic
churches, the gymnasiums of YMCAs, the lobbies of
business buildings, or the auditoriums of dignified,
old theaters. Afternoons are usually ripe with amusement and activities children relish, and by evening,
it's not uncommon to see swarms of young ones with
faces painted and balloons in their hands or funny
hats on their heads. Parades featuring ethnic dancers
or perhaps a unicyclist or two are often part of the
party.

At some First Nights, adults dress in costume. One
First Night in Boston produced audience members
incognito as cats, dogs, and punk rockers, in addition
to a man garbed in a red union suit, a pair of green
running shorts, and an upside-down "S" pinned onto
his chest, calling himself Stupidman.

In the evening the downtown streets swell with
celebrants, and at half hour intervals they can be
seen heading en masse to scheduled shows. At times,
they might stop to stare at living mannequins, mimes,
or musicians in storefront windows. Crowds are large

but rarely rowdy. This is no Mardi Gras. Like it or not, there are no topless women; there is little to instill worry or distress in the mind of a protective parent, even late into the night.

First Night began in Boston, with clones manifesting themselves in big cities across North America like Denver, Buffalo, Vancouver, and Honolulu; yet New England's smaller cities and towns have found themselves fraught with diversity. At a First Night celebration in Keene, New Hampshire, we sampled selections of bluegrass, rockabilly, improvisational, and chamber music in a little over four hours. At the Granite State's **First Night New Hampshire** in Concord, we were entertained over a similar time span with offerings from a big band à la Glenn Miller, a folk quartet, and a jazz ensemble known for making music on an endless array of instruments from countries and cultures around the world.

If we had mastered the art of being in more than one place at one time at either event, we could have taken in Gospel, Motown, swing, pops, classical, Dixieland, and music from Scotland, Israel, French Canada, Elizabethan England, and Vienna, to say nothing of the comics, storytellers, puppeteers, and others performing their hearts out.

Such smorgasbords of talent are not unusual. A First Night in Providence served up sea chanteys, rap, Klezmer music, Irish *ceili* dancing, and Chinese folk and modern tunes, while some of the specialty offerings at a First Night Hartford consisted of West Indian dancing, polkas, Native American music, Afro-Cuban jazz, and music and dance from India.

To enter most First Night performances you simply need to buy a button for a fairly nominal price, which serves as your admission ticket for the whole night. Street performances and storefront window entertainment are usually presented gratis.

The initial First Night in the Hub City was actually an offshoot of the bicentennial brouhaha of 1976. It was born when Zeren Earls, current president and executive director of Boston's First Night, joined some friends of the arts in devising an alternative method of ringing in the year. Earls says: "Many people welcomed it as an appropriate finale to the bicentennial, but it was not considered a one-shot deal from day one. We thought it would become a tradition as an alternative to standard New Year's Eve celebrations."

She recalls First Night's debut: "It was a popular event from day one. We got more people than we anticipated that year. The police estimated 60,000 on the streets.

"We thought it would grow, but not at the pace it has been. It was started very much for the Boston community. But we began getting inquiries from other New England cities in the first five years."

Nowadays Boston's First Night brings 600,000 to the city—from Boston Common to City Hall Plaza to the harbor for fireworks—and thousands more to the downtowns of communities across New England. First Nights can be found in the following New England cities and towns.

Massachusetts

First Night Boston	(617) 542–1399
First Night New Bedford	(508) 993–2911
First Night Worcester	(508) 799–1726
First Night Newburyport	(508) 465–6004
First Night Northampton	(413) 584–7327

Connecticut

First Night Hartford	(203) 728–3089
First Night Stamford	(203) 327–0555
First Night Danbury	(203) 350–8881

Rhode Island

First Night Providence	(401) 521–1166

New Hampshire

First Night New Hampshire (Concord)	(603) 224–1411
First Night Keene	(603) 357–3906
First Night Portsmouth	(603) 431–5388

Vermont

First Night Burlington	(802) 863–6005
First Night Rutland	(802) 747–4505

Maine

New Year's/Portland	(207) 772–9012
New Year's Eve Houlton	(207) 532–4216

(similar event not affiliated with First Night, Inc.)

THE ART OF
SNOWSHOEING

"YOU CAN GO anywhere you damn well please and not follow 50,000 fannies in front of you."

So says a representative of one of the leading snowshoe manufacturers in the nation, when asked why he prefers snowshoeing over cross-country skiing.

The popularity of snowshoeing as a sport is at the spot on the popularity meter that cross-country skiing held a generation ago. Which is the very reason why many don't mind spending an entire winter without clasping a pair of cross-country skis to their feet.

Whereas cross-country skiing became a fashionable social activity in the 1980s, the confirmed snowshoer would rather let the crowds take their Brie cheese and wine and be on their merry ways while he accepts the advice of Robert Frost and follows the road not taken.

"Snowshoers are individualists. They tend to go off on their own," says one ardent snowshoer.

Of course, the snowshoe lends itself to those who wish to trek off into the unknown. Because of its very nature, the snowshoe is used for walking on,

THE BEARPAW, LEFT, HAS ALWAYS BEEN A TRADITIONAL SNOWSHOE WHILE THE NARROWER JUNIOR ALASKAN, RIGHT, IS FOR MORE MODIFIED TASTES.

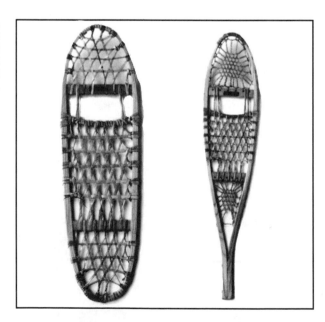

rather than gliding in, snow. You don't need nor want groomed trails; that would defeat the purpose.

Step into these shoes and you are able to reach places skis would never take you. It is possible to walk among the brush and twigs in the dense woods. A cross-country skier will go further than a snowshoer in an identical time span. But if your purpose is to cover a lot of ground in a short amount of time, you should not be on snowshoes. The snowshoer's pace is slower, more deliberate. The snowshoer wants to savor, not gobble.

There was a time when a snowshoe, like a desk telephone or a Model T, came in one form. They were made of wood, New England white ash, usually, and were laced with rawhide.

Enter new technology. Neoprene, a synthetic rubber, replaced rawhide as the lacing material. Then came aluminum, which substituted for wood. And then there was aluminum with neoprene, taking over for both wood and rawhide stitching.

Why these intrusions into the world of winter fun? Basically, these synthetics offered snowshoers more convenience with less maintenance.

Yet many veteran snowshoers will say that real snowshoers don't wear neoprene. And the same for aluminum.

Says a veteran snowshoe manufacturer, "Traditionalists, old-timers, hunters, ice fishermen, and trappers prefer wood. It looks better and they are accustomed to it. The people who buy aluminum are usually college educated and more high-tech oriented."

A Chicago-based company, Sherpa, Inc., was among the first to make aluminum snowshoes. They called theirs "Snow-Claws."

The "claw" can either be a three-sided serrated crampon or one with six triangular teeth one-and-a-half inches long. While aluminum shoes need less maintenance, some snowshoers prefer them because they are lighter than wood ones and the crampon offers more opportunity to tackle icy conditions or steep mountainsides.

One snowshoe enthusiast who swears by Sherpa's aluminum shoes said they are easier to use, with less cumbersome bindings, and are also more durable. He recalled a time when he was walking down a slope and had to bridge a small gap with the toe and heel of his shoe. A wooden shoe would have cracked or warped, he said, but the aluminum shoe showed nary a scratch.

Wooden shoes also have their backers. John

SNOWSHOES ALLOW THOSE IN SEARCH OF WINTER RECREATION THE OPPORTUNITY
TO FOLLOW IN THE WORDS OF ROBERT FROST, "THE ROAD NOT TAKEN."

Summers, owner of Summers Backcountry Sports store in Keene, New Hampshire, recommends wood with rawhide over neoprene. Why?

Replies Summers: "Rawhide has twice the abrasion resistance of neoprene. With enough exposure to hard-crusted snow and ice, the bed of the neoprene snowshoe can be abated to the point that the lacing falls right out of it. Also, rawhide is laced wet into a snowshoe and dries tight. Neoprene is not laced as tight as rawhide."

So both have their supporters. The industry has learned that, too. Sherpa has since released a wooden snowshoe, and Vermont Tubbs, Inc., one of the leading manufacturers of wooden snowshoes, now makes a metal-frame shoe.

The heritage of the snowshoe, however, goes back a long way. It is believed that snowshoes may have their origins in Biblical times. Evidence has been uncovered which causes some to theorize that primitive snowshoes may have been used in Europe and Asia as long as 2,000 years ago.

But the North American Indian was more directly responsible for the development of the snowshoe. Depending where they lived, Indians adapted snowshoes to their topography. Those living in treeless plains tended to use long, narrow, pointed shoes. Indians in forested areas like New England crafted a shorter, wider, rounder snowshoe, making it more maneuverable in underbrush and in the woods.

Beaver tails. Ojibwas. Pickerells. Bearpaws. These are not the names of rock groups or old USFL football teams. They are styles of snowshoes, many of which have been around for a long time and are used for specific purposes.

For example, a New Hampshire hunter who enjoys practicing his hobby in the remote Connecticut Lakes Region of the Granite State's northern fringes takes a pair of beaver tails with him. They are 14 inches wide, about three feet long, and are favored by hunters and trappers because their short length makes them manageable in the brush.

Ojibwas and pickerells are specialty types used for long trail walking or perhaps ice fishing.

But the most popular types today are modified bearpaws and cross-country-style snowshoes. Both are modern adaptations of older traditional styles. The bearpaw was almost round in shape, was used before and during World War II, and became popular almost by accident, according to John Summers.

Says Summers: "The Army ordered two different types of snowshoes, a 10-by-60-inch model called the

Alaskan or Yukon, and the bearpaw. When the war was over, the flat, oval bearpaw came out by the thousands with "U.S. Army" stamped on it. The consuming public said to themselves if it was good enough for the Army, this is what we should use."

The modified bearpaw, also known as the Green Mountain style, is shorter than the bearpaw, elliptical rather than rounded, and turned up about three inches at the toe. It is narrow (ten inches wide) and short (36 inches long), and enables a person to move around with ease in twigs and brush.

Long and narrow, the cross-country style evolved from a traditional longer and wider shoe called the Michigan or Maine model. The cross-country snowshoe, 10 by 46 inches, is a favorite of those who wish to snowshoe for pleasure in wide, open areas.

Such terrain is the place for you if you are trying snowshoeing for the first time. If you are concerned about learning technique, don't be. There isn't any. Advises one snowshoe partisan, "Anyone who can walk can snowshoe."

But you do need to practice a bit. A merchandise distributor at one major sporting goods manufacturer in New Hampshire recommends that novices "out for the first time go to some place that's fairly flat to get the feel of wearing snowshoes, before going up a steep grade. You don't need to know as much about technique as you do with cross-country skiing. The snowshoes become extensions of your feet and you'll have to walk a little bow-legged. It takes some getting used to."

Those purchasing snowshoes like the modified bearpaw or the cross-country might be able to skip the bow-legged walk. Because they are less wide than other more traditional types, it is easier to keep your legs closer together and walk in a more normal gait.

The consensus among snowshoers and sporting goods dealers is that snowshoeing isn't as physically exerting as cross-country skiing. You don't use as many muscles on snowshoes, but you should still be in reasonably good condition. Says a veteran: "After you've finished, you'll feel it."

SNOWSHOE SUGGESTIONS

WHERE CAN ONE find ample ground to wander around in the outdoors with a pair of snowshoes attached to his or her feet? Just about any place where there is a plentiful supply of snow. If you are looking for a few specific ideas, consider these suggestions from some experts in each state.

Connecticut

JOE HICKEY AT Connecticut's Bureau of Parks and Forests reports that because of their elevation, **Bigelow Hollow State Park** and **Nipmuck State Forest** on either side of Interstate 84 near Union tend to hold snow and offer agreeable snowshoe opportunities on foot trails and old forest roads. In both parks, the terrain is fairly flat.

In northwestern Connecticut, **Mohawk State Forest** near Cornwall is another snow miser. Since some of the forest sits on a plateau, there is some challenging up and down topography for the snowshoer. **White Memorial Foundation** in nearby Litchfield (two miles west of the center of town, off Route 202) contains 4,000 acres including both flat, open areas and wooded trails.

Maine

JUST ABOUT ANY state park in Maine, says Marshall Wiebe, Director of Public Information for the Maine Department of Conservation, should prove hospitable to snowshoers in search of recreation, but he suggests that those looking for scenery and snow would be happiest in the state's sparsely settled sections. From much of **Aroostook State Park** in Presque Isle you can see Squapan Lake and surrounding mountains. **Cobscook Bay State Park** in the far southeastern corner of the state gets transitory snowfall but offers stellar vistas of Cobscook Bay.

Lily Bay State Park north of Greenville borders Moosehead Lake, while **Rangeley Lake State Park** promises plenty of unplowed roads along the shore of its namesake lake. **Mount Blue State Park** in Weld, northwest of Farmington, presents views of elongated Lake Webb and nearby peaks.

Massachusetts

PERHAPS THE BEST locale to snowshoe in the Bay State, according to Pauline Stieff, of the Bureau of Recreation Department of Environmental Management, is **Savoy Mountain State Forest** in the Berkshires, where you will find an abundance of both level and hilly ground to roam about. The forest, between Routes 2 and 116 north of Savoy, contains 10,000 pristine acres for your snowshoeing pleasure.

Other choice parcels of earth in the Berkshires for snowshoers include **Mount Greylock State Reservation** (10,327 acres) east of Route 7 and north of Lanesboro, and **Clarksburg State Park** (3,250 acres), hugging the Vermont border north of Clarksburg. Also consider **Monroe State Forest**, north of Route 2 and south of Monroe, and **Mohawk Trail State Forest**, along Route 2 west of Charlemont.

Stieff says it is not essential to journey to the Berkshires, though, to find suitable terrain for snowshoers. In Worcester County, there are 1,950 acres at **Wachusett Mountain State Reservation**, along Route 31 north of Princeton. In the northeast, there are 3,000 acres of medium terrain at **Harold Parker State Forest** in North Andover; 476 acres at **Maudslay State Park** in Newburyport; and well-maintained cross-country ski trails at **Great Brook Farm State Park** in Carlisle.

Sprawling **Myles Standish State Forest** (14,635 acres), west of Route 3, between Plymouth and Cape Cod, is available for snowshoers in the southeastern section of the state. Beginners will find the flat terrain of **Ames Nowell State Park** north of Brockton amiable. The closest area to Boston Stieff recommends is **Wompatuck State Park**, off Route 228 in Hingham. In Bristol County, **Freetown State Forest** is congenial to snowshoers. Freetown consists of over 5,000 acres and is located off Route 24 south of Assonet.

New Hampshire

MUCH OF THE state's land is tailored beautifully for snowshoers. However, Kerri Tracy at the New Hampshire Division of Parks and Recreation particularly recommends **Bear Brook** and **Pawtuckaway State Parks**, with their open fields and woods for both easy and challenging terrain. For mainly challenging territory, Tracy suggests snowshoers head north to **Franconia Notch State Park** or west to **Mount Sunapee State Park**.

The hiking trails around Mount Kearsarge, east of Mount Sunapee, also lure snowshoers. Those who select the trails on the **Rollins State Park** side of the mountain will have a tougher go than people choosing to tackle the wider and smoother trails in

Winslow State Park. In the south, there is **Monadnock State Park**, four miles north of Jaffrey, with a wide range of trails. John Summers recommends **Pisgah State Forest** in Chesterfield and Hinsdale, with its well-marked trails and logging roads.

Rhode Island

THE OCEAN STATE'S concise borders and neighboring bodies of water combine to cause a paucity of acreage for the snowshoer. However, Paul Dolan, principal forester for the State of Rhode Island, recommends that those interested in snowshoeing head to the **George Washington Management Area** north of Route 44 in Glocester (five miles west of Chepachet Center) in the northwest corner of the state. There they can ply the rolling, snow-covered gravel roads used by snowmobilers. Unfortunately, Dolan says, the surrounding woods lack sufficient snow cover most of the time.

Vermont

THE ENTIRE **Green Mountain National Forest,** which runs up and down the spine of Vermont, is filled with sections of inviting snow, according to Ray Auger, director of the Catamount Trail Association, a private, non-profit organization responsible for establishing a 280-mile-long cross-country ski trail that will run the length of the state.

In southern portions of the forest, Ray endorses for snowshoers the Stratton Pond and Little Rock Pond areas, part of the Manchester Ranger District. The fairly flat land of the **Silver Lake Recreation Area**, south of Middlebury and part of the Middlebury Ranger District in central Vermont, should interest beginning snowshoers, while **Chittenden Brook Recreation Area** near Rochester has enticing loop trails.

Apart from the national forest, Auger suggests the series of trails in **Groton State Forest**, a mixture of both flat and rolling land in the Northeast Kingdom. Other northern areas Auger recommends are sections of the **Long Trail** surrounding Camel's Hump, south of Bolton, and **Mount Mansfield**, north of Stowe.

OLD FAVORITES IN THE OFF-SEASON

The lobster traps wear a light slicker of snow. Jagged icicles hang from the roof of the Thomas Oyster House, and there's a crust of ice hugging the bow of the Gloucester fishing schooner *L. A. Dunton*. A duo of well-bundled tourists cross the village green, dusted with snow, and enter the Buckingham House. The warmth of a toasty hearth welcomes them inside and they shut the door behind them.

This is **Mystic Seaport** in the off-season. One of a hearty few indoor/outdoor attractions in New England that remains open year round, the recreated seaside community can be as inviting a place to visit in winter as it is in the other three seasons. If you loathe crowds, it can be even more so. Chances are in winter that you won't be swamped by the busloads of schoolchildren that can inundate the seaport in spring and fall, or the tourists that swarm it in summer.

Mystic Seaport in Winter

SEAPORT SPOKESPERSONS say that on winter weekends the grounds can get somewhat busy, although on winter weekdays you might feel as if you have the whole place to yourself. The village is staffed daily and there are living history demonstrations all seven days of the week. We visited on a January weekday and met guide Juanita Babcock in the Buckingham House kitchen, placing an apple pie in a cast-iron Dutch oven.

"Women back then [the 1830s] wouldn't go through the effort of heating up a bake oven just to bake one item," Juanita explained as she placed the kettle on the fire after spreading embers under and atop the pie.

"Since this is a double crust pie I want it to brown on top and on bottom. If I were baking a single crust pie like a pumpkin pie I'd just put embers on the bottom."

Earlier in the day Juanita had baked bean and barley soup and cornbread, and a little of each was left. Standing in the kitchen, bathed in the warmth of the fire, we felt that there was a singular safety in the woman's domain of hearth and home, especially when compared to the 1830s man's world out in the elements. But Juanita was quick to point out: "Having clothing catch on fire was the second leading cause of death for women back then, second only to childbirth. Staying at home could be dangerous.

Weaving, spinning, soap making, and butter making are all demonstrated at one time or another in the Buckingham House, and if you visit in winter you will have a likelier opportunity to give one of these domestic nineteenth-century tasks a try. "You have a chance to get involved hands on, something we can't offer guests when there are 5,000 people here," said Juanita.

The same idea applies to other Mystic village buildings. Guide Dorothy Brewer in Stone's Store, an 1870s emporium stocking hardware and groceries, let us give the hand-operated coffee grinder a whirl. "There are just too many people here in summer to let anyone do that," she stated.

On winter weekdays you might feel as if you have the whole place to yourself.

Dorothy also revealed some historical facts relating to the season. Men, not women, would have done the family shopping here in winter, because the man of the house drove the horse and carriage in cold weather. She described a typical 1870s scene in a store like this: men sitting about playing checkers or spitting tobacco as they discussed local politics, while a wood-burning stove kept them warm.

The staff at today's Mystic also does its part to accommodate the needs of winter visitors. The Mystic Seaport custom called Mug Up has its roots in the maritime practice of sharing hot drinks on a winter's day at sea. With your paid admission you are entitled to warm up with a free cup of hot chocolate or coffee at the Galley, the seaport's fast-food restaurant.

In addition, daily winter tours and evening winter workshops are regularly scheduled, affording looks at seafaring topics that might slip through the cracks at other times of the year. One winter workshop slate included topics, "Getting the Most Out of Your Sails," "A Historical Perspective on Nineteenth-Century Navigation," and "The Bermuda Race: Behind the Scenes."

The winter tours, said guide Donna Ballantone as we walked along a path of shells and gravel and snow, "give a look at a history of Mystic that visitors who come in the crush of warm weather don't see." Our tour took us into the Henry duPont Preservation Shipyard and the Mystic River Scale Model exhibit.

We entered the visitors' gallery on the upper level of the main shop where a shipwright's tool chest and photos of classic boats caught our attention; then we viewed a 90-foot lathe used for working on wooden ships' masts and spars. Below us a handful of shipyard workers were in the process of restoring a sardine-carrying boat from Maine.

"Boats are like houses," Donna told us. "You can add to or subtract from them and they can be restored to any period."

The acrid scent of varnish hit us like a wooden plank as we stepped inside the separate small boat shop where a shipwright named Bill was refurbishing a Swampscott dory-skiff. He demonstrated the suppleness of wood by taking a piece of white oak that had been warmed with steam and, like magic, bending it back and forth like a piece of cooked linguini. "Steam it for one hour for every inch of thickness," Bill advised. "When you season it, it will become rigid."

After your tour you can board the *Charles W. Morgan*, last of the wooden whaling ships, the *L. A. Dunton*, or the 1882 training ship, the *Joseph Conrad*. Or you can enter the drug store, the cooperage, the bank, the print shop, or any of the exhibit galleries where there are parades of hand-carved ship figureheads, scrimshaw, and ship's models on display.

We opted for a trip to the ship chandlery, where chandler and chanteyman Rick Spencer performed on fiddle and concertina some lasting songs of the sea. Sitting by the pot-bellied stove and surrounded by lanterns, running lights, sextants, compasses, foghorns, and other products of the chandler's trade, Rick, long hair parted in the middle and looking a bit like Ian Anderson of the rock group Jethro Tull, sang a verse from "Blow the Man Down":

> As I was a-rolling down Paradise Street
> A big Irish copper I chance for to meet
> He says: "You're a Black Baller by the cut of your hair.
> You're a Black Baller by the clothes that you wear."

Rick then explained: "These chanteys are extremely entertaining but that isn't the only purpose of singing them here. They are also an anthropological tool that tell of sailors' lives."

Around 1819, the Black Ball line of packet ships became the first to run on schedule—previously ships just sailed whenever they filled—and they hired the toughest sailors they could find. To show they were different, Black Ballers cut their hair short in back and wore red top boots that exposed the red lining of their pants.

"In this song," said Rick, "the cop recognizes the

sailor as a Black Baller and accuses him of theft. The sailor knocks him down—'blow the man down' means knock him down—and receives a jail term."

On weekends you can have a conversation with residents of the year 1876 in the sailors' reading room. There you will find staff persons portraying whaler's wife Anna Ashby, Gloucester fisherman James McCrae, first mate Jim Coulter, or other salty characters discussing life at sea or the loneliness of being away from one's family. All anecdotes told are based on fact, although the persons depicted are composites.

A male tourist visiting from the twentieth century was asked what brought him into the reading room, described as "a moral haven amid the temptations of sailor town." Was he here to write a letter home or did he get into a brawl in the sailor's tavern?

A child might be asked if he'd like to go to sea as a cabin boy. Glenn Gordinier, Mystic research associate who often is found in character as hard-bitten first mate Josiah Gardner, offered: "We'll tell him the responsibilities of a cabin boy, making your own bed, doing your own laundry and your own dishes, and then doing the same for the captain and first mate. Some children do those chores at home anyway and some don't. When we tell them they'd get paid for it, their eyes get real big."

What should one keep in mind before visiting Mystic Seaport in winter? There won't be as many staff persons in the buildings as you will find in summer. And dress warmly and wear comfortable walking shoes. The dirt roads can get muddy after a winter rain, and the wind off the ocean can be brisk. Mystic Seaport Museum, Inc., 50 Greenmanville Avenue, P.O. Box 6000, Mystic, CT 06355; (203) 572–0711.

THREE OTHER FAVORITES IN WINTER

Old Sturbridge Village

NEW ENGLAND'S OTHER well-known nineteenth-century living history village also welcomes visitors in the off-season. Like Mystic Seaport, Old Sturbridge Village is refreshingly free in winter of the masses that jam its country roads the rest of the year. The tinsmith, broom maker, shoemaker, cooper, black-

smith, printer, and other village tradespersons will have plenty of time to afford you individual attention. Meanwhile, the folks over at the Pliny Freeman Farm will likely be splitting logs into firewood, making fence posts, threshing grain, or doing additional chores typical during an 1830s Massachusetts winter.

Special winter evening programs at Old Sturbridge Village afford chances to get a bit of on-the-job training as a nineteenth-century resident. At **Dinner in a Country Village** you can help prepare an evening meal by using a brick oven or the spit in the fireplace, and then dine on your created feast later.

Or listen to a period concert in the meetinghouse before playing Fox and Geese or another once popular after-dinner game as part of a program called **Sturbridge Village by Candlelight**. During **Crafts at Close Range** you will acquire once common techniques like creating a barrel out of wooden staves, or the arts of blacksmithing, tinsmithing, and cabinet making. Old Sturbridge Village, Sturbridge, MA 01566; (508) 347–3362.

Lowell National Historical Park

THE BOAT RIDES cease operation in winter, but otherwise **Lowell National Historical Park** and **Lowell**

Heritage State Park are as active as they are the rest of the year, offering both quick glimpses and thorough inspections into this northern Massachusetts city's trail-blazing place in the Industrial Revolution.

Lowell's trolleys—reproductions of turn-of-the-century cars used on the Boston and Northern Street Railway—do operate in winter, both as parts of tours and as general transportation. You also might be led by foot through the streets or into buildings like the Union Meeting Hall at the Mogan Cultural Center for a presentation on labor in Lowell, and the Suffolk Mill for a look at the workings of a nineteenth-century turbine and an operating power loom.

The stories here are not simply of movements and mechanics, however. They are also of people, and in a program called "Tunes and Tales," Alex Demas will impart labor legends and lore accompanied by the melodies he makes on folk instruments like a mandolin, autoharp, banjo, guitar, or Appalachian dulcimer.

Witness this touching lyric from a song called "Babies in the Mill," written by a man who began mill work at age ten:

> Get out of bed you sleepy head
> And get you a bite to eat
> For the factory whistle is calling you
> And there is no more time to sleep.

To touch your senses as well as your heartstrings, step inside the Boott Cotton Mills Museum, opened in 1991, with its simulated weave room. Here, over 90 belt-driven, rocking, clattering, operating power looms afford visitors a realistic taste of life when an honest week's work meant 72 hours in this environment. Lowell National Historical Park, 169 Merrimack Street, Lowell, MA 01852; (508) 459–1000.

Northfield Mountain Recreation and Environmental Center

IN SUMMER PEOPLE come to this western Massachusetts locale to hike, bicycle, take a guided nature walk, star gaze, canoe, bird watch, or sing rousing old standards around a campfire. In winter, this recreation center, owned and operated by Northeast Utilities at the site of Northfield Mountain Reservoir near the Connecticut River, is just as much a cluster of activity.

The environmental enterprise maintains 40 kilometers of cross-country ski trails, all groomed, and also offers lessons and ski and snowshoe rentals; about ten kilometers of trails can be used by snowshoers.

Guided snowshoe walks, winter companions to those summer nature strolls where we once learned that cattails are good to eat in pancakes, are scheduled regularly. On these you will discover wild flowers that decorate the winter scene or learn which animals left those odd-looking three-toed tracks in the snow.

Often on the slate are a ski orienteering meet, where you will learn to combine the skills of skiing with those of map reading, and an evening examination of the midwinter sky, where guided stargazers eyeball winter constellations. And in late February or early March you can satisfy voyeuristic tendencies by eavesdropping on mating owls.

Then there are other intriguing programs that pop up now and then. One winter evening was devoted to the stories and songs Native Americans created centuries ago to pass the time on long, cold nights. Another session taught cross-country skiers the technique of telemarking, named for the village of Telemark, Norway. Northfield Mountain Recreation and Environmental Center, RR 2, Box 117, Northfield, MA 01360; (413) 659–3713 for a recording, (413) 659–3714 for the office.

MUSH

Sled dog racing isn't reserved for the wild, wild North of Alaska and the Yukon. Right here in New England you can often catch a sled dog race on any given weekend from November into March. Granted, some might not be on snow, as is often the case early in the season or in the southern part of our region, but the race will usually go on.

Actually, real sled dog drivers, whether they are on the 1,157-mile Iditarod Trail Sled Dog Race in Alaska or in Connecticut's own Pachaug State Forest, hardly ever say "mush." The word is likely a corruption of a French word, either *marche* (which means "walk"), or *mouche* (which means "hasten"), reflecting commands given to sled dogs by their French-Canadian owners in days past.

" 'Mush' is too dull," says Bill Hahn, a Connecticut banker who has been racing sled dogs since 1979.

"You need to say something that is sharper, more commanding, like 'hike'. Or 'let's go' or 'all right'.

"I used the word 'mush' in my first race," recalls Hahn, "and people looked at me like, 'What woods did he come out of?' "

However, it is proper to refer to a sled dog racer as a musher, although the word "driver" is used interchangeably.

The World Championship Sled Dog Derby

YOU'LL FIND DOZENS of mushers on hand in Opechee Park in Laconia, New Hampshire, in early February, the setting of the **World Championship Sled Dog Derby**. Most mushers are friendly and will talk with you before a race and explain the intricacies of their passion, although you should use discretion if a driver seems especially busy or preoccupied in hitching up his or her dogs or making other race preparations.

The Laconia event lasts three days, but the crush of matches takes place on Saturday and Sunday. Dog teams are divided into categories based on either the number of dogs per team or the age of the musher. For example, there are a six-dog class, a ten-dog class, and a three-dog junior class for youngsters. The entrants in each of these classes race in two heats, one per day. The team with the shortest total time over both days is the winner.

The featured event, though, is the unlimited class, in which mushers use over ten dogs per team, and sometimes as many as 18 or 20. There are three heats in the unlimited competition, one per day over three days. It is in the unlimited class where you will find the top drivers and fastest dogs.

In theory, the more dogs on a team means the less weight each dog has to pull, and therefore the quicker the team. However, a common axiom heard from mushers is: "You'll only go as fast as the slowest dog on your team."

To the uninitiated all the dogs on a particular team might seem to have the same role, while in reality they each play different positions. The lead dog is the star, like a quarterback or a cleanup hitter, and must possess speed, endurance, and the desire to lead, as well as a strong trust in his musher. Some quick and strong dogs lack the will to be leaders, or are so aggressive that they are prone to fighting. A good lead dog might follow his driver's command without a moment's hesitation, even though the command might at first seem against his instincts.

Usually following the lead is a pair of speedy point dogs, not as strong or commanding as the lead but still capable of helping him out and backing him up. Two steady, reliable swing dogs come next. Finally, there are two muscular wheel dogs, which help the driver steer the sled and keep the lines taut.

While you might recall old-time movies featuring Sergeant Preston of the Canadian Mounties leading a team of Siberian huskies across the frozen northland, you will find that today's mushers use cross-breeds of setters and hounds with Alaskan huskies in short "sprint" races like the championships in Laconia. Stockier and stronger Siberian huskies, usually slower than Alaskans, are used mainly on middle- or long-distance races of 60 miles or more.

All mushers, whether world champions, like Alaskans Susan Butcher and Rick Swenson, or the New England businessperson who dabbles with Siberians on weekends, acknowledge the trusting friendship they form with their dogs. Listen to mushers communicating with their canine teammates and you will likely hear them speaking in plain English. Beverly Bonner, a member of the Lakes Region Sled

SLED DOGS RUSH ACROSS THE WINTRY NEW ENGLAND LANDSCAPE.

Dog Club, sponsors of the world championships, says, "I talk to the dog as if it is a person, and say things like, 'All right, let's go' and 'We're going home'."

Bill Hahn comments: "You have to talk friendly to the dogs and keep them high-spirited. People may think you're crazy but I talk to my dogs and they listen to me."

When standard English phrases aren't used, you will probably hear commands often given to horses, like "gee" to indicate a right turn, and "haw" for a left turn.

Initial training for the racing season begins around Labor Day or whenever daytime temperatures drop into the 50s. Then the dogs are hitched to three- or four-wheeled gigs or, in some cases, all-terrain vehicles. Jack Bicknell, a veteran of sled dog races from the Rangeley Lakes region of Maine, recommends that a dog have 100 to 150 miles of race practice before actually competing in a race each season. Bicknell states that some dogs start racing as young as one year old and that a top racing dog lasts about six or seven years, before losing power and speed. Sled dogs past their prime are often either placed in smaller classes or used in training.

In times of bare ground, the three- and four-wheeled gigs take the place of sleds, but most mushers agree that there is nothing like the feel of a sled on snow. Laurie Merritt, a vice-president of the Yankee Siberian Husky Club, compares it to the difference between taking a sailboat versus a motorboat on a lake in summer. "Racing on snow is so much quieter and seems much more natural," she says.

Others point out how the sled is both lighter and harder to steer than a gig, and therefore makes for a more exciting race.

Races can be cancelled in cases of ice on the race route, which can be rough on dogs' paws. Mushers are required to carry first aid kits during races and to put ointment on tender paws if a dog has suffered abrasions. Some even put little booties on their dogs' paws.

What should a spectator watch for when attending a sled dog race? First, one should peruse the race map and position oneself in a locale offering a wide viewing range. Veterans often recommend spots where the race route curves, or at the base of a hill— settings where mushers and dogs can really show their skills. For the world championships in Laconia, Beverly Bonner suggests a viewing point across from the Office of Developmental Services on Parade Road. For the races in Rangeley, Maine, Jack Bicknell advises spectators to select a spot about two miles east of town along Route 16, where the race route and the highway cross and you can sit in your car and watch the speeding canines charge by.

Most sled dog enthusiasts will tell you to look over the teams before the race and pick a musher to root for, though whether you base your selection for your personal favorite on the driver's personality or the dogs' appearance (or the driver's appearance or the dogs' personalities) is purely up to you. Such a connection will increase your involvement and therefore your enjoyment. Says veteran Bill Hahn: "It's nice when people are waiting at the finish line even if you come in dead last."

During the heat of the action, Hahn suggests you watch the dogs' legs to see if they are moving in rhythm with one another or if any dog is limping, and to listen to the musher's tone of commands to his or her dogs. Laurie Merritt recommends that spectators notice the drivers' legs to see if he or she is properly propelling the sled with his or her foot. "This gives the dogs momentum and a musher should use a flowing type of kick, not a jerky one."

"If you do it right you will be in rhythm with the dogs," opines Beverly Bonner, who also tells onlookers to examine the lines between the dogs to see if they are tight; if lines are dragging it means the dogs are not running well.

Bonner states that hard-packed snow and temperatures between 0 and 10 degrees, while cold for spectators, are ideal racing weather conditions since they will keep the participants from becoming overheated. For viewers, Bonner notes that watching from one's car is a wise choice.

There are several sled dog racing clubs in New England. Bonner's organization, the Lakes Region Sled Dog Club, dates to 1957, although races took place in Laconia as early as 1929. In fact, the World Championship Derby dates its anniversaries from those first matches in 1929, although it wasn't until 1936 that the "world championship" title was adopted. The races were scrubbed just prior to World War II, and during the war some mushers trained dog teams for search and rescue missions in the frigid turf of northern Europe and Greenland.

Since the club's founding in 1957, there have been only a handful of cancelled world championships, all due to adverse weather conditions. Over the course of the three-day derby about 10,000 spectators come to view the contest, although crowding is rarely a problem, since they are spread over the 15-mile race route. A top team in the unlimited class should be able to finish a single heat within an hour. Laconia's event also awards the largest purse in New England, usually ranging between $10,000 and $12,000.

The World Championship Sled Dog Derby takes place in early to mid-February. For further information, contact Lakes Region Sled Dog Club, P.O. Box 382, Laconia, NH 03247; (603) 279–5063 or (603) 524–2165.

OTHER SLED DOG RACES

IN CONNECTICUT, MONTHLY races occur in Connecticut's Pachaug State Forest near Voluntown. Joanne Altieri, Connecticut Valley Siberian Husky Club, 104 Williams Street, Meriden, CT 06450; (203) 238–2532.

In Maine the Down East Sled Dog Club sponsors about five races each winter. Sure things include a 30-mile mid-distance run in Lee around New Year's weekend, and sprint races in late January in Lincoln and in early March in Greenville. For information and exact dates call (603) 382–8584. (No, that is not a typo—the information person for the Down East Club does live in New Hampshire).

The Rangeley Lakes region of Maine is home to two annual meets, one in January sponsored by the New England Sled Dog Club, and one in March sponsored by the chamber of commerce. Rangeley Chamber of Commerce, P.O. Box 317, Rangeley, ME 04970; (207) 864–5364.

There are usually at least two races in Freetown

State Forest in southeastern Massachusetts. Bob Allen, South Shore Sled Dog Club, 714 Pike Avenue, Attleboro, MA 02703.

Another group responsible for New England sled dog races is the Yankee Siberian Husky Club. Susan Kwaitkowski, Yankee Siberian Husky Club, RFD 1, Box 89, Cram Road, South Lyndeborough, NH 03082; (603) 654–6088.

In Rhode Island, frequent races take place in Arcadia Management Area in Exeter. Jeff Johnson, Narragansett Bay Sled Dog Club, 666 Newcombe Road, North Kingstown, RI 02852.

You can also contact state tourism divisions for statewide schedules of sled dog races:

Department of Economic Development, 865 Brook Street, Rocky Hill, CT 06067; (800) CT–BOUND, (203) 258–4290 or (203) 258–4289 in Connecticut.

Maine Publicity Bureau, 97 Winthrop Street, Hallowell, ME 04347; (800) 533–9595, or (207) 289–2423.

Office of Travel and Tourism, 100 Cambridge Street, 13th floor, Boston, MA 02202; (800) 632–8038 or (617) 727–3201.

Office of Vacation Travel, Box 856, Concord, NH 03301; (603) 271–2666.

Rhode Island Tourism Division, 7 Jackson Walkway, Providence, RI 02903; (800) 556–2484 or (401) 277–2601.

Vermont Travel Division, 134 State Street, Montpelier, VT 05602; (802) 828–3236.